A CULTURAL HISTORY OF FAIRY TALES

VOLUME 2

A Cultural History of Fairy Tales
General Editor: Anne E. Duggan

Volume 1
A Cultural History of Fairy Tales in Antiquity
Edited by Debbie Felton

Volume 2
A Cultural History of Fairy Tales in the Middle Ages
Edited by Susan Aronstein

Volume 3
A Cultural History of Fairy Tales in the Age of the Marvelous
Edited by Suzanne Magnanini

Volume 4
A Cultural History of Fairy Tales in the Long Eighteenth Century
Edited by Anne E. Duggan

Volume 5
A Cultural History of Fairy Tales in the Long Nineteenth Century
Edited by Naomi J. Wood

Volume 6
A Cultural History of Fairy Tales in the Modern Age
Edited by Andrew Teverson

A CULTURAL HISTORY OF FAIRY TALES

IN THE MIDDLE AGES

VOLUME 2

Edited by Susan Aronstein

BLOOMSBURY ACADEMIC
LONDON • NEW YORK • OXFORD • NEW DELHI • SYDNEY

BLOOMSBURY ACADEMIC
Bloomsbury Publishing Plc, 50 Bedford Square, London, WC1B 3DP, UK
Bloomsbury Publishing Inc, 1359 Broadway, New York, NY 10018, USA
Bloomsbury Publishing Ireland, 29 Earlsfort Terrace, Dublin 2, D02 AY28, Ireland

BLOOMSBURY, BLOOMSBURY ACADEMIC and the Diana logo are trademarks of
Bloomsbury Publishing Plc

First published in Great Britain 2021
Paperback edition published 2025

Copyright © Susan Aronstein, 2021

Susan Aronstein and Contributors have asserted their right under the Copyright, Designs
and Patents Act, 1988, to be identified as Author of this work.

Series design by Raven Design
Cover image: The Unicorn, 1450, France, 15th Century
(© De Agostini Picture Library / Bridgeman Images).

All rights reserved. No part of this publication may be: i) reproduced or transmitted in
any form, electronic or mechanical, including photocopying, recording or by means of
any information storage or retrieval system without prior permission in writing from the
publishers; or ii) used or reproduced in any way for the training, development or operation
of artificial intelligence (AI) technologies, including generative AI technologies. The rights
holders expressly reserve this publication from the text and data mining exception as per
Article 4(3) of the Digital Single Market Directive (EU) 2019/790.

Bloomsbury Publishing Plc does not have any control over, or responsibility for,
any third-party websites referred to or in this book. All internet addresses given
in this book were correct at the time of going to press. The author and publisher
regret any inconvenience caused if addresses have changed or sites have ceased
to exist, but can accept no responsibility for any such changes.

A catalogue record for this book is available from the British Library.

A catalog record for this book is available from the Library of Congress.

ISBN: HB: 978-1-3500-9448-2
PB: 978-1-3505-9387-9
ePDF: 978-1-3502-8758-7
eBook: 978-1-3502-8757-0
set: 978-1-3505-9409-8

Series: A Cultural History of Fairy Tales

Typeset by Integra Software Services Pvt. Ltd.
Printed and bound in Great Britain

For product safety related questions contact productsafety@bloomsbury.com.

To find out more about our authors and books visit www.bloomsbury.com
and sign up for our newsletters.

CONTENTS

LIST OF ILLUSTRATIONS	vii
SERIES PREFACE	x
Introduction: Once Upon a Time in the Middle Ages *Susan Aronstein*	1
1 Forms of the Marvelous: Fairy Stories, or Stories about Fairies? *Richard Firth Green*	23
2 Adaptation: Like a Fairy Tale *Shyama Rajendran*	45
3 Gender and Sexuality: The Beauties and Beasts of Medieval Romance *Lynn Shutters*	63
4 Humans and Non-Humans: Writing the Fairy, Reading *Melusine* *Sarah L. Higley*	89
5 Monsters and the Monstrous: Tracking Medieval Monsters into Fairy-Tale Worlds *Christine M. Neufeld*	111
6 Space: Place, Non-Place, and Identity in the Medieval Fairy World *Helen Fulton*	135

7	Socialization: Renegotiation and Reconciliation *Usha Vishnuvajjala*	157
8	Power: Patronage, Subversion, Seduction, and Challenge *Melissa Ridley Elmes*	177

Notes	193
References	206
Notes on Contributors	222
Index	225

ILLUSTRATIONS

0.1	Medievalism and Fairy Tale Castles, from Maxfield Parrish, "Puss in Boots" (1913)	4
0.2	The Enchanted Forests of Medievalism, from Maxfield Parrish, *Aucassin and Nicolette* (1903)	11
0.3	Perceval's adventures. Bibliothèque nationale de France, MS Francais 113, fol. 156v (1470[?])	19
1.1	Merlin's mother is impregnated by a demon, from the *Lancelot-Graal*. Bibliothèque nationale de France MS Francais 96, fol. 62v (1450[?]–1455[?])	32
1.2	The infant Lancelot being taken away by the fairy Vivien, from the *Lancelot-Graal*. Bibliothèque nationale de France, MS Francais 113, fol. 156v (1470[?])	36
1.3	Diana and her nymphs, from Christine de Pizan's *l'Epître d'Othéa*. Bibliothèque nationale de France, MS Francais 606, fol. 13 (1407–9)	42
2.1	Illustration from Galland's *The Thousand and One Nights* (date unknown)	46
2.2	Mediterranean trade. Getty Library, MS 13 (85.MS.213) (before 1340)	51

2.3	The Enchanted Horse, from Antoine Galland's translation of *The Thousand and One Nights* (1864)	58
3.1	Courtliness and Beauty of Lovers, from the Codex Manesse. UB Heidelberg, Cod. Pal. germ. 848, fol. 178r: Herr Bernger von Horheim	70
3.2	Knight Coming to the Rescue of a Woman Threatened by Rape, from the Smithfield Decretals. BL Royal MS 10 EIV, fol. 74v	85
3.3	"Courtly" Beauty in *Pretty Woman* (dir. Garry Marshall, 1990)	87
4.1	The Woman in the Wood, Raymondin meets Melusine. Bibliothèque nationale de France, MS Francais 24383, fol. 5v (fifteenth century)	90
4.2	Melusine in her bath. Bibliothèque nationale de France, MS Francais 24383, fol. 19 (fifteenth century)	101
4.3	Melusine flees Lusignan. Bibliothèque nationale de France, MS Francais 24383, fol. 30 (fifteenth century)	108
5.1	Plinian races. Getty Library MS Ludwig XV 4 (83.MR.174) (1277 or after)	114
5.2	Hell mouth. Getty Library MS 30 (87.MN.141.17), fol. 17 (1475)	119
5.3	Perceval fights a hybrid dragon. Bibliothèque nationale de France, MS Français 112, fol. 23 (1470)	124
5.4	Saint Margaret and the Dragon. Getty Library MS 37 (89.ML.35), fol. 49v (1469)	128
6.1	Sea Voyage. Heidelberg, Cod. Pal. germ. 60, fol. 179v (1460)	140
6.2	The Otherworlds of the *Mabinogion*	144
6.3	Urban Landscapes. Bibliothèque nationale de France, MS Français 111, fol. 1 (1480[?])	149

7.1	The Green Knight entering Arthur's court. British Library, Cotton Nero A X, fol. 94v (*c.* 1375–1400)	166
7.2	Warwick Goble, "Dorigen pledging Aurelius," *The complete poetical works of Geoffrey Chaucer* (1912)	172
7.3	Yvain returns. Bibliothèque nationale de France, MS Français 1433, fol. 104r (1320[?]–1330[?])	173
8.1	Melusine in her bath. Bibliothèque nationale de France, Rare Books, RES-Y2-400, fol. 142 (1478)	180
8.2	The Green Knight's Wife with Gawain. British Library, Cotton Nero A X, art3, fol. 129 (*c.* 1395–1400)	186

SERIES PREFACE

Taking a transnational approach, *A Cultural History of Fairy Tales* seeks to deepen our appreciation for and knowledge about a type of *text* (understood in the broadest sense of the term) that is often taken for granted due to its association with children's literature, old wives' tales, and oral peasant culture. Whether we think of the Brothers Grimm or films by Walt Disney Studios, fairy tales are often viewed as naïve and timeless stories with universal appeal, which suggests they are ahistorical, innocent narratives. This series brings together scholars from a diversity of disciplines to challenge many of these preconceptions about the fairy tale, shedding light on its very complex cultural history.

The chapters included in these six volumes foreground how the fairy tale was deployed in different historical periods and geographical locations for all kinds of cultural, social, and political ends that cross categories of class, age, gender, and ethnicity. "Fairy tale" here serves as a broad umbrella term for what more generally could be referred to as "wonder tale," which encompasses but is not limited to texts that feature fairies, witches, enchanters, djinn, and other beings endowed with magical or supernatural powers; anthropomorphized animals; metamorphosis (humans transformed into animals or other objects and vice versa); magical objects; and otherworlds and liminal spaces. "Fairy tale" also refers to texts that may not include any of these qualities but have been received as—that is, read or categorized as or are generally considered to be—a fairy tale.

By moving from antiquity to the present and transnationally, chapters crossing the six volumes foreground, for instance, how ancient animal fables present both continuities and discontinuities with the representation of animals in later wonder tales; how conceptions of fairies, djinn, and other magical characters change across historical periods and geographical locations; and how the very notion of what is marvelous, natural, or supernatural is understood differently across space and time. Chapters showcase the range of different types of characters and themes one can find in wonder tales as well as the multiple forms and functions tales can take. Together these volumes paint a broad picture of the ways in which different national tale traditions interact with and mutually influence each other, giving us a transnational and transhistorical understanding of the fairy tale. Indeed, readers will discover the rich, complex, and often ideologically charged cultural history of texts that can seem so familiar to us, which helps us understand them in new and exciting ways.

All six volumes cover the same eight themes for the reader to gain a sense of continuities and discontinuities between types of characters, narratives, and traditions over time. Readers will move from *forms* of the fairy tale and the ancillary genres that fed into it to the history of *adaptations*, revealing the ways in which tales are always already a blend of multiple local, regional, and national traditions. A genre often focusing on questions related to development and initiation into adulthood and sometimes (less than we might think) concluding with marriage, tales often feature the norms of *gender and sexuality* grounded in a particular culture. Through the prevalence of non-human characters and problematic human figures, the fairy tale allows for the exploration of the boundaries between *the human and the non-human*, as well as between what is considered normal and *monsters or the monstrous*. As a nonmimetic genre, generally speaking, the fairy tale also plays with the delimitations between real and imaginary *spaces*, opening up both utopic and dystopic possibilities. Tales have often been used in the processes of *socialization*, for both children and adults, men and women, articulating class, gender, and ethnic differences. As such, tales cannot be separated from questions of *power* and ideology.

This cultural history of the fairy tale is divided into the following historical periods:

Volume 1: A Cultural History of Fairy Tales in Antiquity (500 BCE–800 CE)

Volume 2: A Cultural History of Fairy Tales in the Middle Ages (800–1450)

Volume 3: A Cultural History of Fairy Tales in the Age of the Marvelous (1450–1650)

Volume 4: A Cultural History of Fairy Tales in the Long Eighteenth Century (1650–1800)

Volume 5: A Cultural History of Fairy Tales in the Long Nineteenth Century (1800–1920)

Volume 6: A Cultural History of Fairy Tales in the Modern Age (1920–2000+)

Readers will come away with a new and fresh understanding of the fairy tale, which indeed enhances our appreciation for a genre that has touched many of us since childhood. Far from being naïve, innocent, timeless texts, *A Cultural*

History of Fairy Tales foregrounds the ways wonder tales are embedded in sophisticated social, cultural, political, and artistic practices across history, anchored in specific cultural contexts that shape their meaning as tales are adapted from one cultural and historical context to another.

Anne E. Duggan, *General Editor*

Introduction

Once Upon a Time in the Middle Ages

SUSAN ARONSTEIN

A FAIRY-TALE PAST

From early editions of Jacob and Wilhelm Grimm's *Kinder-und Hausmarchen (Children's and Household Tales* [1812]) to Disney's princess film *Frozen 2* [2019], idealized medieval castles have translated audiences back to an enchanted fairy-tale past. And yet, while all agree that the Middle Ages are central to fairy tales, many scholars assert that there are no actual medieval fairy tales. This is not to say that these scholars do not recognize the importance of medieval narratives as a proto-fairy-tale trove of themes and motifs—they do; however, most argue, as Jack Zipes does, that *fairy tales* as a distinct genre do not emerge until considerably later. Zipes dates this "later" to seventeenth-century France, and Marie-Catherine d'Aulnoy's *contes des fées*. Ruth Bottigheimer locates it in sixteenth- and seventeenth-century Italy, with Giovanni Straparola's *Pleasant Nights* (two volumes, 1551 and 1553) and Giambattista Basile's *Tale of Tales* (two volumes, 1634 and 1636). And all historians of the genre, wherever they pinpoint its beginnings, acknowledge the key role played by both Charles Perrault's *Tales and Stories of the Past* (1697) and the Grimm brothers' *Children's and Household Tales* in the codification and dissemination of what we now call the fairy tale.[1] Noting the influence of Perrault and Grimm in *Fairy Tales from Before Fairy Tales: The Medieval Latin Past of Wonderful Lies,* Jan Ziolkowski observes, "the fairy tale ends up being understood as the kind of tale that is included in classic fairy tale collections" (2007: 237); this understanding, he notes, generates a central paradox: "fairy tales are often set in a medieval-feudal past, but medieval sources and analogues ... go unmentioned or undervalued" (27).

In his study, Ziolkowski convincingly recovers medieval Latin sources and analogues for several narratives included in *Children's and Household Tales*. In so doing, he demonstrates that even the genre as it is generally understood (and defined by Bottigheimer)—a short tale, firmly based in the world of human beings, in which magic (and marriage) helps achieve the "ending of two people's difficulties and the beginning of a life lived happily ever after" (2009: 6)—can be traced to the Middle Ages. This definition ironically excludes, however, the vast array of popular medieval romances that provide fairy tales with their enchanted castles and magical forests—romances that one could argue have had a far greater influence on the genre than the Latin tales the Grimms' appropriated in their collection. Bottigheimer disqualifies these narratives on several counts: they are too long; they don't always end happily; they dwell—at least for a time—in a fairyland parallel to the human realm rather than introducing supernatural and fairy creatures with no backstories or world of their own, who "enter narratives in order to benefit human beings" (Bottigheimer 2014: 1). "Existentially doubled" tales, such as the medieval romances, "with a fairy world paralleling the human world, into and out of which both fairies and humans move," are not, Bottigheimer concludes, fairy tales; they are fairyland fictions, a subgenre of the magic tale (7).

As we can see from the above discussion, when scholars attempt to define *the* fairy tale, they quickly find themselves in a maze of caveats and contradictions, quibbling about the distinction between oral and literary texts, sorting through themes and motifs, and reducing plots and narratives to the simplest common denominators, leading Zipes to conclude, in the *Oxford Companion to Fairy Tales*, that "there is no such thing as the fairy tale; however, there are hundreds of thousands of fairy tales" ([2000] 2015: xv), and proving, as J. R. R. Tolkien famously asserts, "Faerie cannot be caught in a net of words" (1964: 10).[2] For "*Faerie*," he observes, "contains many things besides elves and fays, and besides dwarfs, witches, trolls, giants or dragons: it holds the seas, the sun, the moon, the sky, and the earth and all of the things that are in it: tree and bird, water and stone, wine and bread, and ourselves mortal men, when we are enchanted" (9). Nevertheless, Tolkien grapples to catch the genre in a net of words; as he does so, he suggests that we recognize a fairy tale when we see it, not by knowing what one *is* but by knowing what one *does*: it enchants. "The presence of enchantment," Marie Tatar writes, echoing Tolkien, "is perhaps the defining feature of the genre" (2015: 4). "Familiar roads with unexpected twists," fairy tales are known by their affect: wonder, marvel, enchantment, awe (1). This affect that does not, in Tolkien's words, "depend on any definition or historical account of elf or fairy, but upon the nature of *Faerie:* the Perilous Realm itself, and the air that blows in that country" (1964: 10). Through *Faerie,* fairy tales enchant their audiences "from the world of reality to provide an alternative world based on naïve morality" (Zipes [2012] 2013: 14). Passed down from one generation to the next (or told and retold) these tales translate us to another land, allowing us to "gain distance, so we can know [our world] as well as ourselves" (20). They "open up the great question of 'what if'," "start conversations," and provide "maps for coping" in the here and now (Tatar 2015: 3; 1999: xi).

For *Faerie* is distant in both space and time; as such the fairy tale's enchanted once upon a medieval time promises to connect us to the lost world, the lost wisdom, the lost innocence of cultural and personal childhoods. In the words of Jacob Grimm, these tales are presented as "all that remain" of a simpler time, preserved in "the places by the stove, the hearth in the kitchen, attic stairs, holidays still celebrated, meadows and forests in their solitude and above all the untrammeled imagination" (quoted in Ziolkowski 2007: 190). In a modern world where "the dreamlands [have] vanish[ed] (at least temporarily) from the earth," Ziolkowski observes, "it is solace that at least the impenetrable woods, mutable fogs, and dragons of fairy tales remain … forests and creatures … [that] still bear the traces of a real or imagined medieval culture (Figure 0.1). Wonder," he concludes, "has migrated out of the general human experience into the more circumscribed experience of childhood and it bears a medieval or pseudo-medieval impress" (2007: 7–8).

But "how," Ziolkowski asks, "did 'once upon a time' come to equal the Middle Ages? How did the landscape of fairy tales come to be peopled with princesses, princes and dwarfs, or dotted with the castles that are associated with the Middle Ages?" (2007: 23). To answer Ziolkowski's cogent question and, indeed, to understand the cultural history of the fairy tale in the Middle Ages, we need to add another question, reversing the terms: "How did the Middle Ages come to equal 'once upon a time'? How did its landscapes come to be peopled with fairy tale princesses, princes and dwarfs, or dotted with the castles that are associated with fairy tales?" In this introduction I will explore both versions of this question, beginning with an examination of the genre's roots in medievalism, "the ongoing process of recreating, reinventing, and reenacting medieval culture in postmedieval times," and then looking at the ways in which medieval fairy tales also imagine an ideal "medieval past" before turning to a survey of the fairy-tale narratives written in the historical period we now designate as medieval (Emery and Utz 2014: loc. 172).

As we begin our examination of the fairy tale, both as a genre set in the Middle Ages and as narratives written during the period that spanned from 900–1500 or so, it is important to note that the Middle Ages are "in us," as Donald Howard once wrote, rather than "in them" (1980: 4); they are "virtually unique," in

FIGURE 0.1: Medievalism and Fairy Tale Castles, from Maxfield Parrish, "Puss in Boots" (1913). Public domain.

Leslie Workman's words, "among major periods or areas of historical study in being entirely the creation of scholars" (1995: 227). In other words, there are no "real" Middle Ages; the period itself is a medievalism, "a construct invented in the fifteenth century by humanists seeking to glorify their own time as a superior 'Renaissance'" (Emery and Utz 2014: loc. 176). Furthermore, from the moment of their invention in the fifteenth century, the Middle Ages have been constantly reinvented by scholars, thinkers, authors, creative and performing artists, game-makers, and a host of others; some "study" them and some "use" them; however, as Workman asserts, "the *study* of the Middle Ages on the one hand, and the *use* of the Middle Ages in everything from fantasy to social reform on the other are the two sides of the same coin" and we can see both sides of this coin in the history of fairy tales and fairy-tale scholarship (1999: 12; my emphases).

As we do so, we also see the process by which the fairy tale comes to equal the Middle Ages—and the Middle Ages, the fairy tale—unfolding. Many of the scholars and enthusiasts who collected and studied fairy tales were themselves medievalists, actively engaged in constructing a suitable past that tells us more about their own dreams and desires than it does the actual historical period that they purport to study; "mess[ing] up" the Middle Ages, in what Umberto Eco asserts is a common practice, "to meet the vital requirements of different periods" ([1976] 1986: 68). As they did so, they constructed a golden medieval past to which fairy-tale authors turned, adapting what Zipes, building on the work of Richard Dawkins and others, calls memes—"the tunes, ideas, catchphrases, clothes, fashions" that "help create and build traditions"—rooted in popular conceptions of the Middle Ages that themselves stemmed from more academic work, reinventing their tales' golden medieval past and rewriting their narratives to respond to what Ziolkowski terms "immediate cultural needs and pressures" (Zipes [2012] 2013: 17, 19; Ziolkowski 2007: 7).

MEDIEVALISTS AND FAIRY-TALE MEDIEVALISM

In this return to an invented medieval past, fairy tales are, and always have been, a form of medievalism. Between them, writers of and about fairy tales collected and retold medieval narratives, solidifying the connection between their fantasy Middle Ages and an enchanted once upon a time. As they did so, they also set the canon of medieval fairy narratives, influencing what texts were preserved and taught and making it impossible to disentangle the history of the fairy tale in the Middle Ages from the genre's post-medieval cultural history. This entanglement is particularly evident—and influential—in three key moments in the history of both medieval studies and the fairy tale: seventeenth-century France, nineteenth-century Germany, and early twentieth-century England. The fairy kingdoms of the aristocratic salons, the primeval forests of the Brothers Grimm, and the fantasy worlds of J. R. R. Tolkien and C. S. Lewis all have their roots in an imagined medieval past, a lost world of magic and wonder, but each also participates in a more general cultural return to the Middle Ages that both inflects their fairy-tale pasts and profoundly influences the academic discussion of medieval texts and history.

Let us begin in seventeenth-century France; in spite of the critical commonplace that traditionally aligns this period of French history with the Enlightenment (and thus classical civilization), scholarly and artistic medievalism, as Alicia C. Montoya asserts in her study, *Medievalist Enlightenment from Charles Perrault to Jean-Jacques Rousseau* (2013), flourished alongside Enlightenment discourses. Publishing records, letters, treatises, and catalogs all attest to the popularity of medieval texts—particularly romances, such as tales of Arthur, Tristan, Lancelot, and the Grail—and in these texts, Montoya observes, scholars both found "a basic continuity, connected with the idea of a national literary tradition" and a way to trace the origins of French literature back to the Middle Ages (2013: 49). "Just as the poems of Homer were the myths of the Greeks and the Romans," Jean Chapelain argued in *La Lecture des vieux romans* (Reading Old Romances), "so our old *romans* are also the myths of the French and the English" (quoted in Montoya 2013: 52; emphasis in the original).

While early academic medievalists, such as Chapelain, saw medieval texts as carriers of France's collective and mythic memories, the aristocratic women whose *contes de fées* launched the late seventeenth century's fairy-tale vogue engaged in an artistic medievalism in which the Middle Ages functioned "as an alternative site—even as an explicit utopia—that allowed [them] to rethink the ideology and poetics inherited from classicism ... and serve[d] as a means to criticize the present" (Montoya 2013: 3). These tales originated in the storytelling games of the salon, an "unofficial institution created and run by women," which, as Anne Duggan asserts, "provided a literary and philosophical forum in which women could legitimate themselves as beings endowed with reason" (2005: 43). In them, "elite women carved out a space for themselves," where they were no longer "wives or mothers but reasonable beings engaged in literary production, as well as in the production of the new social elite" (43, 45). As they published their *contes de fées,* salon women turned to medieval sources—chivalric fiction, romances, and folklore—to create a medieval past that authorized them to inhabit the public space. In prefaces, letters, and the tales themselves, they inserted themselves into French literary tradition, laid claim to a long and continuing genealogy of women writers, and celebrated a community of powerful women.

In her 1696 collection, "The Enchantments of Eloquence," Marie-Jeanne L'Héritier de Villandon, daughter of the royal historian and relative of Charles Perrault, asserts that her "Gallic fables," which "came to me by oral tradition," "come straight from the once famous storytellers and troubadours of Provence" (Bottigheimer 2012: 134, 135); Charlotte Rose de Caumont de La Force echoes this ancient lineage in her preface to "L'Enchanteur," a story included in her 1697 *Les Fées, contes des contes* "declaring that she had drawn her inspiration from 'an ancient gothic book called *Perceval*'" (Montoya 2013: 117). In laying claim to their tales' medieval origins, L'Héritier and La Force not only style themselves as heirs to and continuers of the French literary traditions, they also place that tradition—and its continuance—in the hands of the women storytellers responsible for keeping it alive. L'Héritier identifies her source as "a lady very knowledgeable about Greek and Roman antiquities, and even more erudite in Gallic antiquities, [who] told me [this tale] when I was a child," and assures her readers that she presents her stories to them "entirely in the terms that the storytellers of Provence taught it to our grandmothers" (Bottigheimer 2012: 135, 136)—grandmothers that, in her *Apothéose de Mademoiselle de Scudéry,* L'Héritier traces back to France's medieval past, "recall[ing] the name of Marie de France and the Comtesse de Die to give weight to her thesis of a female literary genealogy extending all the way back to the Middle Ages" (Montoya 2013: 138).

With their turn to the Middle Ages, these fairy-tale writers created a once upon a time of powerful fairy queens, self-actualizing princesses, and the lovers worthy of them, idealizing a medieval past in which, as Duggan's analysis of d'Aulnoy's fairy tales shows, "women obtain and maintain political power without the assistance of men," and contesting the fantasy Middle Ages found in another prominent genre that turned to the medieval period in its later phase, the opera (2005: 213). "By reconfiguring feminine space" and "transform[ing]" seductresses into "good fairies and princesses whose islands offer guiltless pleasure and repose in ways that recall the seventeenth-century salon," d'Aulnoy's tales, Duggan writes, "challenge ... opera's negative representation of the female seductress in her island lair" (236, 237). As they empower fairy rulers and princesses, valorize the medieval past, and trace a connection between that past and the present, between fairy kingdoms and modern salons, these writers seek to "bring back the time of the fairies, when so many perfect people could flourish" (L'Héritier, "Letter to Madame D. G***," quoted in Bottigheimer 2012: 149). They also explicitly connect aristocratic and royal women with the fairies themselves. In d'Aulnoy's dedication of her tales to "Madame" (Princess Palatine, who was the wife of Louis the XIV's brother Philippe), she declares, "Here are queens and fairies, who after giving happiness to whoever was most charming in their time, are coming to the court of Your Royal Highness to seek for whoever is most famous and lovable in ours" and concludes that "undoubtedly, it is great princesses like you ... who lead us to imagine the kingdom of Enchantment" (Bottigheimer 2012: 170).

D'Aulnoy and other women of the court turned to the Middle Ages to reimagine French medieval romances and pen an enchanted fairyland in which, Zipes observes, the "fairies are all power brokers." These fairy kingdoms provided "an alternative to the civilizing process of King Louis XIV's court," and laid claim to a republican queendom in both past and present, but their vision of a fairy-tale Middle Ages did not go unchallenged (Zipes [2012] 2013: 36). The most influential of these challenges came from Abbé Pierre de Villiers and Charles Perrault, who between them shaped the future of the fairy-tale genre. The title of the Abbé's 1699 *Conversations about the Contes de Fées and some other works of our time to serve as an antidote to bad taste, dedicated to the gentleman of the Académie Francaise* says it all; as its fictional dialogue between the Parisian and the Provincial unfolds, the Abbé laments this "heap of *contes de fées*, which have been the death of us for a year or two. If we didn't have so many ignorant people possessed by the desire to write books, we would never have seen so many printed absurdities" (Bottigheimer 2012: 212). Excoriating the tales as "invented by ignorant nurses," written by women, and read by women who "enjoy laziness and triviality," the Abbé condemns them, their authors, and their readers, concluding that the only fairy tales worth reading were those written by his fellow academician Charles Perrault, whose first volume of fairy tales, *Tales of my Mother Goose,* was published in 1697, the same year that d'Aulnoy published her *Tales of the Fairies*. These men's "distaste of the genre," as Duggan observes, is tied up with their opposition to salon culture and women in the public sphere (2005: 121). Thus, it is not surprising that, when Perrault turned to his own fairy-tale medieval past, he found a very different Middle Ages than the one penned by d'Aulnoy and her salon compatriots. Here, instead of fairy queens and independent princesses, we find endless variations on the medieval tale of Patient Griselda, a Middle Ages into which Perrault projects his biases about women to argue, as Duggan writes, that "good, honorable women are located in domestic and abject spaces such as hospitals, attics, hovels" and "preoccupy themselves with domestic labor" not "public and intellectual forms of activity such as judging and writing literary works" (2005: 143).[3] Indeed, Perrault revises his sources to make "women even more abject" (149), and his fairy tales, rather than empowering women, "attempt to lure [them] into submission, suggesting that if they subject themselves to pain and hardship—without resistance and with absolute constancy—they will be rewarded with a prince" (148).

While the fairy-tale authors of seventeenth-century France practiced an artistic medievalism to create a fantasy Middle Ages in which contemporary debates about gender (as well as class and political structures—issues beyond the scope of this introduction) played out, Jacob and Wilhelm Grimm saw themselves as practicing scholars rather than creative authors. As Maria Tatar writes in her introduction to the *Annotated Brothers Grimm,* "When Jacob and Wilhelm Grimm first developed the plan to compile German folktales, they had in mind a scholarly project that would preserve storytelling traditions threatened by industrialization and urbanization ... capture the 'pure' voice of the German people and ... preserve their oracular *Naturpoesie* before it died away" (2004: xxxviii). The Grimm brothers' project, then, was not merely to gather oral tales. Their scholarship served a nationalistic and ethnocentric purpose, and they specifically sought to collect and preserve tales that were "distinctly German and both mirrored and shaped national identity" (xliv).

The Grimm's "recovery" of the Middle Ages "laid the foundations for the study of German language, literature and folklore" (Tatar 2004: 421). In addition to their famous collections of tales, between them they started up the *German Dictionary*, produced the *German Grammar*, and published traditional academic works, such as *Ancient German Law*, an edition of the Old High German *Lay of Hildebrand*, translations of heroic poems, and a monograph on courtly love poetry.[4] Working in a Germany occupied by Napoleonic forces, the Grimm brothers' medievalism served both political and emotional ends. In his autobiography, Wilhelm recollects:

> The days marking the collapse of all previously existing establishments will never be forgotten ... The zeal with which we pursued our studies in older German helped overcome our spiritual depression ... Undoubtedly the world situation and the need to withdraw into the tranquility of scholarship contributed to the reawakening of the long-forgotten literature, but we were not just seeking solace in the past, we also hoped that the course on which we had embarked would contribute somehow to the return of a better day.
> (quoted in Tatar 2004: 426)

Whether they were working as editors, translators, scholars, or collectors, the Grimm brothers' medievalism led them to find an ideal past in a reimagined Middle Ages, a once upon a (German) time capable of creating and sustaining national identity.

"Ever," as Ziolkowski writes, "on the prowl for materials from the Middle Ages that would expand and undergird their understanding of Germany's [medieval] past," the Grimms found that past most powerfully preserved in the fairy tales, passed down by "noble savages who maintained and transmitted traditions, along with traditional narratives [that] embodied all that was beautiful and true in their culture" (2007: 195, 32). For, as "we review the riches of German poetry," the Grimm brothers write in the preface to volume 1 of *Children's and Household Tales*, we "find that nothing of it has been kept alive." "Even the memory of it is lost," they assert. "Folk songs and these innocent tales are all that remain" (2004: 435). These songs and tales, the Grimms argue, "kept intact German myths which were thought to be lost"; in Briar Rose, the Bird with the Golden Feather, and Snow White, the Grimm brothers found preserved the *Eddas*, the *Nibelungenlied*, and the (German) story of *Tristan and Isolde*. However, Ziolkowski demonstrates that, in spite of their claim to have "found" these tales by hearth sides and hedgerows, the stories the brothers published in *Children's and Household Tales* are more artistic medievalism than medieval scholarship. Whether working with actual medieval texts or transcribed oral tales, the Grimms transformed their materials into German *marchen*, "adopting a folksy, old-fashioned and biblical style" that adapted the tales to conform with their idea of medieval oral storytelling (Ziolkowski 2007: 192).

As medievalism, *Children's and Household Tales* offered its initial readers a faithful return to a romanticized Middle Ages—a German past—where readers could find a "shared Germanness," based on "languages and verbal traditions that in [the Grimm's view] reflected a common spirit" (Ziolkowski 2007: 166). It also offered a medieval past that was "in some ways better and more natural than the world in which they lived" (7). And indeed, the Grimms' medievalism is shot through with a persistent anti-modernism, in which the medieval past, in addition to true "Germanness," embodies plenitude, wonder, and innocence. "One discovers," they write in the preface to the first volume of *Children's and Household Tales*, "that the custom [of telling tales] only exists where there is a warm openness to poetry or where the imaginations are not yet deformed by the perversities of modern life"; the tales told here, they proclaim, "are suffused with the same purity that makes children appear so wondrous and blessed to us" (2004: 436). "In the fairy tale," the Grimms promise, "a world of magic is opened up before us, one which still exists among us in secret forests, in underground caves, and in the deepest sea, and it is still visible to children" (426; Figure 0.2):

> As in myths that tell of a golden age, all of matter is alive; the sun, the moon, and the stars are approachable, give gifts and can even be woven into gowns; dwarfs mine metals in the mountains; mermaids leap in the water; birds ... plants, and stones all speak and know how to express their sympathy .... Everything beautiful is golden and strewn with pearls, and there are even golden people there; misfortune, by contrast is a dark power, a dreadful cannibalistic giant who is ... vanquished since a good woman who knows just how to avert misfortune stands ready to help. These narratives always end by opening up the prospect of boundless happiness.
>
> (437)

That Tolkien's later description of *Faerie* so closely echoes this passage is not surprising. J. R. R. Tolkien and C. S. Lewis grew up on fairy tales and medieval literature, imbibing from an early age the Grimms' vision of a romanticized medieval past—a past more natural, more real, more heroic. As they began their careers at Oxford in the wake of the First World War and in a society irrevocably altered by that war, developing technology, and changes in artistic and literary taste, the two men feared that England was in danger of losing this past, and with it, the nation's essential identity; drawing on the same nineteenth-century national and ethnocentric medievalism that runs through the fairy-tale tradition built by the Brothers Grimm, they embraced a deep-seated anti-modernism that underlies all of their academic and popular work. As professors, as scholars, and as creators, the two men sought to preserve and valorize an idealized Middle Ages that ran through

FIGURE 0.2: The Enchanted Forests of Medievalism, from Maxfield Parrish, *Aucassin and Nicolette* (1903). Public domain.

the medieval literature they taught and studied and into the fantasy worlds they created. In "the bitter, depleted world in which Lewis and Tolkien wrote," Norman Cantor argues in *Inventing the Middle Ages*, "they were not prepared imaginatively and intellectually to withdraw and accept defeat. Out of the medieval Norse, Celtic and Grail legends, they conjured fantasies of return and triumph …. A mythopoetic vision of medieval heroism was to be communicated to the masses through fantasy stories. 'That something which the educated receive in poetry,' Lewis wrote, 'can reach the masses in adventure stories and in almost no other way'" (1991: 213). Lewis's quote here identifies his (and Tolkien's) double audience: the educated, who would "receive" their medieval wisdom through poetry, and the masses, who could be reached through fantasy adventures and fairy tales. In other words, Lewis and Tolkien, like the Grimm brothers, played both sides of medievalism's coin. They not only *created* the Middle Ages in their fantasy works, they also *studied* the Middle Ages: Lewis in influential books, such as *The Allegory of Love* and *The Discarded Image*, which promulgated a view of the Middle Ages as a harmonious world of beauty and order; and Tolkien in groundbreaking studies of *Beowulf* and accessible editions of *Pearl* and *Sir Gawain and the Green Knight*. More importantly, in 1931, they implemented what Maria Sachiko Cecire identifies as "Oxford's medieval and Faerie-touched curriculum" (2019: 4). Believing that "literature can express higher truths and convey ideal national character," Tolkien and Lewis designed an English Studies syllabus that was "an academic version of their own writing," one that proposed an "approach to medieval literature through nationalist sentiment and openness to enchantment" (83, 84, 99).

In fairy tales, Tolkien and Lewis found the thread that connected the medieval to the modern, and their study of the genre connects their academic medievalism with their creative *use* of the Middle Ages in their fantasy worlds. For Tolkien, the fairy tale and the medieval are synonymous—his *Faerie* dwells in northern sagas, Arthurian legends, and medieval romances; both his definition and defense of the genre is inextricably tied to a distaste for modernity and the valorization of a lost and idealized Middle Ages. He laments that "fairy stories in our modern lettered world have been relegated to the 'nursery,' as shabby or old-fashioned furniture is relegated to the playroom" (Tolkien 1964: 34). Fairy tales, Tolkien argues, invoke longing. In *Faerie* modern children (and modern adults) hear the call of "the tormented hills and the unharvested seas …. For the heart is hard, though the body be soft." "I desired," Tolkien confides, "dragons with a profound desire" (40, 41). He concludes,

> I do not think that the reader or the maker of fairy-stories need ever be ashamed of the "escape" of archaism: of preferring not only dragons but horses, castles, sailing ships, bows and arrows; not only elves, but knights and

kings and priests. For it is after all possible for a rational man to arrive at the condemnation ... of progressive things like factories, or the machine-guns and bombs that appear to be their most natural and inevitable, dare we say, inexorable products.

(63)

Lewis similarly dismisses the modern in favor of the medieval. "I side impenitently," he proclaims in "On Three Ways of Writing for Children," "with the human race against the modern reformer .... Let [children] at least have heard of brave knights and heroic courage .... Let there be wicked kings and beheadings, battles and dungeons, giants and dragons, and let villains be soundly killed at the end of the book" (Lewis 1966: 31).

Lewis's call for knights and kings, battles and dungeons, giants and dragons encapsulates the connections between medieval literature, an idealized Middle Ages, and fairy tales with which this introduction began. As the fairy-tale tradition developed from seventeenth-century France, through nineteenth-century Germany and into twentieth-century England, it did so in direct dialogue with not only medieval narratives but also narratives about the Middle Ages; this dialogue has had profound consequences for both the fairy tale and our conception and study of the historical period. Beginning with its identification "in the middle"—between classical antiquity and the Renaissance—and continuing through the medievalisms of subsequent centuries, the Middle Ages "is not," as Nadia Altschul reminds us, "a global historical time ... but a local European time span," one that "has gathered its meaning from engagement with particular parts of Europe—mainly France, England and German-speaking countries—to the detriment of the more hybrid, multi-confessional, multiracial societies of the Mediterranean" (2014: loc. 6082). The same is true—until just recently—of fairy-tale and fantasy medievalisms, which, derived from the medieval narratives of Germany, France, and the British Isles, offer a once upon a time sealed-off from the vibrant diversity of the global Middle Ages.[5]

Furthermore, the connection between fairy tales and the Middle Ages, combined with the cultural, political, gendered, and ethnocentric fantasies of the medievalists who both studied and used the medieval past, profoundly influenced both the canon of medieval literature as literary studies developed in the early twentieth century and the continuing fairy-tale and fantasy traditions. "Lewis," Cantor writes, "saw himself, Tolkien and his other Oxbridge friends as spokesmen for 'Old European, or Old Western Culture'" (1991: 210); Cecire provides a comprehensive study of the ways in which these spokesmen's dreams of the Middle Ages shaped the medieval curriculum they developed at Oxford University, "an academic version of their fantasy writing" that "privileged ... medieval languages and literature ... fantastical and allegorical narratives ... [and] Victorian approaches to national identity" (2019: 97). A white, colonial, masculinist curriculum, this medieval syllabus invited students, as Lewis wrote, into a "great rough countryside" where they "could choose [their] own path": "Here's your gun, your spade, your fishing tackle; go and get your dinner .... It is time you learned to wrestle with nature for yourself" (quoted in Cecire 2019: 102). "This vision of scholarly activity in the 'great rough countryside,'" Cecire writes, "captures the youthful, vigorous spirit of Victorian and Edwardian boys' novels but depicts England's cultural history (rather than colonial settings) as the imaginative landscape for exploration, achievement, and transition into idealized male adulthood. Medieval languages and literature are, in this view, what makes the man" (103).

But what medieval literature? As Tolkien and Lewis constructed a syllabus capable of making the man, they established what, for years, would be the canon of medieval literature, one that excluded a whole range of generic and cultural traditions at the same time that it provided the basis for generations of new tales of Faerie. On the syllabus were the texts that evoked what Tolkien fondly called the Northern Imagination (the *Eddas* and the sagas, *Beowulf* and other Old English texts) along with Arthurian Legend (Malory's *Morte D'Arthur* and *Sir Gawain and the Green Knight*), *Sir Orfeo*, and Chaucer (whom, Cecire reminds us, they "recover[ed] as a medieval writer" [2019: 99]). This syllabus invented an Anglo-American Middle Ages in keeping with Lewis's and Tolkien's romance of the medieval past, an age of men and monsters, adventures and dragons, good and evil, at the same time that it either relegated those medieval narratives, such as the *lais* of Marie de France, the Middle English popular romances, and whole non-Western traditions, that questioned this view of the past to the sidelines, or ignored them all together.

Patricia McKillip, whose *Riddle Master* trilogy (1976–9) was one of the first modern tales of Faerie to explore what she terms "the rich and strangely unmined possibilities for female heroes, which glittered with color and the wealth of tales for the taking" (1999), discusses the fairy-tale tradition she had inherited from Grimm and Perrault, Tolkien and Lewis in her novel *Stepping from the Shadows* (1982). The novel follows two sisters, Frances and the first-person protagonist, growing up in the late 1950s and 1960s; in it, the sisters find escape from the real world in the fantasy realm Frances spins in stories—a realm where two sisters find beauty and adventure in the chase of an enchanted stag. And then Frances reaches her teens, and the stories change:

> Then her pencil began to slow. It stopped completely one day in mid-sentence ...
>
> "Where did the stag go?" [I asked] ... "I want to go where the stag went."
>
> "You can't." She said shortly and started writing again. But her pencil lead snapped. She leaned back tiredly ...
>
> Why not?

"Because." She was quiet for a long time, while I read through her stack of school paper full of stories. I finished finally, my head full of secret kingdoms, forests, wishes, all the stuff of fairy tales. I felt strange, satisfied, but bewildered.

Who are all these princes? Where are the sisters?

Back in the house in the woods. They never leave.

Why not?

They just don't. The sisters never leave the woods. The princess never leaves the tower. The queen leaves the castle only if she is going to run away to the woods and get married. So I had to use princes. It's in all of the books.

All those he's? He went there. He did this. He did that—

"It's in the books," she said patiently ....

She said finally, softly, with a strange kind of shame, "I can't hear their voices, I don't have their voices in my head. The women's voices. I have only the men's voices. That's all I can find .... I don't even know how to try. The sea, horses, swords, dragons, songs, churches, magic words, ships, and stars—I don't have any other way to think about them. All of the storytelling words belong to men."

(1982: 86–7)

McKillip's search for the women's voices in the fairy-tale tradition in the 1980s speaks poignantly and powerfully of Perrault's and Abbé de Villiers's success in wresting the fairy-tale tradition away from the women who founded it. It also speaks to the state of the English curriculum in the early 1970s, when McKillip received her BA and MA in English from San Jose State University. Much has changed in medieval studies since Frances's despairing statement, "it's in all the books," however, and that change has expanded the range of medieval tales of Faerie from which we construct our own fantasies of the medieval past. Alongside the Northern heroic and chivalric narratives favored by Tolkien and Lewis, students now read a wider range of fairy romances, from Marie's *lais*, through *Melusine*, to tales clearly aimed at a more popular audience; not all tales are heroic, and many portray powerful women from self-actualizing maidens to fairy mistresses. Additionally, geographical boundaries have expanded, and tales from non-Western traditions, such as *The Thousand and One Nights*, are—if too slowly—coming into medieval curriculums.

FAIRIES, MAGIC, AND FAIRY NARRATIVES IN THE MIDDLE AGES

The authors, from d'Aulnoy and Grimm to Tolkien and Lewis, who returned to the medieval past to pen modern fairy tales may have desired an enchanted past of dragons and faeries, but they did not believe in a world—even a medieval one—in which such beings had actually existed. This, however, may well not have been the case for the medieval authors of heroic tales and fairy romances, as Richard Firth Green convincingly argues in *Elf Queens and Holy Friars* (2016). Then, "fairy belief was sincerely held," Green writes, "and we should do them the courtesy of taking their beliefs seriously" (2016: 2). If such beliefs had not existed, he asserts, if "the fairy machinery of medieval romance … [was] nothing but a convenient narrative device," then there would have been no need for the church to wage a sustained campaign against the belief in fairies (33). Indeed, much of the literature addressing fairies in the Middle Ages is not fiction at all; treatises and sermons explore, affirm, and contest the existence of these supernatural (or extra-natural beings). Some writers record eye-witness accounts, others seek geographical and topographical proof, yet others attempt to define them within a taxonomy of beings, stretching from God, through the angels and humans, to beasts and plants; the church flatly dismisses them as devils and demons. "People in the Middle Ages were [clearly] themselves far from indifferent to truth claims about fairies" (33).[6]

How, we might ask, does this fairy belief (however contested) inflect the fairy narratives of the Middle Ages? It does so through a medieval medievalism; even if the authors of these narratives believed that fairies (or dragons, or trolls) once existed (or may have existed), they also were very much aware that the world that contained such numinous beings was disappearing—if not already all but gone (Green 2016: 33). The woods may once have been full of fairies, but medieval tales about them, like modern fairy tales, themselves are artistic medievalisms (and remember that these authors would have had no sense of themselves as living in the Middle Ages); set in a nostalgic once upon a time when heroes battled monsters, beautiful fairy queens enriched impoverished knights, and fairy lovers entertained imprisoned wives, these tales reconstruct a past to serve the needs of the present. In this, as both James Wade and Tara Williams have recently argued, medieval fairy narratives function in much the same ways as modern fairy tales: they transport their audiences, in Wade's terms, to a "possible world," "to explore issues and achieve narrative effects" (2011: 1). These *effects*, Williams asserts, are based on *affect*, on the wonder and marvel the tales evoke in both their fictional human protagonists and their audiences, allowing their fairy worlds to "both reflect and oppose the human one," as they raise questions and explore ethical concerns (2018: 7).

Their sense of a world rich in what Helen Fulton, speaking of the medieval Welsh tales, identifies as "magical naturalism" sets these tales apart from medieval genres such as the more straightforward historical chronicles and *chansons de geste*. In these fairy narratives, "the fantastic is a naturalized form of reality," and magic is not agential, not the result of spells and charms, but innate, simply *there* (Fulton 2013: 25). This magical naturalism may reside, as Bottigheimer asserts, in the doubled world of fairyland, or it may reside in the primary world itself, one in which, to borrow the distinction that Noel Carroll makes between fairy tales and the horror genre, monsters, trolls, dragons, and fairies are "ordinary beings in an extraordinary world" (Carroll 1990: 16). As such, medieval fairy narratives are also distinct from the period's other supernatural genres, saint's lives and miracle tales, in which God (or his angels) make their presence known—an extraordinary event in an ordinary world.

Medieval fairy narratives range across six centuries and numerous linguistic and cultural traditions; they appear in epics and sagas, Arthurian and popular romances, Breton lays and short prose tales, Latin schoolbooks and historical chronicles. For our purposes here, I have attempted to sort this vast expanse of tales into subtypes, knowing that—as with all taxonomies—the categories are imposed (and others could be proposed) and the stories themselves do not always fit (or stay) neatly in their assigned categories. However, these subtypes provide a provisional organization and a framework within which to begin thinking about the complex and vast body of medieval narratives that inform the cultural history of the fairy tale.

Magic and Wonder Tales

Let us begin with the short narratives closest to the modern definition of the fairy tale in which a human protagonist's encounter with the "impossible"—talking animals, shape-shifting demons, supernaturally giant vegetables—leads to their improved fortune. While the characters and events of these tales (their human protagonists, helpful animals and jinns, wily demons, vengeful sorceresses, impossible wealth, and mostly happy endings), all "feel" like fairy tales, their settings do not. Their once upon a time is not a now-lost enchanted past; rather, these tales take place in a mundane world in which magic only temporarily intervenes. For instance, the medieval Arabic tales collected in *Tales of the Marvelous* and the earliest surviving manuscript of *The Thousand and One Nights* recount marvelous *occurrences*—magical brass lions and ebony horses, transformations of men into animals (and vice versa), and interfering demons—but these occurrences take place in this world.[7] The same is true in the short tales adapted for schoolboys that Ziolkowski identifies as source-material for *Children's and Household Tales*; in these tales, the magic is a one-off that mainly lies in enchanted—or unusually large—animals or vegetables, not a sustained state of being. Even when magic tales have come into contact with the narrative tropes of fairy romances, such as in a medieval version of the Jewish tale, "Solomon's Daughter in the Tower" (arguably influenced by Marie de France's *Yonec*), the "magical" lover is not an otherworldly lord who can transform himself into a bird, merely her divinely fated husband, carried to her by an improbably huge bird (see Bottigheimer 2014: 55–7).

Heroes and Monsters

These are the tales that provide the dragons Tolkien so profoundly desired. *Beowulf*, which comes to us from the ninth century, exemplifies this subtype.

In a world filled with monsters—Grendel and his mother, who invade the mead hall, slaughtering men; sea serpents, who lurk beneath the waves; the dragon, who destroys farms and towns—Beowulf proves his prowess and, even in his tragic ending, protects his people from the monsters outside (the monsters within are another story).[8] Other medieval hero and monster tales are found in the thirteenth-century Norse narratives collected in the *Prose* and *Poetic Eddas*, such as the story of Sigurd (Siegfried) and the dragon.[9] King Arthur also battles the monsters who threaten his kingdom, most famously the Giant of Saint Michael's Mont in an episode that appears in several medieval Arthurian narratives, including Geoffrey of Monmouth's *The History of the Kings of Britain* (c. 1136; Faletra 2008) and the *Alliterative Morte D'Arthur* (late fourteenth or early fifteenth century).[10] While the modern fairy tale discards the complex political world of these medieval narratives, it retains the monsters, the dragons, giants, and trolls who threaten towns and maidens, and against which the hero tests his worth.

Faerie Adventures

While the hero and monster tradition has its roots in what Tolkien calls the Northern Imagination, faerie adventures find theirs in Welsh and Irish tales of the otherworld, such as those found in the four branches of *The Mabinogi* and the tales of Bran and Cuchulain (see Davies 2008). In these tales, the hero, either deliberately or accidentally, leaves behind the "real" world and enters into the realm of Faerie, where he (and, in the medieval texts it is almost always he) encounters a series of wonders and marvels, giants and enchantresses; his adventures in this realm test (and prove) his worth, allowing him to return triumphantly to court, usually in possession of a wife and a fortune. These adventures lie at the heart of Arthurian romance, beginning with Chrétien de Troyes' twelfth-century French narratives (*Cliges, Lancelot or The Knight of the Cart, Yvain or the Knight of the Lion, Erec and Enid* and *Perceval*; see Staines 1991; Figure 0.3).

The fact that these romances were adapted and translated into Welsh, English, German, and Dutch, along with the long history of more popular versions of both Chrétien's tales and the faerie adventures of new heroes (such as the Middle English *Adventures of Arthur* and *Lybeaus Desconus*, itself a version of the French tale, *Le Bel Inconnu,* and the various versions of *Sir Gawain and the Green Knight*), speaks to the incredible popularity this genre enjoyed in the Middle Ages as the tales extended across class and linguistic borders (see Aronstein 2012; McDonald 2004; Radulescu and Rushton 2009). These tales of faerie adventures, for the medieval audiences, provided a testing ground for their chivalric heroes, a place where they could prove their worth, at the same time that their faerie forests challenged (and usually proved) the values of the courtly world. Post-medieval fairy-tale heroes still venture into

FIGURE 0.3: Perceval's adventures. Bibliothèque nationale de France, MS Francais 113, fol. 156v (1470[?]). Bibliothèque nationale de France, with permission.

enchanted forests, and their adventures there still prove their worth; however, in these tales, the human world the hero leaves behind is further removed from the "real" world of the audience; its castles and knights are themselves made of fairy tales.

Fairy Mistresses

If tales of faerie adventures affirm the courtly and chivalric values of their mortal courts, tales of fairy mistresses both critique and disrupt that court. Take, for example, the tale of Sir Lanval, first found in Marie de France's twelfth-century *lai* and translated into Norse and Middle English (see Waters 2018). Leaving the court impoverished and in despair, Lanval encounters beautiful women who summon him to meet their mistress, a fairy queen who is beautiful and rich beyond compare; she offers Lanval herself, riches, and status, on the condition that he keep her very existence secret. And, even though Lanval violates this condition, she returns to him and whisks him away from the corrupt court to live happily ever after. For Lanval, and others (like the anonymous knight in the Chaucer's *Wife of Bath's Tale*), fairy mistresses are the means of the ultimate wish fulfillment; they provide their chosen humans with everything they lack in the "real" world.[11] As such, they are the ancestresses of both d'Aulnoy's powerful fairy queens and the multiple gift-bestowing fairies and elves of the post-medieval fairy tale.

Fairy mistresses in the medieval world, however, can be more problematic; they can lure a hero, such as Thomas the Rhymer, to a dark fate, or bedazzle, tempt, and ensnare him, as do the many fairies/demons that hapless knights encounter in the faerie forests of Arthurian romance, all intent on seduction and destruction.[12] They can also entrap kings, granting power and profit, endowing their descendants with an ambiguous heritage, desirable and demonic, as we see in the fourteenth-century political romances of *Melusine* and, more darkly, in the romance *Richard, the Lion-Heart* (see Urban, Kemmis, and Ridley Elmes 2017, 2020; Wade 2011: 109–46; Williams 2018: 58, 60–1). These fairy mistresses also continue into the modern fairy tale, often translated to witches and sorceresses, such as the Wicked Queen in "Snow White," whose apparent outward beauty veils their true, haggish nature.

Fairy Lovers

Fairy lovers, like fairy mistresses, threaten the established order; however, while fairy mistresses can be benign, and indeed are the prototype for the helpful fairies of later tales, fairy lovers—that is the fairy kings who come to mortal women, always threaten the human world. Even in Marie de France's *Yonec*, where the fairy lover appears when the princess in the tower calls for him, loves her, frees her, and through their son, provides her with belated vengeance on her tyrannical husband, that very act embodies the threat fairy lovers pose to the patriarchal order. In Marie, this threat clearly functions as a wish-fulfillment fantasy, but in most tales of fairy lovers, it's not love and escape the fairy knight offers but seduction and rape, often leaving behind sons of mixed heritage, who struggle to find their place in the human world. In those, such as *Sir Orfeo* and *Sir Degare*, where women encounter fairies in the forest, the line between fairy and demon lover is thin indeed. While darker modern fairy-tale retellings, such as Susannah Clark's *Jonathan Strange and Mr. Norrell* (2004) and Sarah J. Maas's *Court of Thorns and Roses* series (2015–17) adapt this medieval motif, in most modern fairy tales, if it exists at all, it's as a subplot to the hero's own journey, in which he rescues the maiden from fairy enchantment.

TOWARD A CULTURAL HISTORY OF THE FAIRY TALE IN THE MIDDLE AGES

The same questions that plague scholars of the post-medieval fairy tale complicate any attempt to pin down the cultural history of the medieval fairy tale. First, as we can see from the above, there is the question of genre. If we limit our definition of the fairy tale to short narratives, with magic, that lead to a happily ever after, not only are we left with only a handful of tales but also those tales themselves seem to lack that essential sense of "faerie" first proposed by Tolkien. Beyond that, there is the vast difference between the Northern monster tales and the Celtic otherworld narratives, between Arthurian romances and tales of dangerous fairy mistresses, enchanted kingdoms and hellish realms. Then, there is the ever-vexed question of origins, complicated by the tendency, inherited from the Brothers Grimm, to value the oral over the written. Tales traveled in the Middle Ages; they moved with invading armies, displaced populations, brides, pilgrims, and traders; manuscripts, scribes, and storytellers were also on the move, and a story told or written in the Levant could appear first in Venice and then in England. Stories also traveled between languages: Welsh to French and back again, French to German, Latin to English, Arabic to Italian to English, Spanish to Arabic, French to Hebrew—the list could (and does) go on. They moved from oral, to written, and back again, as they traveled up and down the class structures and through all levels of society.[13]

As they did so, medieval fairy tales, like all fairy tales, adapted themselves to their cultural moment, each version of the tale returning to an enchanted past to explore the wishes, desires and fears of their present. And while no volume can possibly capture the vast array of tales told across the six centuries we typically designate as "medieval," in the following chapters, you will find an introduction to these tales, one that will give you a glimpse of the richness and variety of the ways writers in the medieval past themselves returned to an enchanted once upon a time, as well as an exploration of what individual tales can tell us about magic and wonder, power and gender, identity and anxiety, tales and tellers in the Middle Ages.

CHAPTER ONE

Forms of the Marvelous

Fairy Stories, or Stories about Fairies?

RICHARD FIRTH GREEN

The conviction that our ancestors were more attuned to the supernatural (or less charitably, more open to superstition) than we are ourselves may well be universal: the idea that in some primaeval period we walked and talked with gods is at least as old as the *Book of Genesis*. There must once have been a world, we seem to feel, where natural and supernatural could exist side by side, a world before the eating of an apple initiated not only the knowledge of good and evil but also a profound separation of the human and the divine. For the sociologist Max Weber and the historian Keith Thomas, however, the disenchantment of the modern world began rather more recently than Eden, with the Protestant Reformation. For them, medieval people might still be imagined as inhabiting what Weber, writing of Eastern religions, called the "great enchanted garden in which the practical way to orient oneself, or to find security in this world or the next, was to revere or coerce the spirits" ([1922] 1956: 270). And, in medieval Europe, not all such spirits were Christian; many people evidently believed that the caves, forests, and lakes that surrounded them were populated by a quite different order of beings. The attitude of official culture (that is to say, the attitude of the church) to such beings—they went by a multitude of names, though we shall simply refer to them here by the generic term "fairies"—was far from tolerant, and as we shall see, there were forces at work uprooting their corner of the great enchanted garden long before Luther.

Nevertheless, there can be no question that the sixteenth and seventeenth centuries witnessed a paradigm shift. "Divers writers report," wrote Reginald Scot, a celebrated fairy skeptic, in 1584, "that in *Germanie*, since Luthers time, spirits and divels have not personallie appeared, as in times past they were woont to doo" (1972: 87); and the readers for whom Scot's contemporary, Edmund Spenser, composed his *Fairie Queene* evidently no longer regarded fairies as, to borrow M. W. Latham's term, "credible entities" (1930: 13). As Jacques Le Goff puts it, they were merely "aesthetically resuscitated" (*récupérées esthétiquement*), and their beauty had become, in a phrase he borrows from Michel de Certeau, "the beauty of the dead" (*la beauté du mort*) (1985: 106). Around 1620, then, when Richard Corbett, a future Anglican Bishop of Norwich, wrote his delightful poem, "The Faeryes Farewell," it must have been quite clear to most members of civil society that fairies were mere products of the imagination:[1]

> By which wee note the *Faries*
> Were of the old Profession;
> Theyre Songs were *Ave Maryes*;
> Theyre Daunces were *Procession*.
> But now, alas, they all are dead,
> Or gone beyond the Seas,
> Or Farther for Religion fled,
> Or elce they take theyre Ease.
>
> (1955: 51; italics in the original)

Fairy beliefs continued to live on in the English countryside, of course, and Corbett ends his poem with a charming tip of the hat to one "old *William Chourne* ... of Stafford Shire" (about whom almost nothing is known):

> To *William* all give Audience,
> And pray yee for his Noddle,
> For all the *Faries* Evidence
> Were lost, if that were Addle.
>
> (1955: 52; italics in the original)

"It seems that commentators have always attributed [fairies] to the past," writes Keith Thomas (1971: 726), and he traces this tendency back as far as the opening lines of Geoffrey Chaucer's *Wife of Bath's Tale* (lines 857–64):

> In th' olde dayes of the Kyng Arthour,
> Of which that Britons speken greet honour,
> Al was this land fulfild of fayerye*.   **filled with marvels*
> The elf-queene, with hir joly compaignye,
> Daunced ful ofte in many a grene mede*.   *meadow

> This was the olde opinion*, as I rede*;   *belief   *read
> I speke of manye hundred yeres ago.
> But now kan no man se none elves mo*.   *any more elves
>
> (Chaucer 1987: 116a)

But it is important to note that Chaucer's passage is doing a very different kind of cultural work than that of Corbett. Corbett's fairies were, in a very real sense, in the past; Chaucer's (however convenient it may have been to pretend otherwise) were not. Moreover, Corbett's fairy nostalgia draws, however lightly, upon Protestant antipathy to the perceived superstition of the old religion; the Wife of Bath, by contrast, is claiming that her fairies have been exterminated at the end of a drawn-out battle with that very same religion. Throughout the length and breadth of England, she says, there is not a single room—from the halls and chambers of the nobility to the humblest cow barn and dairy—that has not been blessed (in other words, decontaminated) by a horde of holy friars; it is this that "maketh that ther ben no fayeryes" (line 872).

What has changed in the two centuries between these two passages is the degree to which people believed in the very existence of fairies. Corbett could assume skepticism on the part of his readers (though evidently not in William Chourne and his friends); Chaucer, on the other hand, lived in a world in which for many people (and not just not old wives like Alice of Bath) fairies remained credible entities (though as a skeptic he himself was something of an exception). Such belief is very difficult to document directly since the literate were understandably reluctant to express an opinion on the matter, and the nonliterate rarely had the chance to record views of any sort. In fact, I know of only one such record. In the first stage of her trial in Rouen, Joan of Arc was questioned about her attendance at the springtime festivities around a "fairy tree" near her village; she replied "qu'elle ne veit jamais fee, *qu'elle saiche*" ("that she had never seen a fairy, *as far as she knew*"), but "a ouy dire a une nomme Jhenne, femme du maire de la ville de Dompremy, sa marraine, *qu'elle les avoit veues la*" ("she'd heard Jeanne, the mayor's wife and her own godmother, say that *she had seen them there*") (Tisset 1960: 66; my emphases).

On the literate side of the fence, we meet clerical authorities who are keen to add authenticating details to their stories of fairy sightings. Thus, when Walter Map tells the story of a man called Eadric the Wild who married a beautiful fairy bride, he feels obliged to add that she was seen by William the Conqueror, as if mention of this royal witness added credibility to his story (Map 1983: 156–7). So too, William of Newburgh tells of a drunken Yorkshireman who stumbled upon a fairy feast and managed to get away with a valuable drinking vessel. William informs us that he himself had visited the spot where the feast was said to have taken place, and he relates the subsequent history of the goblet in detail (it was given to Henry I, later passed on to King David of Scotland, and finally returned to Henry II)—again, evidence that he wished to be taken at his word (William of Newburgh 1988: 119–20). William was certainly no credulous chronicler—he is famous for having doubted the existence of King Arthur, for instance (35)—so such efforts to authenticate his story suggest that fairy belief remained an open question in his day. In the later Middle Ages at least one writer, Jean d'Arras, Chaucer's contemporary and the author of *Mélusine*, is prepared to defend explicitly the idea of fairies as credible entities: "*Et croy que les merveilles qui sont par universel terre et monde sont les plus vrayes, comme les choses dictes faees comme de pluseurs autres*" ("And I believe that the marvels that are found throughout the land and the whole world are the most true, such as so-called fairy activities and many others") (d'Arras 2003: 112).

To show that people believed in fairies is rather easier than to say what precisely it was they believed in. For one thing, local beliefs, orally circulated, must have been far more heterogeneous and unsystematic than our surviving written records tend to make them appear. Carlo Ginzburg's analysis of the trial records of those who believed in the *benandanti* (the "good walkers") in sixteenth- and seventeenth-century Friuli (northeastern Italy), for instance, shows us court officials going to great lengths to try to make sense of a host of confusing and self-contradictory witness statements. The first text to represent itself as something like an anthropologist's field report is the mid-fifteenth-century *Distaff Gospells*, and, before this, accounts of fairy activities, whether secular or religious, tend to be formulaic and derivative, but from them and narrative accounts we can piece together a generalized picture of medieval fairy beliefs. The physical appearance of medieval fairies differed in a number of ways from that of their early modern successors: they were always strikingly beautiful (except in those religious accounts that represent them as hideous devils). Their size was not noticeably smaller than that of their human neighbors; the fairy king who invites King Herla to his wedding feast in Walter Map's *Courtier's Trifles* is described as a pigmy, and Auberon (the ultimate model for Shakespeare's Oberon) in *Huon of Bordeaux* is child-sized, but there is nothing to suggest that either was thought of as typical. Certainly, nothing in the Middle Ages corresponds to the insect-scale fairies of Shakespeare's *Midsummer Night's Dream*, still less to the "little atomies" of Mercutio's Queen Mab speech in *Romeo and Juliet*. Unsurprisingly, then, medieval fairies are nowhere supplied with wings, although they might appear in a variety of colors (not always green), were able to change their shape, and could make themselves invisible. Most important of all, they were never, ever, cute; at best they are awe-inspiring, at worst downright terrifying, as the respectful tone of popular nomenclature implies; they are "the ladies from outside," "the fair folk," "the good neighbors." Their societies tended to mimic those of the human lifeworld (just like their feudal counterparts, medieval fairies attended dances and feasts, went hawking and hunting, even rode off to war), but in one respect their political structure appears to have been quite distinct: we hear far more of fairy queens, such as Morgan la Fée, than we do of fairy kings, and many medieval accounts leave us with the distinct impression of fairyland as a gynarchy. No doubt this was in large part because the local conduit for much fairy lore appears to have been female—particularly the "old wives" (e.g., Chaucer's Wife of Bath), whose tales were dismissed by hostile churchmen as the ravings of *aniles* and *vetulae* ("hags" and "crones"). Finally, medieval fairies played a far larger role in the everyday lives of ordinary people than they were to do later. Among other things, they might seduce them, father their children, abduct them, or steal their babies; they might reveal the future to them; they might furnish them with (or withhold from them) the benefits of wealth or good health; while they might lead them astray on their travels, or expose them to inclement weather, they might also (as with King Arthur's Avalon) offer them a refuge from suffering—even, perhaps, from death.

FAIRY BELIEF AND THE MEDIEVAL FAIRY TALE

This widespread medieval belief in fairies—or at least the willingness to entertain the idea that they might be credible entities—has important generic implications for our understanding of the fairy story; our horizon of expectation, as the *Rezeptionsästhetiker* (reception theorists) would say, has been profoundly distorted by post-medieval attitudes to fairies and the stories we tell about them. The *Oxford English Dictionary* gives two main definitions for the term "Fairy Tale" (possibly a calque on the French *conte de fées*): the first, whose earliest citation is 1635, is "a tale about fairies; a tale set in fairyland"; the second, dated only thirty-six years later, is "something resembling a fairy tale in being unreal or incredible" (OED Online 2020). The first of these, as the OED recognizes, has been watered down over time, and has come to refer more generally to tales "having folkloric elements or featuring fantastic or magical events or characters"—so much so, indeed, that, as Derek Brewer pointed out, "few actual fairies, of whatever kind, appear" in them (2003: 16). The second, by contrast, has retained its potency, and the OED quotes the *Atlanta Journal and Constitution* from 2011: "there are rules to what can be admitted as evidence, and ridiculous fairy tales and lies are not allowed!" (OED Online 2020). Thus, we have been conditioned by post-medieval attitudes to fairies to construe any story containing them as a literary fantasy, and we tend unreflectively to project such conditioning back upon our medieval ancestors. However, while modern fairy narratives, such as Sylvia Townsend Warner's *Kingdoms of Elfin* or Susanna Clarke's *Jonathan Strange and Mr. Norrel*, are conventionally assigned to the genre of fantasy fiction, it is far from clear that that is how their medieval forerunners should be read.

Francophone scholarship has been very much more diligent than its Anglophone counterpart when it comes to considering the formal role of the fantastic in medieval literature.[2] The key figure here is the structuralist, Tzvetan Todorov, whose *Introduction à la littérature fantastique* (*Introduction to the Literary Fantastic*, 1970) will serve to establish the ground rules—I will cite his French text rather than the somewhat flawed English translation (1975).[3] According to Todorov, the fantastic is an evanescent genre, occupying a shifting and unstable territory between the *le merveilleux* (the marvelous) on one side and *l'étrange* (the weird) on the other; or, rather more pragmatically, between experience of *le surnaturel accepté* (the supernatural-accepted) and the *le surnaturel expliqué* (the supernatural-explained) (1970: 47). Just as an explicable mystery would not be particularly mysterious, so, conversely, an everyday marvel would not be particularly marvelous. Readers of the fantastic are kept in a constant state of hesitation unless, or until, they are able either to account for the fantasy (in which case it becomes merely weird) or to meet it on its own terms (in which case it will be marvelous). The litmus paper in this experiment is always the degree to which the events in the story appear to conform, or can be made to conform, to the reader's own experience of the world. In other words, the fantastic text "obliges its readers to consider the world of its characters as a world of living human beings and to vacillate between a natural and a supernatural explanation of the events related" (37). It follows, then, that, from the perspective of their enchanted garden, medieval readers and listeners would have been far more prepared than we are to welcome the supernatural-accepted and predisposed to favor the marvelous over the fantastic. And indeed Todorov himself, in a rare foray from the synchronic into the diachronic, suggests that the true literary fantastic enjoyed only a comparatively brief flowering, from the end of the eighteenth century to the end of the nineteenth (174–5), its most gifted exponents including writers such as Edgar Allan Poe, H. P. Lovecraft, Henry James, and M. R. James. Emboldened by Todorov, Jacques Le Goff can confidently assert that in the medieval period "there was no fantastic" (1985: 37).

How is it then that one of the most substantial (it runs to over 1,100 pages) recent books on the supernatural in medieval French romance is titled *Aspects fantastiques de la littérature narrative médiévale* (*Fantastic Aspects of Medieval Narrative*, 1991)? Since its author, Francis Dubost, is well aware that his use of this terminology is controversial, his defense of it is worth considering. The fourth criterion by which Dubost distinguishes the medieval fantastic from the marvelous, and the one he regards as decisive, is that of the *illusion référentielle* (the appearance of conforming to reality) (1991: 133–6). What is at play in the fantastic narrative, he claims, is neither historical, social realism nor the truth of everyday experience, but its psychological and mythic substance. Like Todorov's, his fantastic seems to demand hesitation: "medieval narrative," he says, "oscillates between two kinds of writing, representation ...

and symbolisation" (134–5). The example he gives, from the French *Prose Lancelot*, concerns the hero's encounter with a white stag escorted by six lions in a magical forest, and Dubost juxtaposes a naturalistic marvel (the lions denying their own carnivorous nature) with a spiritual one (the stag as a symbol of Christ) (135–6). But Todorov would surely reject such a reading as fantastic on the grounds that it is purely allegorical: "if what we read describes a supernatural event yet fails to take the words literally but gives them a meaning which has nothing to do with the supernatural, it leaves no further room for the fantastic" (1970: 69). It is surely pointless to counter that Dubost is juxtaposing two modes of supernatural here, for his white stag/Christ figure clearly belongs to Todorov's category of the supernatural-explained. On the whole, Dubost's position appears to create more problems than it solves, and it seems safer to stick with more conventional accounts, such as Daniel Poirion's (1982), which regard the supernatural events of medieval romance as belonging solidly within the domain of *le merveilleux*.

Had Dubost been writing in an Anglophone context, he might of course have asked, with G. K. Chesterton (1930: 29), why the fantastic should only employ disturbing supernatural elements and never beneficent ones? In fact, it was just such a question that gave birth to the genre of fantasy as it is now understood in the Anglophone world, the genre of works such as C. S. Lewis's *Chronicles of Narnia*, J. R. R. Tolkien's *Lord of the Rings*, and J. K. Rowling's *Harry Potter* series. Yet, if none of these remotely conforms to Todorov's definition of the fantastic, neither, despite their authors' overt medievalism, do they truly return us the marvelous of medieval fairyland. Lewis's Narnia may bear a superficial resemblance to the world of the Lancelot-Graal cycle (Aslan as a version of the *Prose Lancelot*'s white stag), but, lacking any real access to the great enchanted garden, its fantasy can only seem escapist and its allegory contrived. By contrast, the medieval marvelous possessed an acknowledged materiality that kept it firmly within the ambit of the human lifeworld; it told not fairy tales but stories about fairies—credible beings whom one might actually encounter, as Joan of Arc's godmother attested, around a fairy tree.

"THEY BEN ALL DEUYLLS": THE CHURCH'S WAR AGAINST THE FAIRIES

I would not wish to give the impression that medieval people were excessively naïve or credulous (the pains taken by Walter Map and William of Newburgh to authenticate their tales suggests otherwise), but the room left for alternative explanations was clearly far more restricted in this period than it was later to become. Even Albert the Great, a comparatively empirical thinker, accepted the existence of natural phenomena that no modern empiricist would take seriously for a moment. For these chroniclers, fairies were a naturalistic marvel, which, considering Dubost's distinction between naturalistic and spiritual marvels, raises an interesting question: what role did the cultural elite, specifically the medieval church, play in shaping the way the marvelous (particularly the marvelous realm of fairyland) was understood? In church doctrine, the marvelous occupied a contested territory between the miraculous, on the one hand, and the diabolical, on the other. While churchmen would sometimes accept without question the existence of natural marvels beyond their ken—for instance in the Wonders of the East tradition (Friedman [1981] 2000)—closer to home they were always ready to demonize anything that could not be made to conform with orthodox doctrine. So it was with fairies. If direct evidence for the existence of fairy belief is difficult to document, the church's *Kulturkampf* (culture war) against it is not, and in fact the very presence of such a *Kulturkampf* is all the proof we need for the widespread medieval acceptance of fairies as credible entities. Since the church unquestionably believed in both devils and hell, it proved that it must have believed in fairies as well by its readiness to demonize them and infernalize their dwelling places, even if the spin it put on this belief was not one shared by ordinary people.

We see this spin in an early fourteenth-century version of a popular late eleventh-century theological *vade mecum* (handbook) called the *Elucidarium*, updated by French Dominicans as the *Second Lucidaire*. Here, from an early sixteenth-century English print, is what the *Second Lucidaire* has to say about fairies (interestingly, a topic on which the original *Elucidarium* had been silent):

> And vnto the regarde of the feyryes the which man sayth were wonte to be in tymes past, they were not men ne women naturalles *but were deuylles* the whiche shewed themselfe vnto the people of that tyme, for they were paynyms, ydolatres and without fayth. And the sayd feyryes chaunged theym into many fourmes, as of an hors or of a dogge or otherwyse, the which is impossyble vnto nature .... Wherfore thou mayst well thynke that theyse feyryes that in suche wyse shewid them in dyuers fourmes and k<yn>des ne were men ne women ne other thynge naturall, *but were deuylles* that in suche wyse shewed them and the whiche put them in theyr idolles and spake and sayd some thynges for to come by some coniectures as by the influences of the bodyes celestyalles; for otherwyse *the deuyll* hathe no knowledge of thynges for to come .... And in regarde of these [deed (dead)] and of these spirits and elues, and also of many other vysyons that men say that they se by nyght, *they ben often deuylles* that put theym in fourme of some deed body in faynyng his voyce to tempte the persone of some thynge .... But elues, and gobelyns and helquins the which men se by nyght, as men of armes trottynge on horsbacke with grete assembles, *they ben all deuylles* the whiche ben amonge vs, the whiche sheweth them in suche a fourme and in many other fourmes ... for to tempte the man of some vyce and for to make hym erre in the faythe.
>
> (Morrison 2013: 53–5; my emphasis)

The list of fairy activities mentioned here (shape-shifting, fortune-telling, associating with the dead, and riding to war) is far from exhaustive, and indeed its omission of three of the commonest—abducting mortals, having sex with them, and stealing their children—is somewhat surprising. However, there is no mistaking the author's determination to impress upon his audience the essentially demonic nature of fairies (Figure 1.1).

The *Second Lucidaire*'s position on fairies is entirely conventional. William of Auvergne, bishop of Paris in the early thirteenth century, devotes a lengthy section of his encyclopedia, *De Universo (On the Universe)*,[4] to "*hiis substantiis, quae apud Graecos cacodemones & diaboli, apud nos vero maligni spiritus communiter nominantur*" ("those bodies called by the Greeks 'demons' and 'devils' but by us generally, 'evil spirits'"), and in it he spends a surprising amount of time discussing popular superstitions, including the belief in fairies (William of Auvergne 1624: 1.1015). Here is a typical passage, which comes from a section in which William is discussing the ways in which the names of demons match their natures:

> *Sic & doemon, qui praetextu mulieris cum aliis de nocte domos & cellaria dicitur frequentare, vocant eam Satiam a satietate, & et Dominam Abundantia pro abundantia quam eam praestare dicunt domibus quas frequentaverit. Hujusmodi etiam doemones, quas dominas vocant vetulae, penes quas error iste remansit, & a quibus solis creditur & somniatur, dicunt has dominas edere & bibere de escis & potibus, quos in domibus inveniunt.*

> (So, too, they call the demon who is said, with others, to visit houses and cellars by night in the likeness of a woman, Satia, from satiety, and Lady Abundance, because of the abundance they say she confers on the houses that she has visited. Also, old wives (amongst whom this error persists and by whom alone it is believed and dreamed up) call demons of this kind Ladies, and they say these ladies eat the food and drink the beverage which they find in the houses.)

> (1624: 1.1036)

Different in tone, but based on the same premise, is the final section of Thomas of Cantimpré's *Bonum Universale de Apibus* (*The Universal Good of Bees*, 1627), an allegorical depiction of the well-ordered society that ends with an account of various demons under the guise of wasps, hornets, and other noxious insects. Thomas is particularly fascinated by the demons who seduce monks and nuns, but he includes plenty of other fairy lore, including a description of a magic boulder in the Breton forest of Brocéliande with the power to summon up storms (this boulder also features in Chrétien de Troyes's romance *Yvain*). Thomas says that he had asked a fellow Dominican, Henry of Marsburg, for an explanation and was told it worked "*ministerio demonum, qui ad tempestates et pluvias aera possunt impellere et concitare cum volunt*" ("by the agency of demons who can

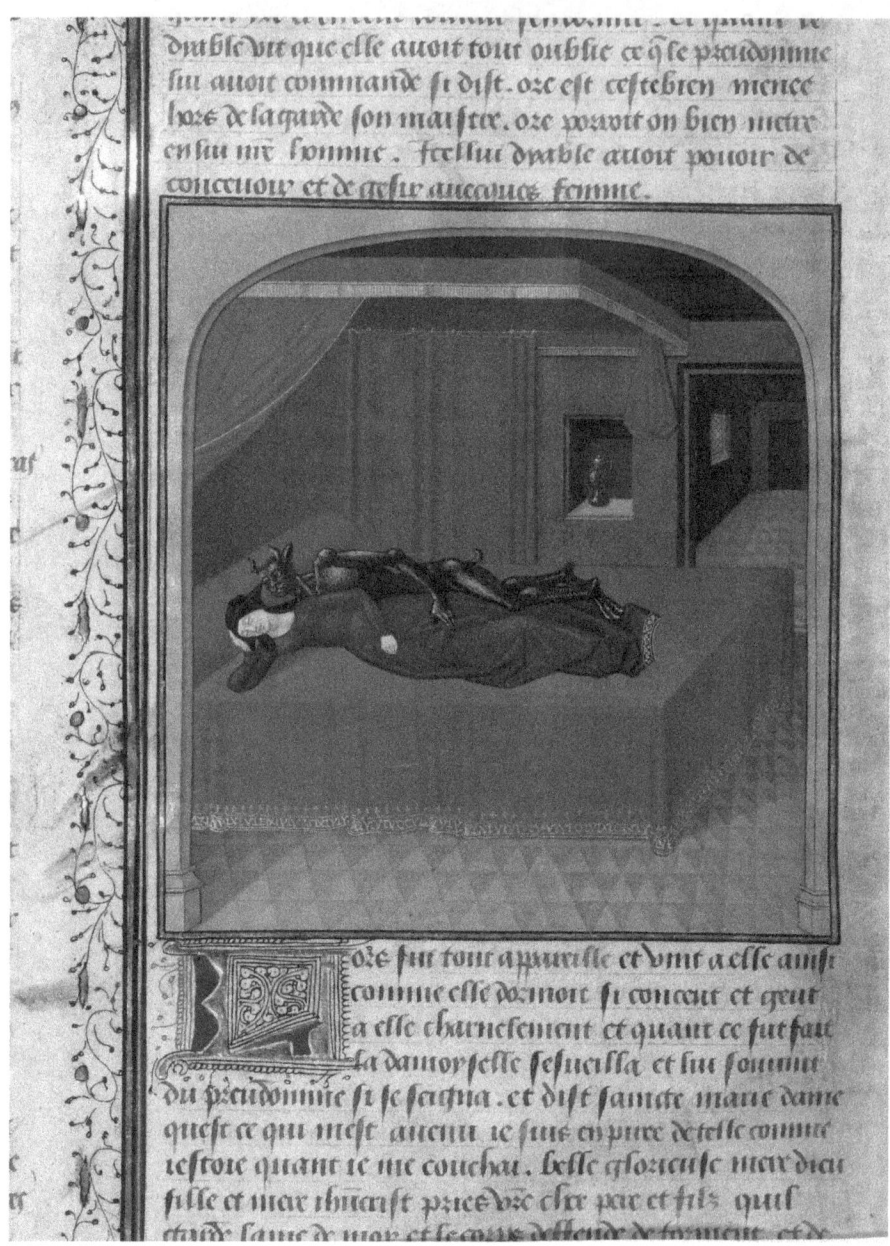

FIGURE 1.1: Merlin's mother is impregnated by a demon, from the *Lancelot-Graal*. Bibliothèque nationale de France MS Francais 96, fol. 62v (1450[?]–1455[?]). Bibliothèque nationale de France, with permission.

direct storms and stir up rainy weather"; Thomas of Cantimpré 1627: 560). Brocéliande was a famous haunt of fairies, and the fairies' ability to manipulate the weather was notorious.

The idea that fairies were really demons was not only disseminated in the learned treatises of schoolmen; we also find it reaching further down the social scale in pastoral manuals written for preachers and confessors. Local cunning men and women (the Middle English term for them was *tilsters*) often invoked fairy aid to effect cures, provide love spells, find lost objects, detect thieves, and so on, and whenever these manuals condemn such superstitious practices, they will generally treat them as a branch of *sortilegium* (literally, fortune-telling). Despite the etymological connection of the French word *fée* (fairy) with the Latin *fata* (the fates), divination (the root meaning of *sortilege*) seems to have played a relatively small part in medieval fairy lore; "in the image of the fairy," writes Laurence Harf-Lancner, "the erotic generally dominates the prophetic" (1984: 17). The offense most commonly condemned under the heading of *sortilegium* was the use of spells and charms.

For who-so be-leueth in the fay*	*believes in fairies
Mote* be-leue thus by any way:	*must
That hyt ys a sleghthe of the del*	*sleight of the devil
That maketh a body to cache el*.	*commit evil
... ...	
So wyth cha[r]mes & wyth tele*,	*spells
He ys i-broȝte aȝeyn to hele*.	*Hell

(Mirk 1974: 87–8)

Owst's (1957) survey of this literature is still useful, and there is a chapter on *sortilegium* in a convenient recent edition and translation of one such pastoral manual, Ranulph Higden's *Speculum Curatorum* (*Mirror for Curates*) (2012: 102–7).[5]

It is rare that we can gain much insight into the reaction of the common people to this clerical crusade against their traditional beliefs. However, one manual, the Dominican John Bromyard's *Summa Predicantium* (*Compendium of Preachings*), offers us a tantalizing glimpse into their intransigence. When it is pointed out to them that charms to recover stolen goods involve invoking the devil, Bromyard observes, "*dicunt non per diabolum, sed pulchrum populum, nec a diabolo didicimus talia nec ei credimus, sed pulchro populo*" ("they say that it is not [done] by the devil but the fair folk; and we have not learned such things from the devil, nor do we believe in him, but in the fair folk"; 1614: 375).

In the early fifteenth century, the Parisian theologian Jean Gerson, believed he detected an alarming increase in this belief in the fair folk, and, while he argued that this increase was driven principally by demonic deception (*ex daemonum suggestione et illusione*), he was in no doubt that one of its chief conduits was the literary discourse of fairyland; it arose, he said, "*ex lectione quorumdam Romanciorum id est librorum compositorum in Gallico, quasi poeticorum, de gestis militaribus, in quibus maxima pars fabulosa est, magis ad ingerendum quamdam novitatem & admirationem quam veritatis cognitionem*" ("from the reading of certain romances, that is books of so-called poetry composed in French about knightly deeds, of which the greatest part is fabrication, more for the sake of purveying novelty and wonder than the apprehension of the truth"; 1706: 1:206). Gerson is arguing that stories about fairies are not only fairy tales, in the sense of the OED's second definition—fantasies and lies—but also that these stories serve the devil's purposes.

Gerson's account also reveals how much of an uphill battle the church had on its hands as it struggled to eradicate its parishioners' belief in fairies; here we see how closely the late Middle Ages held skepticism and credulity in balance when it came to the phantasmic. In this, the period anticipates the post-Reformation process of disenchantment that was to generate the instabilities of Todorov's fantastic, playing a key role in the development of the fairy tale. If stories of fairies were ever truly, in Todorov's sense, fantastic (as opposed to being simply marvelous) it can only have been at the very end of the Middle Ages as the widespread belief in fairyland began to break down. Perhaps Jean d'Arras's *Mélusine*, a tale that, as we have seen, actually raises the question of fairies as credible entities, rather than the works of Poe and Lovecraft, would be a good place to start in the quest for the birth of the fantastic; it is certainly noteworthy that A. S. Byatt uses this story to evoke the late-Victorian gothic in her novel *Possession* (1990).

DISPLACEMENT, CENSORSHIP, AND DISGUISE: LATE MEDIEVAL FAIRY NARRATIVES

Writing his romance of *Mélusine* for a powerful patron like Jean, Duc de Berry, in the early 1390s, Jean d'Arras may have had little to worry about as he recounts his fairy narratives, but this was not true of all his contemporaries. Given the church's studied opposition to popular fairy beliefs, and what Gerson saw as the ideological bias of these late medieval "poetic concoctions" (*ex Poetarum confictione*), this period saw a significant shift in the ways in which authors told their stories about fairies. Even twelfth- and thirteenth-century writers, who seem to have felt relatively little embarrassment over clerical opposition to their material, often exiled fairies to distant lands—for instance, in *Draco Normanicus* (*The Norman Dragon*) Arthur's fairy kingdom is located in the Antipodes—and to distant times—Oberon in *Huon de Bordeaux* is the son of Julius Caesar—suggesting a measure of discomfort with the notion that fairies might seem to have a contemporary relevance. A particularly good example is the Middle English lay of *Sir Orfeo*, which not only grafts its tale of fairy abduction onto the classical legend, but also, after telling us that Orfeo was king of Thrace, adds the charming detail that "Winchester was cleped tho (then called) / Traciens with-outen no (without doubt)" (Bliss 1966: 6). While offering us relatively uncensored accounts of the fairy world, other brief *lais féeriques* (fairy lays) of the High Middle Ages show similar signs of such displacement, for instance in the "Lai de Guingamor": "*En Bretaingne ot.I. roi jadis*" ("once upon a time there was a king in Brittany"; Micha 1992: 64). However, in some other respects authors and storytellers display a degree of open resistance to the dominant culture; the contrast between Chrétien de Troyes and Paien de Maisieres offers us a particularly striking instance. Chrétien is typically circumspect, revealing a habitual "uneasiness with folkloric beings" (Carasso-Bulow 1976: 83): Melegeant's carrying off Guinevere to the land of Gorre in the *Chevalier de la charrette* (*The Knight of the Cart*), for instance, is clearly modeled on a tale about fairy abduction, yet, despite some obvious manifestations of the marvelous (as with the famous sword bridge that Lancelot must cross to enter it) Gorre is never acknowledged to be fairyland,[6] though Vivian, the lady of the lake, who had raised Lancelot, is once mentioned as a *fee* (Figure 1.2). In marked contrast, the *Mule sans frein* (*The Mule with no Bridle*), by the aptly named Paien (Pagan) de Maisieres, abounds in fairy marvels and looks as if it may have been meant to make fun of Chrétien's (Christian's) characteristic wariness.

By the fourteenth century, however, there is clear evidence that writers were becoming more guarded as increasingly insistent expressions of clerical disapproval throughout the fourteenth and fifteenth centuries drove those who wrote about fairies to ever more elaborate expedients in their efforts to deflect criticism. At one extreme we find romances where supernatural forces, even ones that clearly reflect fairy conventions, are represented as diabolical, and at the other, characters who are treated as completely human, even when they exhibit behavior we would normally associate with the fairies. Writers might try to pass off supernatural events as instances of natural magic and replace the machinations of fairies with the ingenuity of astronomers and magicians. Or they might classicize their fairy stories, throwing as it were a learned *cordon sanitaire* around them by substituting nymphs, pans, and satyrs for *fées* and elves. Finally, they might express skepticism about the very existence of fairies and present them as merely amusing figments of the imagination, vehicles for aesthetic exploitation, a move that anticipates our modern perception of them. Such self-censorship might even extend to humble scribes, who were not, on occasion, above bowdlerizing texts whose fairy implication they found objectionable.

The changing ideological imperative is well exemplified by two so-called Breton lays, one French from around 1200 and the other English from two

FIGURE 1.2: The infant Lancelot being taken away by the fairy Vivien, from the *Lancelot-Graal*. Bibliothèque nationale de France, MS Francais 113, fol. 156v (1470[?]). Bibliothèque nationale de France, with permission.

hundred or so years later. The numerous formal parallels between the *Lai de Tydorel* and *Sir Gowther* were pointed out many years ago (Ravenel 1905), but their full cultural significance has remained unexplored.[7] In *Tydorel*, a queen of Brittany, after ten years of happy but childless marriage, is seduced by a handsome knight who lives on the far side of a wide lake deep in a forest (Micha 1992: 152–79). While this knight is never explicitly said to be a fairy, his non-human nature is mentioned more than once, and the first child (Tydorel), begotten from his liaison with the queen, betrays his fairy paternity by his inability to sleep at night. The relationship continues happily for more than twenty years and results in a second child, a daughter; it only ends when the couple are surprised in bed by an old knight, and the fairy lover returns to his homeland for good. The king, however, never learns of his wife's love affair and complacently leaves the kingdom in the hands of her half-fairy son on his death. Tydorel rules the land with conspicuous justice for ten years, but when he learns the secret of his paternity from his mother, he too disappears, leaving to join his otherworldly father, and he too is never to be seen again. Although it makes little of it, the *lai* hints at a fairy foundation myth (like *Mélusine*) when Tydorel's half-fairy sister marries a Breton count of Brittany and gives birth to two sons called Conan and Alan (both traditional first names for the historical Dukes of Brittany).

The author of *Sir Gowther* says that he had long studied "a la[y] of Breyten" (Brittany) before composing his own tale, and if this lay was not *Tydorel* itself, it must have been one very similar to it, such as some precursor to the Norman legend about Robert le Diable (Mills 1973: 148–68).[8] Instead of a story about fairy seduction with a happy outcome, however, here we are given a tale of demonic miscegenation resulting in social mayhem, only terminated through the assistance of the pope. The Duchess of Austria, trapped in an unhappy and childless marriage, has her ill-considered prayer for pregnancy answered by a "felturd fend" (shaggy fiend) who, in a manner reminiscent of the begetting of King Arthur, "As lyke hur lorde as he myght be— / He leyd hur down undur a tre." This union is never repeated, but its monstrous progeny (Sir Gowther) wreaks havoc throughout the duchy until, on learning of his paternity from his mother, he is miraculously converted. Gowther sets off for Rome to confess his sins to the pope, and only after a lengthy period of atonement can he return to his homeland, learn to rule wisely, and finally receive a Christian burial.

The contrast between these two fairy/demon offspring, then, is dramatic. When the King of Brittany dies,

De Tydorel firent seignor.
Onques n'orent eü meillor,
tant preu, tant cortois, tant vaillant,
tant large, ne tant despendant,

ne miex tenist em pes la terre;
nus ne li osa fere guerre.
De puceles ert molt amez
e de dames molt desirrez,
li sien l'amoient et servoient,
e li estrangé le cremoient.

(They made Tydorel their lord.
They never had a better,
nor one so gallant, courteous, brave,
generous, and open-handed,
nor one who better kept the peace of the land
so that no one dared make war upon him.
Much loved by maidens
and desired by ladies,
his people loved and served him,
and outsiders feared him.)

(Micha 1992: 164)

Gowther, on the other hand, institutes a reign of terror as soon as he becomes Duke of Austria. In addition to indiscriminate rape and murder, he takes particular pleasure in pushing friars off cliffs and setting fire to hermits and widows:

All that ever on Cryst con lefe*,	*believed in Christ
Yong and old, he con hom greve*	*afflicted them
In all that he myght doo.	
Meydyns' maryage wolde he spyll*	*he ruined virgins' marriages
And take wyffus ageyn hor wyll*,	*raped married women
And sley hor* husbandus too.	*slew their
And make frerus to leype at kraggus*	*friars leap off precipices
And persons* forto heng on knaggus*,	*priests *hooks
And odur prestys sloo*.	*slew
To bren armettys* was is* dyssyre:	*burn hermits *his
A powre wedow to seyt on fyre,	
And werke hom mykyll woo*.	*cause them much misery.

(Mills 1973: 153)

The church's campaign to demonize fairies clearly underlies the evolution from beneficent Tydorel to diabolical Gowther, and this campaign found a willing ally in medieval misogyny, as well as the period's regimen of patrilineal inheritance. It was not just in relation to church doctrine about the demonic nature of fairies that medieval fairy tales reveal their subversive side; a feminist bias, distinctly in contrast to the church's teachings about the role and nature of women, also lies at the very heart of the medieval fairy tradition. In Chaucer's *Wife of Bath's Tale*, a rapist knight must be taught his lesson by his shape-shifting fairy bride, and even as late as Shakespeare, Oberon can only best Titania by the use of magic. In this tradition, the fairy influence in Tydorel's world is not only generally benign but also strongly feminized. The queen of Brittany falls in love with her handsome fairy visitor and spends twenty guiltless years in an adulterous relationship with him; moreover, it is through her daughter's marriage to the Count of Brittany that this fairy good fortune is perpetuated throughout the land. By contrast, Sir Gowther's world is a world of men. Gowther is forced to confront the question of his paternity by an old earl, a pope gives him his penance, and he receives absolution only after fighting for a Christian emperor against the sultan; moreover, he arranges for his guilt-stricken widowed mother to marry the earl, and though he himself marries the emperor's daughter, we hear nothing of their begetting an heir together.

While *Sir Gowther* demonizes the fairies of his source text, other medieval adaptors simply write the fairy out of their narratives, a self-censorship that can be detected in a popular fifteenth-century romance called *Thomas of Ercledoune*. Thomas seduces a beautiful woman he encounters on a hillside in the Scottish borderlands, and finds himself carried off by her to a distant country where she rules as queen; after a three-year sojourn (which seems like a mere three days to Thomas himself) he is returned to Scotland, where he discovers he has acquired the gift of prophesy. This story was still being recalled by ballad-singers in the nineteenth century and the version of "Thomas the Rhymer" printed by Walter Scott in his *Minstrelsy of the Scottish Borders* makes it abundantly clear that Thomas's abductress is the fairy queen and the land she takes him to is fairyland. Even if this version, supplied to Scott by the celebrated Mrs. Anna Brown of Falkland, has been adulterated,[9] its underlying fairy motifs are unmistakable, yet remarkably none of the five medieval manuscripts of its original, *Thomas of Ercledoune*, ever uses the actual words *elf* or *fairy*. Where, for example, the ballad says explicitly, "I am but the queen of fair Elfland, / And I'm come here for to visit thee" (Child 2001: 436), the earlier romance had simply read, "I am of a nothere contre, / Thowgh I be perlyd (apparelled) moste in pryce" (Nixon 1980: 33). And so, too, the ballad's splendid quatrain,

> And see not ye that bonny road,
> Which winds about the fernie brae?
> That is the road to fair Elfland,
> Whe[re] you and I this night maun gae*.   **must go*
> (Child 2001: 437)

turns out to derive from some variant of the romance's

> Seist thou yonder that fayre castell.
> That standyth hye upon that hyll?

> Of townys and towris it berys the bell*, *wins the prize
> On erthe is lyk non other tyll*. *nothing like it
>
> (Nixon 1980: 43)

—a much less pointed topographical reference.

It is even possible to demonstrate such bowdlerization occurring at a scribal level. In the romance of *Sir Degaré*, when the hero's father encounters his mother-to-be deep in the woods, an early-fourteenth-century manuscript (Edinburgh, Advocates MS 19.2.1) gives his first speech to her as,

> Damaisele, welcome mote thou be*! *be thou welcome
> Be thou afered of none wihȝte*; *fear no (strange) creature
> *Ich* am comen here a fairi knyȝte.* *I
> Mi kynde* is armes for to were, *nature
> On horse to ride with scheld* and spere; *shield
> Forthi* afered be thou nowt. *therefore.
>
> (Schleich 1929: 62; my emphasis)

However, the same passage in a fifteenth-century manuscript (Oxford, Bodley MS, Rawlinson Poetry 34) reads:

> Madame,   God the see*; *God preserve you
> Be noughtt adrad*, thou swete wyght*, *afraid *you sweet thing
> *Y am come to the* as a knyght;* [my italics] *thee
> My kynd* ys armys for to bere, *nature
> On horss to ryde wyth scheld and spere,
> Be dradd* of me ryght noughtt*. *afraid *not at all

A similar suppression occurs in another fifteenth-century manuscript of the poem (Cambridge, University MS Ff. II. 38). There can be little doubt that the Rawlinson scribe (or an intermediate scribe in the textual tradition) has deliberately bowdlerized this passage: not only is the reference to fairyland suppressed but also the knight now greets the lady in God's name. Lest we should be tempted to attribute this to a simple scribal slip, a few lines later, when the lady abandons her newborn child, she furnishes him with a suitable identification token. In the Advocates MS this is "a paire of gloues / That here lemman [lover] here sent *of fairi londe*,"[10] but in the Rawlinson MS this has become a simple "peyr of glovys / Hur lemman to hur for to sonde" (Schleich 1929: 68; my emphasis).

Clerical pressure on the humbler, often anonymous, composers of popular romance is one thing, but there are even signs that more refined courtly writers were conscious of it. Of course, not all of them were interested in what Dryden was to call "the fairy way of writing"—Chaucer, for instance, was clearly skeptical about the very existence of fairies—but those who were, could always neutralize opposition by resorting to the classical world. That the demi-gods, the nymphs and fauns who inhabited the Greek and Roman countryside were really demons had been early established by writers such as Augustine and Cassian, but for Christian writers in the later Middle Ages they nonetheless offered a useful vehicle for exploring the marvelous with less risk of incurring clerical disapproval. Their appearance offers us an early instance of Le Goff's "aestheticization" of the fairy world.

An association of classical nymphs and fauns with actual fairies was readily made. In Guillaume de Machaut's *Fontaine Amoureuse* (*The Lovers' Spring*), for instance, Venus and Cupid are shown constructing an ornamental fountain in order that

> *les nimphes et les fees*
> *Y faisoient leurs assamblees*
> *Et qu'encor souvent y venoient*
> *Et leur parlement y tenoient,*
> *Leurs gieus, leurs festes, leurs caroles*
> *Et leurs amoureuses escoles*

> (the nymphs and the fairies
> might make their gatherings there,
> and come there often
> to hold their parliaments,
> their games, their feasts, their dances,
> and their courts of love.)

(Machaut 1921: 193)

When Stephen Scrope came to translate Christine de Pizan's *Epistre Othea* (*Letter of Othea*) in mid-fifteenth-century England, he regularly rendered *nymph* as *fairy* (Figure 1.3). "*Galathee fu une nimphe ou une deesse*," writes Christine (de Pizan 1999: 283), which Scrope renders as "Galathe was a fairye and a goddess" (1970: 73); and when Acteon sees Diana bathing naked "*avironnee de nimphes et deesses qui la servoient*" (de Pizan 1999: 296), Scrope writes that she was "envirouned with feiriys and goddesses the which serued hir" (1970: 83). Indeed, the association between classical nymphs and contemporary fairies was evidently so widespread in the late Middle Ages that in *De Genealogia deorum* (*On the Genealogy of the Gods*), Boccaccio feels obliged to deny any such connection. At the end of a long section on "Nymphs in General" (*De nymphis in generali*), he writes somewhat disingenuously: "*Quod et si claro homini atque erudito plurimum credi possit, non sic propterea deliris mulierculis et agrestibus ignaris asserentibus absque rubore vultus se ex fontibus formosissimas mulieres, quas ipsae Lammias vocant, prodeuntes vidisse*" ("Even if much of this may be believed by famous and learned men, it owes nothing to the silly young girls and ignorant rustics who report without blushing that they have seen the most beautiful women, whom they themselves

FIGURE 1.3: Diana and her nymphs, from Christine de Pizan's *l'Epître d'Othéa*. Bibliothèque nationale de France, MS Francais 606, fol. 13 (1407–9). Bibliothèque nationale de France, with permission.

call fairies, emerging from springs"; Boccaccio 1951: 349). Ironically, Boccaccio had earlier written a classicized fairy tale, *Il ninfale fiesolano* (*The Nymph of Fiesole*) (1960), himself.

In this regard, the comparison between Geoffrey Chaucer and his friend John Gower is instructive. Gower evidently felt attracted to the fairy way of writing (Lewis [1936] 1958: 204), and he recognized that the classical demi-gods offered him a handy vehicle for expressing it. In his *Tale of Narcissus*, for example, when the hero sees his face reflected in pool: "He sih the like of his visage, / And wende ther were an ymage / Of such a nimphe as tho was faie" ("he saw the reflection of his face and thought he saw the image of the kind of nymph that was a fairy in those days"; Gower 1900–1901: 1:98)—an allusion to the proverbial beauty of medieval fairies (Rieger 1994).[11] Throughout the *Confessio Amantis* (*The Lover's Confession*) Gower exploits the nymph/fairy playing up the motifs traditionally associated with both nymphs and fairies, such as springs and woodlands. For instance, "Nimphes of the welles" (Gower 1900–1901: 1:99) help to bury the dead Narcissus; Acteon surprises Diana bathing naked, "with many a nimphe, which hire serveth" (45); Acis, at the prayer of Galathea (only identified as a nymph in the Latin sidenote, not in the text), is "into a welle / Transformed, as the bokes telle, / With freisshe stremes and with cliere" (135); Calistona seeks to protect her virginity by taking refuge with "wodemaydes" and "with the nimphes ek also / Upon the spring of freisshe welles" (Gower 1900–1: 2:117); and even in the story of the comic Faunus whose absurd obsession with Hercules's lover, Eolen, is the reason "That he forsok the nimphes alle" (135). When Gower provides us with a lengthy account of the classical cult of satyrs and nymphs in book five of the *Confessio Amantis* (1900–1: 1:438–39), he seems to be making a conscious attempt to dissociate his own fairy way of writing from any kind of contemporary experience.

Chaucer, by contrast, was evidently a fairy non-believer, and rather than classicizing the genre, he dismisses it. Indeed, it is tempting to see Chaucer's incongruous introduction of Pluto, "kyng of Fayerye," along with his wife Proserpyna, into the *Merchant's Tale* (1987: 166a) as a parody of this convention (the French fabliaux that provided him with a model occasionally feature fairies—as in *Le Chevalier qui fist parler les cons* [*The Knight who could make vaginas speak*] and *Le Mantel mautaillé* [*The Badly-cut cloak*]—but never classical gods and goddesses). He makes his old wives' tale (the tale told by Alice of Bath) a story of fairy transformation; in his tale of *Sir Thopas* he openly mocks the fairy themes to be found in popular romance; and in a tale that its teller, the Franklin, describes as a Breton Lay (in other words, a *lai féerique*), Chaucer attributes its central marvel to natural, not fairy, magic (Chaucer 1987: 183a). He even expresses skepticism about the very existence of that great magnet for fairy legends, the court of King Arthur: "This storie is also trewe, I undertake," says his Nun's Priest, "As is the book of Launcelot de Lake, / That wommen holde in ful greet reverence" (258a–b).

Chaucer's great contemporary, William Langland, had no interest in either classicized fairies or parodied fairy writing. Evidently a cleric in minor orders, not only is his treatment of fairies in *Piers Plowman* entirely conventional— for instance, in a description of the Harrowing of Hell he calls one of Satan's lieutenants *Gobelyn*, and several times he uses the word *pouke* (puck) as a generic term for "devil"—but he also censored the "fairy" out of his own work. *Piers Plowman* has come down to us in three versions (A, B, and C), conventionally assumed to be successive revisions of one another. The A and B versions of the poem begin with the narrator falling asleep besides a tumbling stream and dreaming a wonderful dream: *"Me bifel a ferly, of Fairye me thouȝte"* (Langland 1975: 227). In this period, the English word *fairie* (from the French *féerie*, meaning "fairyland") had the primary meaning of "a marvel" (the commonest native term for an actual fairy was *elf*, and for fairyland, *elvenland*). Langland, then, clearly intends us to understand the line as meaning, "I experienced a wonder; it seemed to me a marvel," but by the time he came to revise this passage for his C-text he had evidently had second thoughts. Worried that his readers might think he was saying that his vision came from fairyland (which in the eyes of some would mean that it was demonic), he altered the line to "Me bifel for to slepe, for werynesse of walked" ("I fell asleep, tired out with walking"; Langland 1997: 197)—doctrinally less risky, no doubt, but hardly an artistic improvement.

As this overview of medieval fairy narratives demonstrates, when thinking about the cultural history of the fairy tale, it is important to recognize that the Middle Ages maintained a living belief in fairies; this recognition can help us readjust the way we read the cultural and generic role of the marvelous in medieval romance. While many have argued that there were no fairy tales in the Middle Ages, there were stories about fairies. However, in the later Middle Ages, the church's *Kulturkampf* against fairy belief transformed them, banishing fairies from the narrative in much the same way the Wife of Bath's friars banished them from Britan, and it would be another two hundred years before Edmund Spenser could write unselfconsciously about "aesthetically resuscitated" fairies. The OED's two definitions of a fairy tale—"a tale about fairies" and "something ... unreal or incredible" (OED Online 2020)—would have constituted a wholly inadequate classification for such a term (had it existed) in the Middle Ages. Few people (Chaucer is an obvious exception) would even have recognized the second sense,[12] but many would have assumed the existence of a third: "an unorthodox tale about demons." Saints at one extreme and demons at the other were easily accommodated, but anything between, unless it could be categorized as a natural marvel beyond the reach of human experience—interestingly, the way Jean d'Arras explains his half-fairy Mélusine (2003: 816)—might fall under official censure. As long as a belief in the existence of fairies remained pervasive in medieval society those who wrote about them as credible entities—were reluctant, that is, to portray them as demons—felt themselves under pressure to conform to a clerical norm, and as long as fairy tales continued to be primarily tales about fairies, their tellers were obliged to resort to displacement, evasion, and fabrication to exploit their particular corner of marvelous. We should remember this whenever we are tempted to relegate medieval fairy tales to the merely fantastic.

CHAPTER TWO

Adaptation

Like a Fairy Tale

SHYAMA RAJENDRAN

The European fairy tales of Charles Perrault and the Brothers Grimm—and of their countless adaptations, from Andrew Lang's collections to Walt Disney's films—translate their audiences to a medieval past of enchanted forests and adventurous princes, a world of benevolent fairies and happily ever afters. But there is another fairy-tale tradition, one that has come down to us through the tales spun by Scheherazade in *The Thousand and One Nights*. Featuring enchanted cities, lucky fishermen, vindictive sorceresses and malevolent demons, these tales also translate their audiences to an enchanted past, but it is not the western European one. The stories gathered here, from Arabic, Persian, and Indian traditions, establish our Anglo-European vision of the Eastern fairy-tale past. We need to remember, however, as Karla Mallette observes in her study *European Modernity and the Arab Mediterranean: Toward a New Philology and a Counter-Orientalism*, that "Scheherazade entered Western letters at a precise moment, and not in the foggy distance of the Middle Ages but at the cusp of modernity" and, furthermore, that the version of *The Thousand and One Nights* upon which we have based our idea of Arabic fairy tales is not really Arabic at all (Mallette 2010: 21). Instead, it is "the product of Western Orientalism (and Arab philologists living in the West)" (Mallette 2013: 105). Antoine Galland may have based his early eighteenth-century work, *Les Mille et une nuits, contes arabes traduits en français* (*The Thousand and One Nights, Arab stories translated into French*) on a late medieval Syrian manuscript, but he did not simply translate this source; he adapted and expanded it into "a motley crew of fantastic tales from

FIGURE 2.1: Illustration from Galland's *The Thousand and One Nights* (date unknown). Public domain.

the most various sources" and, by so doing, fabricated an Eastern Middle Ages for his Western audience (Mallette 2013: 105; Figure 2.1).[1]

But the *The Thousand and One Nights* may well have made, in Mallette's words, "the Mediterranean crossing" before Galland adapted it for an eighteenth-century French audience (2013: 109). Not only do we get glimpses of the text in works from late medieval Italy such as Giovanni Sercambi's (1348–1424) *Novella* and Ariosto's *Orlando Furioso* (1516), she argues, but also in the wildly popular tale "The Seven Sages of Rome." The latter adapts the Sindbad narrative and provides evidence, along with these other examples, that "Europeans transformed the narrative raw material ... they imported from the Arabic to suit their own purposes" (Mallette 2013: 110). Moreover, as Mallette and others recognize, because *The Thousand and One Nights* seems to "have been enjoyed as oral literature but did not generate a substantial textual tradition" it may be more difficult to pin down the circulation of narratives—to prove that say Geoffrey Chaucer or Giovanni Boccaccio adapted Arabic sources in their own "groaning board[s] of narrative drawn from a variety of sources"—but that does not mean Western authors were not familiar with them (Mallette 2010: 23; 2013: 105). This chapter argues that they were, reexamining the relationship between the medieval Western and Arabic traditions as we see it play out between *The Thousand and One Nights,* Boccaccio's *Decameron,* and Chaucer's *Canterbury Tales.* This reexamination begins with a discussion of the ways in which nineteenth-century studies of the medieval vernacular literatures read them into a nationalist narrative, dictating a linear and progressive relationship between Arabic sources and Western texts that framed subsequent discussions. I will then extract the medieval literary tradition from this nineteenth-century frame to reconsider the circulation, adaptation, and translation of narratives in a mobile Middle Ages, where the border between the Islamic East and the Christian West was permeable, and hybridity in literary traditions (and languages) was not at all uncommon. This will allow us to use modern adaptation theory to consider medieval translations and adaptations in a new light, one that will allow me to reexamine Chaucer's relationship to Boccaccio, and Boccaccio's to the *The Thousand and One Nights* through a reading of Chaucer's "Squire's Tale" as an adaptation of the latter that uses its exotic setting both to construct cultural difference (like Galland's eighteenth-century adaptation) and to suggest cultural proximity (unlike Galland).

CONSTRUCTING NATIONAL LITERATURE: LITERARY STUDIES IN THE NINETEENTH CENTURY

As literary studies and philology developed in the nineteenth century, both fields were motivated by a desire for origins, tracing national languages and literatures back to their roots in an imagined Middle Ages. This "philological desire," Simon Gaunt argues, resulted in a "tendency to concentrate on a single language or tradition in order to place it centre-stage and then to put other traditions and languages in subordinate positions" (2013: 44). As they did so, scholars not only valorized texts written in vernacular languages (French, English, Italian, for instance, as opposed to Latin), emphasizing their national—or proto-national—character, but also placed these texts in a progressive narrative: "national" authors elevated themselves to literary "greatness" as they perfected their sources and analogues. Their studies, then, were both linear and progressive, often resulting in what Suzanne Conklin Akbari calls "a crude model of linguistic and literary succession, in which one dominant culture wiped out the other like waves on a beach" (2013: 5) that had a profound influence on our understanding of both the ways in which stories and texts circulated in the Middle Ages and the relationship between European and Arabic literary traditions. This nineteenth-century progressive, nationalist narrative, as Maria Rosa Menocal famously argued, both "others" the Middle Ages and "repress[es] ... the 'Arabic role' in the history of the medieval 'West'" (quoted in Kinoshita 2013: 25); as it argues that national literatures are born when the medieval moves toward the modern, the oral toward the literary, and the popular toward the learned, it equates Arabic literatures with the medieval side of this series of binaries: non-modern, oral, and popular.

We can see the effects of this narrative of linguistic and literary succession, of the relationship between European and Arabic literatures, and of the valorization of the proto-national and the modern in Anglo-American academic discussions of the relationship between *The Thousand and One Nights*, *The Decameron*, and *The Canterbury Tales*. In these discussions, Chaucer stands at the high point, the English literary genius who realized the potential of his lesser (non-English) sources. The story goes like this: Chaucer, who spent some time in Italy, was clearly influenced by the Italian writer Giovanni Bocaccio, and Giovanni Boccaccio, in turn, was clearly influenced by *The Thousand and One Nights*. There is ample evidence for this chain of influence. All three works use a storytelling frame to bind together a series of stories drawn from multiple traditions and genres. In *The Thousand and One Nights*, Scheherazade seeks to save herself and her people by spinning tales to enchant and educate the husband who has vowed to wed and murder a new wife each day; in *The Decameron*, young nobles spend afternoons telling stories to pass the time while they wait the plague out in their country retreat; and in *The Canterbury Tales*, the pilgrims vie to win a prize for the best story told on the road to Canterbury. Moreover, A. C. Lee's classic study *The Decameron: Its Sources and Analogues* "cites parallels from the *Arabian Nights* to six tales in the *Decameron*" (Mallette 2013: 40), and many of *The Canterbury Tales* adapt tales from Boccaccio and/or contain echoes of tales, themes, and motifs found in *Nights*.

Katherine Gittes's article *"The Canterbury Tales* and the Arabic Frame Tradition" (1983) reads this relationship between Chaucer and his sources through the nationalistic narrative discussed above; while acknowledging the fact that the frame narrative comes from the Arabic literary tradition, she asserts that "it remained for Chaucer to bring the genre to its fullest flowering." Furthermore, she insists that *The Canterbury Tales* is a Western, English work:

> The consideration of the *Canterbury Tales* within the context of an Arabic tradition is not meant to deny Chaucer's debt to Western culture or to downplay his peculiarly English talent. But the fact remains that the genre in which he was working played a part in the form and design of the *Canterbury Tales*. Seeing this, one will avoid imposing on the *Canterbury Tales* qualities of form and design that are alien to its tradition, a tradition that originated not in European villages but at distant Bedouin campsites.
>
> (1983: 249–50)

Here, Gittes reiterates her progressive narrative of literary influence, contextualizing Chaucer within "Western culture" and evoking the Arabic literary tradition with the use of a homogenizing (and medievalizing) cultural stereotype that dismisses the fact that Arabic literary and scientific traditions were in full bloom by the time Chaucer began to write in England.

Robert R. Edwards, on the other hand, asks us to consider a more complex model of literary influence in his discussion of the relationship between Chaucer and Boccaccio (and, by inference, Chaucer and Arabic sources). "Whether Chaucer returned from [his two trips to Italy] with *The Decameron* in manuscript or as a remembered text," Edwards writes, is a "debated conjecture," especially as "the work does not appear as a whole in English until the 1620 translation" (2010: 8). He continues, "The present consensus is that *The Decameron* returned with Chaucer as a literary model, as an idea for a framed collection of stories grounded in an experience of the contemporary world" (9).

However, Edwards does not go from this conjecture to an analysis of Chaucer's "genius" in bringing the "idea for a framed collection of stories" to its full potential. Instead he argues that the way we measure *The Decameron*'s influence on *The Canterbury Tales*

> follow[s] from debates in practical criticism over what counts as a source or how we might construe influence. Consciously or not, these inquiries proceed from what is finally a disarticulated but tenacious model of periodization. "Chaucer and Italy," in its various modern formulations, is Chaucer's "Italian Period" detached from a master narrative that portrays its subject advancing purposefully through stages of influence toward a consummate realization of his powers …. This narrative, as Nick Havely points out, was an invention

of Victorian para-professional scholarship in the 1870s, and it expressed the nationalism of an age that saw Chaucer as a "poet of the people" despite his foreign borrowings.

(Edwards 2010: 4–5)

Edwards highlights that, within the invention of "canonicity" as far as canons are about creating a "national" literature—here, the so-called "English literary canon"—Chaucer's status as an English poet means that any "foreign" influence must be disavowed or subjugated beneath his "Englishness."

Chaucer's trips to Italy, the questions these trips raise about the connections between *The Canterbury Tales* and *The Decameron*, and Edwards's analysis of how nationalist narratives have framed our understanding of literary influence all ask us to rethink our understanding of medieval literary history, particularly the complex ones of places such as the medieval Mediterranean. In this rethinking we will see that not only is it very likely that Chaucer was influenced by Italian writers but also that the Italian writers or writings that he encountered were likely influenced by Arabic writings.[2] Furthermore, we will see that, as Mallette writes in her analysis of *The Decameron,* "the presence of Arab characters and settings and even the use of Arab tales as source texts is something of an inevitability given the Mediterranean milieu" in which many of the tales are set and "given the environment in which their author lived" (2010: 40).

TRAVELING ACROSS THE SEA: CULTURAL EXCHANGE IN THE MEDIEVAL MEDITERRANEAN

In the introduction to Akbari and Mallette's edited collection, *A Sea of Languages: Rethinking the Arabic Role in Medieval Literary History*, Akbari notes that literary history's commitment to national literatures, together with its "unwillingness to acknowledge the permeability of the cultural veil that separated Christian and Muslim communities" in the Middle Ages has meant that the field has been "slow" to reexamine its assumptions and to recognize the "need to place literary and linguistic histories in their broader context, one that emphasized inter-cultural and extra-linguistic exchange" (2013: 5, 3). The essays in *A Sea of Language* seek to provide this larger context, reminding us that the "interconnected seascape" of the Mediterranean was, in Sharon Kinoshita's words, "a transnational space—a contact zone of commercial exchange and cross-confessional interaction" (2013: 36; Figure 2.2). "The more closely one looks at this space," Kinoshita observes, "the more muddled the lines between East and West, self and other, medieval and early modern appear" (7).

Mallette provides this closer look at "the realities of [Mediterranean] regional history." "The Arabs," she reminds us, "occupied Spain, Sicily, and Malta for extended periods of their medieval history [and] immigration and

FIGURE 2.2: Mediterranean trade. Getty Library, MS 13 (85.MS.213) (before 1340). Courtesy of Getty.

trade patterns ... kept those regions in contact with the Arab world beyond that era of occupation" (2010: 31). While the Iberian Peninsula "became a center for cultural production under Arab domination," its libraries and scholars preserving, disseminating, and commenting on both Arabic and classical texts,

> the social and political structure of the Italian communes and their economic ambitions created a dynamic [in which] ... merchants, diplomats, crusaders, pilgrims, and humble sailors— traveled out to the Arab ports of the Mediterranean and returned with tidal regularity through the long centuries; they haggled over, purchased, transported, picked apart, repackaged, and remarketed the intellectual products of the Islamic Mediterranean.
> (Mallette 2010: 39)

Given this long history of occupation, mercantile trade, and cultural exchange, Mallette concludes that "influence," the standard term used to discuss the relationship between Arabic and European literatures, is wholly inadequate:

> It misrepresents the curiosity of the Christians who set out to possess the culture of the Muslims and the Muslims who agreed—for different reasons in different times and places—to supply their needs. It disavows the urgency of those cultural transactions and the revolutionary impact of the knowledge and technologies thus acquired. And it understates the banality of the transaction, the familiarity—by turns comforting, wearisome, or noxious— with which Muslims and Christians at times approached the other's culture.
> (2010: 40)

Thus, Mallette and the essayists in *A Sea of Languages* argue that, instead of focusing on influence—on linear, national literary histories—we need first to recognize the essential hybridity of medieval literary productions and then to develop, as Simon Gaunt argues, a "critical language ... equipped to conceptualize material and literary objects of multiple provinces, often the products of cultures which prized eclecticism as an expression of political or civilizational strength rather than of aesthetic weakness" (Gaunt 2013: 44).

To develop the new critical language that Gaunt calls for, we need to recover the oral-written spectrum on which many medieval stories likely circulated. The Middle Ages, as Jan Ziolkowski observes in his study *Fairy Tales Before Fairy Tales*, "was the site of much back-and-forth exchange between the oral and the written": "tale-telling took place at all levels of society ... [and stories] could originate in one group and migrate very easily into another" (2007: 5). As they did so, they could also migrate from oral to written and back again, and, in the end, "where the tales happened eventually to be recorded does not necessarily indicate anything about where they originated" (5). By recorded, of course, Ziolkowski means *written down*. As Ziolkowski outlines the process, it is clear that the ways in which medieval tales circulated closely resembles the oral-written-oral circuit that is also evident in the cultural history of the fairy tale. Like fairy tales, medieval narratives find what Jack Zipes calls "the genre's vital progenitor" in the oral tradition; also like fairy tales, the "evolution and dissemination" of these medieval stories encompassed a "symbiotic relationship of oral and literary currents" (Zipes 2012: 3). Therefore, we must, as Zipes does for the fairy tale, reject "the useless dichotomies such as print versus oral that some scholars are still promoting to paint a misinformed history" of the relationship between European literatures and their Arabic sources (3).

To do so, we must follow Menocal's attempt, in her groundbreaking study on the Arabic role in medieval literary history, to undo what she calls "the myth of Westernness." While Menocal herself acknowledges that this attempt indulges in a bit of mythmaking of its own, it does, as she asserts, have "several advantages ... [I]t does not shy away from the concept of a mixed ancestry for western Europe that until recently has seemed largely unimaginable and insupportable ... [and] I believe that it enriches rather than impoverishes the recounting of the story we already work with, the readings of texts we have already agreed on" (1987: 16). I believe that Menocal's vision of a hybrid Middle Ages, combined with the more recent work rethinking medieval literary histories discussed above, opens the way for us to rethink the relationship between *The Canterbury Tales*, *The Decameron*, and *The Thousand and One Nights*. Taken together, these works ask us to recognize that literary histories are always already entangled, despite retrospective efforts to "nationalize" them—and to undo western European attempts to marginalize the Arab role in medieval literary production.

TRANSLATIO AND ADAPTATION: ENTANGLED LITERARY HISTORIES

Tracing the circulation, translation, and adaptations of medieval narrative poses the same challenges as following the literary and linguistic fortunes of the modern fairy tale; however, while modern concepts of literary originality separate out translations and adaptations from more literary endeavors, as we think about the entangled histories of stories in the Middle Ages, we should remember that translation was actually central to medieval literary practice. Indeed, *"translatio studii et imperii* (the transferal of learning and empire) was a concept that was of basic importance to medieval reflections on the relationship between present and past cultures, and on the means by which cultural value and authority was transmitted from one period to another" (Evans et al. 1999: 317). Medieval authors engaged in the process of *translatio* didn't just translate however, as they did so, they also adapted texts and traditions to their own languages and cultures; as such, Linda Hutcheon's explication of what we think of as adaptation in the modern world, which resonates strongly with the medieval understanding of *translatio*, provides us with a productive lens to examine the movement of narratives between languages and cultures in the Middle Ages. Hutcheon asserts that "the phenomenon of adaptation can be defined from three distinct but interrelated perspectives." First, as a *"formal entity or product,"* an adaptation functions as a "transposition of a particular work or works"; second, as a *process of creation*, the act of adaptation always involves both (re-)interpretation and then (re-)creation"; and finally, as a *"process of reception*, adaptation is a form of intertextuality," invoking other works that have come before it (Hutcheon 2006: 7–8; my emphasis). Adaptations, in other words, go beyond translation; they interpret and recreate, making works "suitable" for new audiences. As they do so, they speak to both audiences who are unfamiliar with the original work (for instance, you do not have to have read *Emma* to enjoy *Clueless* as a high school rom-com), and to what Hutcheon calls the "knowing audience," who recognize the intertext. Adaptation, Hutcheon tells us, is "repetition without replication, bringing together the comfort of ritual and recognition with the delight of surprise and novelty" (173).

Medieval authors saw themselves as adaptors; they wrote in a culture where originality and individual genius had not yet been valorized by the Romantics. Authors, including Chaucer, repeatedly reference other authors and other tales, assuring their audiences that they are following "old stories." And yet, as Rita Copeland demonstrates, the relationship between these authors and their texts is much more complicated then these references suggest. These same writers often assert *their* authorship by creating "secondary" translations: "Rather than representing themselves as translations in the service of authoritative sources, these texts tend to claim for themselves (either directly or implicitly, through the irony of disclaimers) a kind of originary discursive status, as if the translation, once achieved, displaces the source by assuming a certain canonical authority of its own" (Copeland 1991: 95). In other words, they *adapt* their sources, using material from other cultures, time periods, and traditions to write "new" texts in their own languages (rather than in Latin) that ultimately claim authorship (or authority) over the original text.[3] Their secondary translations, like adaptations, are "a derivation that is not derivative–a work that is second without being secondary" (Hutcheon 2006: 9).

SOUNDING HIS STYLE: *THE THOUSAND AND ONE NIGHTS* AND *THE SQUIRE'S TALE*

Once we recognize "the vibrant multifaceted culture of the medieval Mediterranean"—a culture in which Boccaccio, who lived and worked in a port city, was immersed, and with which Chaucer, who traveled widely first as a soldier and then as a diplomat, would have been familiar—and acknowledge the fact that stories in the Middle Ages circulated widely in both oral and written form, we can embrace the possibility that both authors may well have been familiar with oral versions of the tales from the *The Thousand and One Nights*, which they then adapted in their own works (Mallette 2010: 53). Furthermore, thinking about these works through the lens of adaptation theory allows us to productively revise our usual approach to the relationship between *The Thousand and One Nights*, *The Decameron*, and *The Canterbury Tales*. In the rest of this chapter, I seek to make such a revision. I read Chaucer's "Squire's Tale" as an adaptation of a story from the *Nights*; rather than focusing on the linear transmission of sources and analogues, I examine the ways in which Chaucer reinterpreted his Arabic sources to make them suitable for his audience, creating a new hybrid text: a derivation, to repeat Hutcheon's formulation, without being derivative. By so doing, I hope to arrive at a more expansive definition of what "adaptation" can mean in retelling and remediating stories, one that will reopen historical questions of Chaucer's influences potentially drawn from the Arabic literary tradition, allowing us to reconsider the ways in which Chaucer's text calls our attention to the construction of cultural difference.

For his contribution to the storytelling contest, the Squire regales the pilgrims with an example of what Larry Benson identifies as the newly fashionable "fantastical ... chivalric romance," a genre that "emerged from the meeting of the Saracen and the crusader" (Benson in Chaucer 1987: 13; Hefferman 2003: 1). His tale's Eastern influences have long been recognized, and indeed have become part of Chaucer's nationalist literary narrative: Chaucer may have worked here from multiple Arabic sources but "the resulting composite romance can be said to be Chaucer's own" (Hefferman 2003: 68). Within this narrative, as Kathryn Lynch notes, scholars have long attempted to trace the sources Chaucer transformed into this "unique composition." "What all [their] theories of origin share," she observes, "is the centrality of the Oriental motif to the Squire's Tale; the tale wraps itself in an aura of exotic alterity, an insistent Orientalism in much the same sense that Edward Said has defined the term" (Lynch 1995: 531). As such, Chaucer's adaptation of his sources seems to be a precursor of Antoine Galland's eighteenth-century edition of *The Thousand and One Nights*; an early example of a text that transfers its Arabic sources into a Western fairy-tale genre, a translation that allows its author to construct the East as a place of "exotic alterity."

Galland, like Chaucer, began with an Arabic source—in his case, a mid-fourteenth Syrian manuscript, but as he translated, he not only adapted that source to the generic framework of "the *contes des fees* ... that enjoyed an immense vogue in the salon culture of late seventeenth-century France"; he was also driven to "complete" the text—to provide a full one thousand and one nights of stories (Mallette 2010: 36). To do so, he first added tales from other medieval Arabic traditions (such as the Sindbad stories) and then incorporated entirely new stories (told to him by Hanna Diyab, a Christian

Syrian), including those of "Aladdin and his Magic Lamp" and "Ali Baba and the Forty Thieves." Thus, by the time that Galland had finished his edition, it was not an edition at all; rather it was "the product of Western Orientalists (and Arab philologists living in the West)," and "the *Nights*, a framed tale, ha[d] itself been captured within an interpretive frame which has become perversely difficult to separate from the text itself" (Mallette 2010: 20). Within this interpretive frame, the Western vision of a fairy-tale Eastern world constructed an exotic other, a "Baghdad—where genies popped from bottles, willow-waisted maidens were transformed into moon-faced cows, and monarchs in disguise went on nocturnal rambles to get acquainted with the populace, a wonderland marvelously exterior to the chill light of reason that suffused [France in] the eighteenth century" (36).

If *The Thousand and One Nights*' "proximity to the oral tradition makes it peculiarly fluid and therefore peculiarly vulnerable to modern manipulation," blurring "the line between the provinces of the premodern author and the modern textual critic" and allowing Galland to freely adapt, add to, and orientalize the text, the same can be said of Chaucer's engagement with his Arabic sources in "The Squire's Tale" (Mallette 2010: 20). The tale, "characterized by an interest in exotic oriental detail, complex plots involving numerous characters, magic blended with realism, and family plots," does indeed manifest "many of the features of Orientalism" that Lynch asserts "were clearly present in Chaucer's day" (Heffernan 2003: 63; Lynch 1995: 531). Through this narrative, the Squire relocates his listeners to the world of Genghis Kahn, to the past, to the "east," to a scene of magic—and he does so by centering on the oral (rather than written) nature of his story. He begins by setting the scene in "Tartarye"; he praises the Khan's fame, honor, and courage, tells us of his similarly admirable family, and then focuses in on the Khan's birthday celebrations. A knight "suddenly" appears in the hall "upon a steed of brass" (line 81), stuns the court into silent "marvel" (line 87), salutes the king, queen and all the lords, with "heigh reverance" (line 93), and delivers a message:

> After the forme used in his langage,
> Withouten vice* of silable or of lettre.   *fault
> And for his tale* sholde seme the bettre,   *speech
> Accordant to* his words was his cheere*,   **in accord with/expression*
> As techeth art of speche, hem that it leere*,   *learn
> Al be that I kan not sowne* his stile,   *express
> Ne kan nat clymben over so heigh a style.
> Yet seye I this as to commune entente*,   *general purposes
> Thus muche amounteth al that ever he mente,
> If it so be that I have it in mynde.
>
> (lines 100–9)

While the Squire's narration here seems innocuous enough, his focus on the fact that the knight communicates his message in another language, one that the Squire cannot imitate is important for our purposes. The knight delivers the message to the court, while the Squire is delivering it to the assembled listening pilgrims and to the reader, and in his account of this moment, the Squire invokes orality several times—both the knight's and his own in attempting to "sound" the knight's "style," concluding that he is only capable of paraphrasing the specific message that the knight delivers to the court ("Yet seye I this as to commune entente, / Thus muche amounteth al that ever he mente"; lines 107–8).

The story, then, is mediated through the Squire, with all his proclaimed flaws, as its teller, and the Squire's dilemma—his inability accurately to translate the foreign speech and "style" of the magical knight—not only calls our attention to the fact that the written text itself preserves its own orality but also suggests the process of adaptation at work in Chaucer's tale. Given the Squire's claim that his English is *not enough* to completely faithfully render his tale for his listeners, and his profession that he does not have the skill as a storyteller, the Squire himself gestures to the fact that his tale is more of an adaptation than a translation. Further, "The Squire's Tale," as we have seen, is less a self-contained entity and more a patchwork weaving of already existing stories; it names and claims a plethora of different historical and literary traditions as its own.[4] Its amalgamation of several sources and its gestures to multiple textual traditions turn the story into an intertext itself, one brings its multiple traditions together, adapting its various sources, written and oral, into a fairy-tale romance that serves, like Galland's *Nights*, to construct an exotic cultural other (Figure 2.3).

In my discussion, I will focus on this process of adaptation in the first part of "The Squire's Tale," whose source has been traced to the story of the Ebony and Ivory Horse in *The Thousand and One Nights*. In the Arabic tale, three wise men present the king of Persia with magical gifts: a spy-killing golden trumpet, a quaint living peacock clock, and a flying horse made of ivory and ebony, operated by winding a pin. The man who brings the horse tells the king that the horse can take his rider anywhere he wants to go, and can do so in a single day, even if the journey would normally take a year. A convoluted tale of promised princesses, jealous brothers, and high adventure—in which the magical horse plays a prominent role—follows, ending as the horse enables the son of the Persian king to free his beautiful princess-lover from an unwelcome royal suitor, fly home, and live happily ever after. "The Squire's Tale," however, is incomplete. Indeed, the horse in this tale never even flies, let alone takes anyone, princely or otherwise, on an adventure. What makes it interesting as an adaptation of *The Thousand and One Nights*, then, is not its reimagination of

FIGURE 2.3: The Enchanted Horse, from Antoine Galland's translation of *The Thousand and One Nights* (1864). Bibliothèque nationale de France, with permission.

plot and characters but, rather, the ways in which Chaucer, through the Squire, uses his adaptation here to meditate on the difficulties of translating other cultures and languages and to construct the cultural other. The Squire begins by transposing his Arabic sources into a genre with which his audience would have been familiar; the opening sequence discussed above closely resembles various Arthurian romances, including *Sir Gawain and the Green Knight*: the idealized king, the rich and beautiful court gathered for a sumptuous feast, the crowd-stunning marvel, the promise of subsequent adventures. In fact, the Squire's narration here explicitly reminds the audience of this generic frame; he says that not even Gawain, if he were to return from Faerie, could compare with the mysterious knight to "in speech and appearance" (lines 95–7) and, as he turns to the court's flirtations, he concludes that no one but "Lancelot, and he is dead" could possibly describe them (line 287).

Adapting his sources within the familiar framework of the Arthurian romance serves, as did Galland's similar use of the *contes des fees*, two purposes. First, it provides the audience with a way into the tale, but second, and more importantly, it allows the Squire to construct the Mongul court, the knight who comes from the King of Arabia and India, and the marvelous gifts he brings as the exotic—and untranslatable—Other. From the very beginning of his tale the Squire draws our attention to the fact that something is untranslatable—and thus *different*—about the Kahn's court. He claims to have insufficient skill, storytelling talent, and English to adequately describe Canacee's beauty ("But for to telle yow al hir beautee / It lyth nat in my tonge, n'yn my konnyng; / I dar nat undertake so heigh a thing. / Myn Englissh eek is insufficient"; lines 34–7). Similarly, he declines to describe the feast that the knight gate-crashes: he will not tell us of their "strange" soups, or of their "swannes" or "heronsewes," or of "some mete" that is considered very dainty (lines 67–70). Here, his use of the rhetorical trope, *occupatio*, indeed emphasizes what he pretends not to talk about: the exotic otherness, the strangeness of the Mongol court.

As he tells his tale, the Squire constructs levels of cultural mediation: first, the Mongol Court, and then the otherworldly knight, who comes from even further East. Genghis Kahn's court may be a site of exotic excess, but the knight who interrupts their feast is even more exotic—of fairy, a marvel, a supernatural creature whose language is so foreign that, as we have seen, the Squire is utterly unable to translate it. And this knight presents four equally marvelous gifts: a steed of brass that can—in one day—take the king anywhere he wants to go, in any weather conditions, without harming the rider (lines 116, 119–20); a mirror that will show the king future political and personal adversities, reveal who is his friend and who his foe, and—when used by a lady bright—will disclose whether or not her new lover will be true or false; a ring that grants its wearer understanding of the speech of birds and complete knowledge of healing herbs; and a sword capable of cutting through any armor to inflict a grievous wound that can only be healed by the sword itself. This cornucopia of magical objects, drawn from various sources, each suggests an individual adventure to be undertaken as the tale continues; however, the Squire never does finish his narrative, and apart from the ring in part two of the tale, we never actually see any of these magical gifts in action.

In fact, much of the remainder of Part 1 describes the court's attempts to fathom the magical objects, which along with the otherworldly knight, have disrupted their feast. When the royal officers find that they are unable to move the brass horse to a tower with all of the other gifts ("it stood as if it were glued to the ground"; line 182), a large crowd of people swarms in to stare at the magical metal equid, desperately trying to make sense of this marvel in their midst (line 189). On the one hand, it is a horse: "high," "broad," "long," and "well-proportioned" (lines 191–92). In *form* the horse is perfect, the Squire assures us: "Certainly, from his tail to his ear / Neither Nature nor Art could correct anything about him" (lines 196–97). On the other, it is foreign, strange, cunningly made of brass, seemingly inoperable. The court requires a framework within which to understand it, and they resort to other tales of the marvelous. The Squire describes the onlookers' opinions of the horse: it is "a fairye" (which carries multiple meanings: a fairy, an enchantment, a supernatural contrivance), "like Pegasus," or—more mundanely—like the Trojan horse (lines 201, 207). Similarly, they attempt to understand the mirror, sword, and ring through the perspective of what they know, books and stories—arguing, judging, and speculating before resuming their feast. After dinner, they return to marveling over the horse of brass, finally giving up and asking the knight to reveal the secret of operating it. Like the ivory and ebony horse in *Nights*, the solution is relatively simple. The horse operates by turning three screws: one to make him ascend, the other, to descend, and the third to disappear. Once the king (and court) understand how the horse works, they all relax and happily return to their reveling; the horse's bridle is carried off to the tower, and the horse itself mysteriously vanishes from both the court (presumably to return when the king calls) and the Squire's narrative.

The amount of time that the Squire spends describing the magical horse is quite startling, especially given his refusal to describe Canacee, and this discrepancy creates a narrative tension between what can and cannot be described, drawing our attention to the fact that the Squire is translating this tale for his audience and asking us to consider how his/Chaucer's adaptation of the beginning of the tale of the ebony and ivory horse functions. Alan Ambrisco argues that Chaucer, in this opening, makes the Eastern court familiar by removing "cultural boundaries between his exotic subject and his domestic audience," positioning the Mongols as "pseudo-Europeans" against whom the "exoticism of the emissary ... denied full coherence or articulation" is constructed. The court, as it reacts to the knight, "stands in" for the audience, "encouraging" them to identify with the Kahn and his followers (Ambrisco 2004: 210, 213). Here, Ambrisco reads the Squire's use of *occupatio*, his refusal to describe Canacee's beauty or the strange stews, as the deliberate occlusion of "Mongol culture, language, and point of view ... replaced by a European norm that is absent and present at once" via the comparisons used in the text (209, 211). While I agree with Ambrisco that the Squire "employs tropes of similitude" in his description of the Court (and, I would add, in his generic frame), I think the Squire's use of these tropes functions more complexly. Rather than simply "turning the cultural other into the self, thus negating differences between self and other," the Squire (and Chaucer) engage here in a particular kind of rhetorical construction of cultural difference; his use of the dynamics of similitude are meant to strike his listeners (and us) as simultaneously familiar and unfamiliar (212).

Thinking about how adaptations embed difference in similarity can help us highlight the importance of Chaucer's potential Arabic sources without backsliding into a nationalistic reading of his work and to complicate a strictly Orientalist reading of "The Squire's Tale." This tale exemplifies Hutcheon's characterization of the ways adaptation functions; it "brings together the comfort" of Arthurian romance with the delight of surprise and novelty" in the Eastern knight and his exotic gifts (2006: 173). As it does so, it does not displace its source; rather it reinterprets and recreates it to produce a new text, a hybrid one that makes the Arabic source legible—suitable—to a new audience, demonstrating what Hutcheon calls "the adaptive faculty," "the ability to repeat without copying, to embed difference in similarity, to be at once both self and other" (173–4). Furthermore, I would suggest that, since, in the words of Michael Taussig, "the human compulsion to behave *like* something or someone else marks a paradoxical capacity to be Other" (1993: 19), the Squire's (and Chaucer's) audience are also being encouraged in this adaptation of an Arabic tale to see *similitude* rather than *sameness*. The Squire's construction of the exotic worlds of the East—of the Kahn's court, the foreign emissary and the brass horse—as *like* the otherworlds of fairy tale and romance may not merely function as an orientalizing gesture creating those worlds as Other. Instead, by calling attention to the proximities between Arabic tales and European narratives, they may also call attention to those between the domestic self and the foreign other. As it meditates on these proximities—and attempts to translate the narrative speech Arabic tales for an English audience, Chaucer's adaptation of "The Squire's Tale" provides us with a window into the dynamic circuit of cultural and narrative exchange at work in the medieval Mediterranean where stories and people—merchants, pilgrims, and diplomates—circulated, along with goods, both across the Mediterranean and between Europe and England.

CHAPTER THREE

Gender and Sexuality

The Beauties and Beasts of Medieval Romance

LYNN SHUTTERS

Fairy tales exist everywhere and nowhere in the Middle Ages. When twenty-first-century people do not imagine the Middle Ages as an era of ignorance and atrocities, they idealize them in "fairy-tale" terms: knights, ladies, castles, and chivalry all shape modern-day perceptions of the medieval past. These tropes are largely drawn from romance, the preeminent genre of the era, which features the additional "fairy-tale" elements of quests, magic, and marvelous encounters. The medieval literary corpus imaginatively combines with modern-day cultural associations to render the "Middle Ages" and "fairy tales" metonyms, such that they frequently—and often reflexively—stand in for each other.[1] Yet, even as the Middle Ages are a fairy tale, there are no fairy tales in the Middle Ages, at least not according to many accounts of the genre, which locate the emergence of Western classic fairy tales in the early modern period in works by Giovanni Francesco Straparola (*c.* 1480–1557); Giambattista Basile (1566–1632); Charles Perrault (1628–1703); the 1690s *conteuses*, the most notable and enduring being Marie-Catherine d'Aulnoy (1652–1705); Jeanne-Marie Leprince de Beaumont (1711–76); and in the nineteenth century, Jacob (1785–1863) and Wilhelm (1786–1859) Grimm.[2] Ironically, a common feature of the classic fairy tale is its setting in "a magical elsewhere of possibility," an elsewhere often coded as "medieval" (Warner 2018: xxviii). We arrive then, at a paradox, which Jan Ziolkowksi succinctly conveys: "[fairy] tales are ... set in a medieval feudal past, with castles and kings; but medieval sources and analogues ... go unmentioned or undervalued" (2009: 27).

Medievalists are well positioned to correct this omission and extend the cultural history of the fairy tale back to our own area of study. Doing so, however, results in a second challenge: what material should be identified as "medieval sources and analogues" of fairy tales, or selected for a chapter like this? Even limiting ourselves to the Western Middle Ages, we have, temporally, a thousand years to cover (500–1500 CE) and, geographically, an array of cultures spanning across the European continent. In this chapter, I focus on medieval romance, a term that, most broadly, refers to literature written in vernacular languages beginning around 1100 CE. Although never strictly defined, romance came to be associated with certain narrative structures and literary conventions, including idealized, aristocratic characters; legendary, temporally distant settings; adventures centered upon an individual knight; magic and the marvelous; and love.[3] As evasive as the term romance might seem, modern readers "often know it when they see it," a recognition rooted through familiarity with the fairy-tale genre (Fuchs 2004: 2). Romance conjures up "that fairy-tale feeling," as Barbara Fuchs states (2).

"That fairy-tale feeling" is nowhere more present than in romance constructions of gender and sexuality. At first glance, medieval romance rigidly adheres to archetypical gender roles. The knight protagonist is handsome and brave, and he single-handedly vanquishes his enemies. Conforming to what seems like a medieval version of compulsory heterosexuality, he loves a beautiful lady who is often in need of rescue. To readers today, these gender roles seem one-dimensional and dated, so much so that the "knight in shining armor" and "damsel in distress" operate as modern-day shorthands for traditional gender types. Even as we dismiss these models of gender and sexuality as leftovers from a bygone era, they continue to circulate, trading on nostalgia to shape beliefs about how gender and desire ideally work. This tension—between historical difference and distance, on the one hand, and recognition and continuity, on the other—establishes one of the key values in studying gender and sexuality in medieval romance. In what follows, I hope to demonstrate how focus on romance constructions of gender and sexuality both allows us to better understand these texts within specifically medieval contexts and fosters new perspectives on gender and sexuality today.

Methodologically, I will identify key tropes governing gender and sexuality in romance and underscore the creativity with which romance authors deploy them. The four tropes I examine—courtliness, virtue, the marvelous, and rape—each govern a section of the chapter, although my discussion of individual tropes also ranges across sections. The simultaneous isolation and synthesis of tropes is necessary, I believe, because through combination each trope both affects and is affected by the others. We might imagine romance constructions of gender and sexuality as a medieval tapestry, containing multiple images and motifs, each of which demands scrutiny, even as the viewer must step back to appreciate the interplay of elements and contemplate how they function as a whole. Or, in terms of gender and sexuality studies, we might reference the concept of intersectionality, the notion that all aspects of a person's identity—gender, sexuality, race, class, etc.— are mutually constitutive.[4] When writing, however, it is hard not to separate out categories, for "the structures of language require us to invoke race, gender, sexual orientation, and other categories one discursive moment at a time" (Carbado 2013: 816). I similarly conceive of courtliness, virtue, the marvelous, and rape as "intersectional" tropes, tropes that we must separate out for the purposes of identification but which constantly call back and forth to each other.

Our "tapestry" is further complicated by the dense intertextuality of the romance genre. The corpus of medieval romance is extensive, and romance representations of gender and sexuality are by no means monolithic. However, the frequent referencing in one romance of characters and episodes from others means that there is a greater degree of consistency across romances than one might expect. Even when an author departs from romance conventions, he (for the authors of medieval romances were predominantly men) does so not to efface prior conventions but to recollect them, with the assumption that audience members will recognize and appreciate this process of adaptation. As a result, romance constructions of gender and sexuality are both highly stylized and remarkably idiosyncratic, as stock conventions are redeployed to new effect. Here, too, modern gender theory is useful, for we might describe this phenomenon as "repetition with a difference": each individual romance is simultaneously a citation or performance of gender and sexuality conventions from prior romances and an idiosyncratic iteration of them; it is not despite but *through* repetition that romances reconceptualize gender and sexuality.[5] Consequently my goal in this chapter is to consider gender and sexuality in romance not as a list of tropes but as an ongoing process of adaptation. To illustrate this process, I examine three exemplars of the genre, described in detail below: the twelfth-century French romance *Le Bel Inconnu*; the fourteenth-century English romance *Lybeaus Desconus*; and the fourteenth-century French *Mélusine, ou La Noble Histoire de Lusignan*, a generic hybrid that includes romance elements. These texts speak to each other, sometimes quite directly, with *Lybeaus Desconus* being a later, English retelling of the French *Bel Inconnu*.[6] I am less concerned with direct borrowings, however, than I am in capturing the comparative, often nonlinear practices that medieval audiences would employ when "reading" a medieval romance. My goal throughout is to help modern readers appreciate how seemingly stock, simplistic figures come alive, how romance constructions of gender and sexuality gain their complexity, and how such constructions might continue to circulate in the modern world.

SUMMARIES OF PRIMARY TEXTS

Li Biaus Descouneüs (*Le Bel Inconnu* in Modern French, *The Fair Unknown* in Modern English; referred to hereafter as *Le Bel Inconnu*) is a late twelfth-century Arthurian romance by Renaut de Bâgé.[7] A knight of unknown patrimony arrives at Arthur's court and entreats the king to grant him a future challenge. Arthur agrees, takes the knight into his service, and names him "Fair Unknown" on account of his remarkable beauty. The maiden Helie then arrives at court and reports that the lady she serves is in peril; Helie asks Arthur to dispatch his most accomplished knight to rescue her. This feat, Helie observes, will require that the knight face the challenge of the "Fearsome Kiss." The Fair Unknown volunteers to undertake the adventure, and Arthur awards him the quest. Because the Fair Unknown is untested, Helie is greatly displeased. The two face many perils en route to rescuing Helie's lady, including fierce knights and rapacious giants, all of whom the Fair Unknown handily defeats. Helie and the Fair Unknown arrive at the Golden Isle, where a beautiful fairy, the Maiden of the White Hands, resides. The Maiden and the Fair Unknown fall in love, but the Fair Unknown secretly departs from the Golden Isle to complete his quest. Eventually he arrives at Sinadoun, the city where Helie's lady is held captive by a pair of sorcerer brothers. The Fair Unknown enters her castle, defeats the sorcerers, but then encounters a huge, hideous serpent. The serpent kisses the Fair Unknown and departs. A disembodied voice reveals the Fair Unknown's identity: he is Guinglan, the son of Gawain and Blanchemal the Fay. A beautiful lady then appears and informs Guinglan that she is Blonde Esmeree, the daughter of the King of Wales. The sorcerers transformed her into a serpent when she refused to marry the elder of the two. By withstanding the Fearsome Kiss, Guinglan broke the spell. Blonde Esmeree offers Guinglan her hand in marriage and her kingdom. Guinglan consents so long as King Arthur agrees to the match. Guinglan then recollects his love for the Maiden of the White Hands, returns to her, and begs her forgiveness. The two are reconciled; Guinglan, however, learns of a tournament to be held in Arthur's court and, against the Maiden's wishes, leaves to attend it. He wins the tournament. Arthur approves of the marriage of Guinglan and Blonde Esmeree and oversees their wedding. The romance ends unconcluded as to whether Guinglan will remain with Blonde Esmeree or return to his true love, the Maiden of the White Hands.

Lybeaus Desconus is a fourteenth-century Middle English romance, questionably attributed to Thomas Chestre, providing a shorter, more streamlined account of the Fair Unknown narrative.[8] As in the French romance, Guinglan, who does not know his identity, seeks a boon from King Arthur and sets out with Elene (Helie) to rescue her lady, the Lady of Sinadoun, who has been transformed into a serpent. Major departures from the French romance include recasting the Maiden of the White Hands as the Dame Amoure, an overtly evil sorceress who uses love-inducing enchantments to detain Guinglan in her kingdom. *Lybeaus Desconus* also differs from the French romance in that the lady in need of rescue is transformed not into a serpent but into a serpent-lady hybrid: she has the body of a serpent but a human face. Finally, the conflict between romantic love and social duty that the French hero faces is absent from the English romance; upon rescuing the Lady of Sinadoun, Guinglan falls in love with her and willingly marries her, with Arthur's approval.

The third text that concerns us here is Jean d'Arras's *Mélusine, ou La Noble Histoire de Lusignan* (*Melusine, or the Noble History of Lusignan*, hereafter *Mélusine*) written in the late fourteenth century for the French duke Jean de Berry to provide an origin myth for his family, the House of Lusignan.[9] The work is a generic hybrid, combining romance, history, and crusader adventures; it thus demonstrates how romance constructions of gender and sexuality could be harnessed to political ends. Jean traces the origins of the Lusignans back to the marriage of Raymond, a Poitevin nobleman, and Mélusine, a beautiful fairy. Mélusine weds Raymond on the condition that he allow her to withdraw to a private chamber on Saturdays and never attempt to spy on her. Raymond agrees, and the two embark upon a marriage that is both personally fulfilling and politically successful. Mélusine possesses great wealth and supernatural powers; she constructs the city of Lusignan and is beloved by her people as a wise and benevolent ruler. She and Raymond have ten sons, who take part in their own adventures and expand the family holdings abroad. This happy marriage comes to an end, however, when Raymond breaks his vow to respect Mélusine's weekly withdrawal. Spying on Mélusine, Raymond discovers his wife in hybrid form: a beautiful woman from the waist up, a serpent from the waist down. Mélusine transforms into a dragon and flies away.

COURTLINESS

Fairy tales, according to Marina Warner, are "one-dimensional, depthless, abstract, and sparse" (2018: xxvi). Protagonists such as Snow White and Prince Charming fit this description, for they require little in the way of character development; they simply are good, virtuous characters, beautiful on the inside and out and worthy of the wealth and status that their happy ending confers. Much the same can be said of the knights and ladies of medieval romance, although, in this genre, these attributes—beauty, virtue, lovability, wealth, and status—are folded into a single concept: "courtliness." Because the romance genre developed in aristocratic courts, it is no accident that the versions of femininity and masculinity celebrated in romance are specifically courtly. This cluster of courtly attributes naturalizes class distinctions: attributes that might seem arbitrary—wealth, noble birth—combine with beauty and the capacity to love, qualities believed to reflect individual worth. Beauty and love therefore confirm aristocratic status, both reflecting and creating the social hierarchies upon which that status depends. If physical beauty and the inherent disposition to love (and be loved) naturalize class distinctions, we might also expect them to naturalize gender distinctions; that is, we might expect beauty and love to be constructed along different lines for women and men. This, however, is not necessarily the case, for either courtly beauty or courtly love.

The overlap between beauty and courtliness, and its resultant blurring of gender distinctions, is demonstrated by the opening of *Le Bel Inconnu*, when two strangers arrive in King Arthur's court: first, an exceptionally beautiful knight, the titular "Fair Unknown," then an equally beautiful maiden. Both characters' beauty is superlative; regarding the knight, we learn that "All those who saw him readily agreed / that they knew of no man so fair as he" (lines 99–100). The maiden, Helie, is similarly described: "So lovely a creature had never been seen" (line 138). The Fair Unknown and Helie are also similar in that their beauty encompasses not only their actual bodies but also their clothing and accessories. For the Fair Unknown's "perfect beauty" to signify in court culture, his beauty must encompass the speech, manners, and rich clothing through which that culture is defined. Notably, the court's high appraisal of the Fair Unknown's beauty does not occur immediately upon his entrance but after he dons a "fine cloak" (line 94) that enhances his beauty: "Thus arrayed he was a handsome young man indeed" (line 96). This interplay of somatic and sartorial beauty also occurs in the initial description of Helie,

> who was lovely of form and face.
> She was beautifully dressed in samite;
> So lovely a creature had never been seen.
>
> (lines 136–8)

Although this description first notes Helie's physical features, the observation of her rich clothing immediately follows to suggest that form, face, *and* clothing equally contribute to the high assessment of her beauty. The continued description of Helie further underscores this point, for while six lines are devoted to her somatic beauty (lines 139–44), twice as many are devoted to her accessories, which include "a golden circlet, / whose stones were worth a king's ransom" (lines 145–6); a horse "as beautiful as that of any king or count" (line 148); and horse tack fashioned of gold, gems, and silk (lines 149–56).

What, we might ask, do these descriptions indicate about gender? Notably, for both men and women, rich clothing is indispensable. Beauty cannot exist without the luxurious silks and gems that romances so lovingly describe. As James Schultz notes, beauty and courtliness, the somatic and sartorial, are indistinguishable elements of "a single image ... combin[ing] a noble body, courtly virtue, splendid clothing, and the visible mastery of courtly skills" (2006: 91). Furthermore, there is no categorical difference between masculine and feminine beauty. Medieval constructions of beauty and gender therefore differ from their later Western counterparts, which distinguish masculine and feminine beauty through cultural evaluations of secondary sex characteristics: beautiful women possess long, frequently blonde hair, delicate facial features, and shapely breasts and hips, while handsome men typically have shorter hair, with dark hair coloring being more acceptable, "strong" facial features, a tall stature, and a broad chest and shoulders. Such gender dimorphism does not, however, hold true in medieval romance, for, as Schultz observes, "the bodies of [beautiful men and women] turn out to be virtually the same" (22). Beauty, for both genders, requires conformity, and exceptionality is established through differences of degree, not kind. Romance writers often draw wry attention to these conventions, establishing the superior beauty of one lady, for example, by comparing her to another romance heroine, who, within her own narrative, is the most beautiful (Figure 3.1).

If women are distinguished from each other in terms of degree of beauty, female beauty is distinguished from men's by the kind of narrative description it attracts. Returning to the Fair Unknown and Helie, we might note that while both are beautiful, the man's beauty is established by the brief affirmations of Arthur and his court. Helie's beauty, by contrast, is established extradiegetically, through the observations of the narrator, and at greater length, by way of a blazon, an itemized description of a woman's features. As Schultz comments, "these differences [in describing men and women] do not reflect a structure of bodies so much as they reflect a structure of looking at bodies, and this is determined by the gender hierarchy that structures court life" (2006: 37). The narrator's lingering gaze focalizes and eroticizes Helie, not just as a woman "lovely of form and face" but as a comprehensive vision of courtliness.

That Helie is lovely also renders her lovable, for love in romance entails the recognition and affirmation of courtliness: the beauty and courtliness of the lover renders him capable of appreciating those qualities in his beloved. This chain of associations is nicely captured by the Old French term *fin amor*: *amor* of course means "love," while its modifier *fin* encompasses a range of meanings, including "delicate, fine," "pure, refined," "perfect, splendid," "true, sincere," and "noble, virtuous" (*Anglo-Norman Dictionary* 2021). *Fin amor* refines, ennobles, and elevates its practitioners even as it is, paradoxically, a mode of loving only attainable by those who are already refined, noble, and elevated.[10] Because *Fin amor* is a condition of nobility, aristocrats who do not love are worthy of blame. For example, in *Le Bel Inconnu*, when Guinglain reveals to his squire Robert his love for the Maiden of the White Hands, the squire responds:

> I am not an expert in knightly matters
> but there should be no knight
> who wishes never to be in love;
> and he who has not set his heart on Love
> should not increase in honor.
>
> (lines 3765–9)

FIGURE 3.1: Courtliness and Beauty of Lovers, from the Codex Manesse. UB Heidelberg, Cod. Pal. germ. 848, fol. 178r: Herr Bernger von Horheim. Courtesy of Wikimedia Commons.

Robert presents the connection between honor and love as a universally acknowledged dictum, but he also recognizes his own lack of expertise in such matters due to his lower social status.

Fin amor is paradoxical on numerous counts: it is both cause and effect of courtliness, and it both affirms and undermines the social structures on which courtliness, as an expression of feudal aristocracy, otherwise depends. It is worth noting that while *fin amor* is not always antisocial, its most famous practitioners—Lancelot and Guinevere, Tristan and Isolde—engage in adulterous affairs that result in the suffering of both the lovers themselves and practically everyone to whom they are connected; in many versions of the Lancelot and Guinevere legend, the lovers' adultery precipitates the fall of Arthur's kingdom. Key to celebratory accounts of *fin amor* is class-based mystification, as Stephen Jaeger explains: "tragic and destructive though it is, [*fin amor*] also raises status, confers virtue, and recognizes inner worth .... The ennobling force of passion is like a product that you can't afford if you have to ask about the price" (1999: 191). In the many romance renditions of these stories, authors vacillate in their treatment of *fin amor* between celebration of an erotic, ecstatic passion and recognition of the social and spiritual woes in which that passion results. Assessing *fin amor* poses a challenge, then, not just to modern-day readers but to medieval authors and audiences, for whom the paradoxes of *fin amor* served as bases for both ethical inquiry and aesthetic effect. Narrative outcomes of *fin amor* narratives, outcomes that range from social integration to social destruction, are imbricated with constructions of gender and sexuality, as we shall soon see.

VIRTUE

In examining love, beauty, and courtliness as mutually constitutive, I have focused on attributes that knights and ladies were imagined to share. I now wish to examine how medieval romances distinguish between masculinity and femininity. This leads to my second trope: virtue. While the gender-neutral concept of courtliness is itself a virtue, the plot of romance requires that courtliness manifest as action, and action bifurcates virtue along gendered lines. The knight, in romance, takes center stage: his adventures organize the plot and establish his prowess, virtue, and renown. Female characters, conversely, provide the situations and opportunities through which masculine identity is established. To serve these designated roles, knights and ladies possess different characteristics, which romances encode as masculine and feminine virtue.

Between masculine and feminine virtue, masculine virtue might appear more straightforward: romance plots center on a quest, which the virtuous knight fulfills. The *need* to complete quests, however, exists in uneasy tension with the allegedly innate goodness of the aristocratic knight. We see this in

Le Bel Inconnu, when, despite the Fair Unknown's remarkable beauty, an indicator of his courtliness and worth, both Helie and King Arthur doubt the knight's ability. Helie's appraisal of the Fair Unknown is especially scornful:

> [T]his knight is too young.
> I want only a proven knight
> of the highest reputation;
> as for this fellow, let him stay where he is.
>
> (lines 237–40)

Helie suggests that beauty is not sufficient to indicate a knight's abilities; a knight instead follows a developmental trajectory in which youthful inexperience gives way to proven worth. After the plot of the romance gets under way, masculinity shifts from an innate quality signaled by the knight's outward beauty to a series of performances. As formulated in Judith Butler's classic study, masculinity is "tenuously constituted in time ... through a stylized repetition of acts" (1990: 120). The need for "stylized repetition" is reflected in the structure of the romance genre, which tends to be episodic, composed of an interlaced sequence of "aventures." Thus, on his way to rescue Helie's lady, the Fair Unknown fights multiple opponents, and with each chivalric performance Helie's estimation of him rises, progressing from deep skepticism to qualified admiration to full endorsement. "I have measured him well along our route," she comments, "by the harsh combats I have seen him undergo. / In truth, I know of none better than he" (lines 2720–2).

For these "combats" to count as worthy performances of masculinity, they must be undertaken for a worthy cause, and in the service of an esteemed individual. That individual is typically either a lady, who requires rescue or whom the knight seeks to impress, or a lord, such as King Arthur, to whom the knight owes fealty. Ideally, the knight's duties to his lady and lord overlap, and Arthurian romance is in fact structured to facilitate their convergence. These romances conventionally open and close in Arthur's court, a sort of homosocial "home-base" for the knight's adventures in service of a lady. The opening of *Le Bel Inconnu* conforms to this structure, for the plot commences when Helie arrives at the court to implore aid for her mistress. In the many adventures that follow, the Fair Unknown demonstrates his devotion not just to Helie and her mistress but to other ladies as well: he fights two giants to rescue a lady from rape and wins a sparrowhawk for another lady, thereby reinstating her reputation and avenging her lost love. In serving these ladies, the Fair Unknown also serves King Arthur, and upon defeat of each adversary sends his vanquished foe to Arthur's court to report the Fair Unknown's deeds. The circulation of the Fair Unknown's accomplishments in this public setting establishes his reputation and, since he is a knight of Arthur's Round Table, the reputation of the Arthurian community more broadly.

In sum, masculine deeds circulate within and across an array of overlapping social structures, and a single chivalric performance might signify in multiple ways: as a deed performed by an individual man for an individual woman, as an act representing chivalric service to women more generally, as feudal service of a knight to his lord, and as a metonymy for the virtue and valor of the Arthurian court. These formulations ideally coincide but can also conflict, particularly when a knight's lady and lord make incompatible demands. The negotiation of this conflict distinguishes between the French and English versions of the Fair Unknown narrative. In the French romance, the Fair Unknown twice deserts his beloved lady, the Maiden of the White Hands, first, to complete his quest to rescue Blonde Esmeree, and later, to attend a tournament hosted by King Arthur. Although both instances, particularly the first, could be interpreted as the Fair Unknown's virtuous fulfillment of his chivalric duties, the Maiden sees things differently. When, after first abandoning the Maiden, the Fair Unknown returns to beg her forgiveness, she upbraids him in the most stringent of terms: "You treated me with utter scorn / like a boor [*vilains*] and a man without shame" (lines 4050–1). The Old French *vilains* is particularly biting: it demotes the Fair Unknown in class, from courtly knight to rude peasant, and because the mode of chivalric masculinity to which the Fair Unknown adheres is inextricably linked to his class, it denigrates his masculinity as well.

Even as the Fair Unknown lowers himself in his mistress's eyes, he elevates himself in Arthur's. Upon abandoning the Maiden for the second time, the Fair Unknown participates in a tournament at Arthur's court. Defeating a host of adversaries, he wins both the tournament prize and the admiration of the homosocial community, as signaled when King Arthur "embrace[s] him, / clasping him in his arms" (lines 6113–14). In accordance with Eve Sedgwick's classic formulation of homosociality, Arthur's court routes affection between men through the exchange of women, specifically through the exchange of Blonde Esmeree, whose marriage to Guinglan Arthur negotiates upon the tournament's conclusion. As heiress to the kingdom of Wales, Blonde Esmeree is quite a prize, for Guinglan most directly but also for Arthur, who, as Guinglan's liege-lord, would likewise expand his authority through this strategic match. Motivated by duty toward and affection for Arthur, the Fair Unknown agrees to the marriage; internally, though, he despairs, as his heart remains loyal to the Maiden. The *Bel Inconnu* closes at this point, leaving unresolved the fate of the Fair Unknown, who is torn between devotion to Arthur and the Maiden, and therefore, too, between two imperatives of chivalric masculinity. The Middle English *Lybeus Desconus* notably sidesteps the conflict between amatory and feudal allegiances: the Dame Amoure, the character who roughly conforms to the Maiden of the White Hands, is evil; Guinglan only temporarily falls prey to her seductions; and upon rescuing the Lady of Sinadoun (corresponding to the French Blonde Esmeree), Guinglan falls in love with her. The political marriage that concludes the romance is therefore also a love match, and amatory, political, and homosocial allegiances neatly coincide.

If masculine virtue involves a complex negotiation of allegiance and performance, then what, we might ask, does feminine virtue entail? On several accounts, one of the great accomplishments of medieval romance is its conceptualization of female virtue outside the bounds of virginal sanctity. Within Latin Christian contexts, men and women were fallen beings, subject to the corruption of human flesh and the compromised status of human will and desire. Sexuality was both a product of and metonymy for postlapsarian humanity. Women, however, were more strongly associated with sexuality than men. The female body was allegedly prone to sinful urges that women were not well equipped to control, and a woman's beautiful body risked leading men astray as well. From the perspective of Christian exegetes, the Bible was replete with examples of dangerously seductive women, including Eve, Delilah, and Bathsheba, as was classical myth, which featured women such as Dido, Medea, and Deianira. According to anti-feminist stereotypes, seductive beauty is not merely a female characteristic but a weapon manipulated at will: duplicitous women trade on their beauty to win the love and loyalty of virtuous men and then bring about their downfall. The only virtuous women in this tradition are virginal women, female saints and above all the Virgin Mary, whose beauty indicates their purity and holiness.

Medieval romance, by contrast, celebrates the beautiful, erotic lady, devotion to whom constitutes the knight's virtue, not his downfall. As the desired object rather than the questing subject, the lady must be worthy of the knight's allegiance. She must therefore be beautiful and courtly, and she must also be a loyal lover, a status that neither requires marriage nor precludes adultery. Celebration of such women in medieval romance has long fueled celebration of the genre itself, on the grounds that the romance heroine constitutes a step forward in Western accounts of femininity. Recent scholarship is more skeptical of the pedestal upon which romance heroines are placed.[11] Howard Bloch, for example, argues that the genre's celebration of women marks not a departure from earlier anti-feminist traditions but their continuation. "No less than the discourse of misogyny," he claims, "does that of courtly love reduce woman to the status of a category; and no less than the discourse of salvational virginity does it place the burden of redemption upon the woman who ... finds herself in the polarized position of seducer and redeemer" (Bloch 1991: 196). Many romances nonetheless register awareness of the misogyny to which they subject women and simultaneously celebrate and eroticize courtly femininity even as they interrogate the bases and biases of these conventions. The English *Lybeaus Desconus* and *Mélusine* aptly illustrate such stances; both texts evoke and unsettle the romance associations of feminine beauty, eroticism, and virtue, although they do so to very different effects.

Lybeaus Desconus features a female character, the Dame Amoure, whose beauty, duplicity, and wickedness locate her squarely within anti-feminist tradition. A sorceress who seduces Lybeaus and temporarily delays him from his quest, the Dame Amoure is described in the briefest of terms: she is beautiful, unchaste, and skilled in sorcery, a recipe for disaster for any questing knight. The precise nature of the Dame's power is nonetheless left intriguingly uncertain. Initially, the narrator attributes her power to her beauty—Lybeaus capitulates to her "For she was bright and shene" ("Because she was radiant and lovely"; line 1475)—but then draws attention to her sorcery: "For the faire lady / Cowhte more of sorcerye / Than other suche fyve" ("For the fair lady knew more of sorcery than five others like her"; lines 1485–7). The Dame Amoure's actual practice of sorcery, however, falls disappointingly short of these grandiose claims, consisting of little more than the beauty one would expect of any aristocratic lady:

> Whan he sawe hir face
> Hym thought that he was
> In paradice on lyve;
> With false lies and fayre
> Thus she blered his eye:
> Evill mote she thryve!
>
> (When he saw her face
> He thought that he was
> In an earthly paradise;
> With fair and false lies
> She thus blurred his eye:
> May evil befall her!)

(lines 1492–7)

Seduction and deception in an earthly paradise: these features cannot help but recollect original sin, the transgression in Eden, and the original seductress, Eve. While such references are predictable if not overdetermined in misogynist tradition, this passage nonetheless raises a number of questions: is the Dame Amoure's sorcery nothing more than her remarkable beauty? Or, is her remarkable beauty an illusion resulting from her sorcery? Are all beautiful women sorceresses of sorts, presenting a beautiful outward illusion that belies their inner evil? Or is the duplicitous Dame Amoure manipulating a link between beauty and virtue that elsewhere obtains? Because multiple interpretations are possible, this episode illustrates the semiotic ambivalence of female beauty and its manifestation as a point of interest and anxiety in the romance genre.

While medieval authors often employ the tropes of female beauty and magical deception to anti-feminist ends, they occasionally do so to challenge misogynist thinking, as we see with the fairy Mélusine. At first glance, the fairy's secret, snaky tail does not bode well: long-standing Christian traditions associating serpents with sin cast Mélusine's hybridity in a negative light, as do late medieval visual representations of the biblical Fall from Eden, in which the Genesis serpent frequently bears a woman's face and is thus a hybrid figure much like Mélusine herself.[12] Yet Raymond's marriage to Mélusine marks an auspicious turning point in the nobleman's life: the two build a powerful kingdom, have ten sons, and live happily for many years. Their happiness ends, however, when Raymond's brother suggests that Mélusine's weekly withdrawal masks an adulterous affair. Raymond, fueled by his brother's vitriol, spies upon his wife and discovers her secret, but not the one he suspects: he sees Mélusine, alone, in her hybrid form, bathing and combing her hair. We might expect Raymond to turn on his supernatural wife, but he instead blames his brother and himself: "Thanks to your false and treacherous rumor," Raymond exclaims, "I have broken my promise to the being who, after the one who bore our Lord, is the best, most loyal lady ever born'" (D'Arras [*c*. 1392] 2012: 182). As E. Jane Burns notes, Raymond's comments locate Mélusine in a Christian context, but rather than comparing Mélusine to Eve or the Genesis serpent, Raymond "align[s] this half-woman half-serpent with the Virgin Mary" (Burns 2008: 187). Paradoxically, the discovery of Mélusine's hybrid body reinforces Raymond's belief in her virtuous integrity, as expressed when he laments her loss: "Now I have lost beauty, goodness, sweetness, affection, wisdom, courtesy, charity, humility, all my joy, all my comfort, all my hope, all my happiness, my prosperity, my worth, my valor, because all the modest honor God had lent me was by way of you, my sweet love" (D'Arras [*c*. 1392] 2012: 182). As Raymond's lengthy enumeration of his wife's virtues makes clear, Mélusine's beauty, regardless of her weekly transformation, accurately represents her inner state, and it is Raymond's beauty that proves misleading, as Mélusine observes in her own lament: "Oh, if only I had never seen your [Raymond's] graceful body, your gracious manner, or your handsome face! Would that I had never desired your beauty, since you have so perfidiously betrayed me!" (191).

Raymond's surveillance of his wife and its devastating effects indicate that the problem here lies not with women's waywardness but rather with social structures that formulate femininity in these terms. While Raymond's suspicions are in keeping with the misogynist thinking of the later Middle Ages, it is worth noting that such thinking was not the only available stance on women. The institution of marriage underwent dramatic transformations in this era, particularly regarding formulations of wifehood, which in turn revised constructions of femininity. Although marriage remained a hierarchical institution, the conjugal bond was increasingly described in terms of mutuality, and while wives were still represented as inferior beings requiring spousal supervision, they were also imagined as partners capable of contributing to the well-being of their husbands and the conjugal household. As Glenn Burger notes, conduct literature from the era when *Mélusine* was written encourages wives to advise their husbands on both household management and transactions further afield. To fulfill this conjugal role, the good wife must possess "a certain degree of female agency" (Burger 2018: 97). The fairy Mélusine is a good wife precisely along these lines, frequently advising her husband and using her powers to his benefit. It is when Raymond follows advice from his brother, and therefore from outside the conjugal unit, that disaster results. Consequently, this romance provides not only a marvelous origin myth for the House of Lusignan but also endorses a specifically late medieval model of marriage and femininity.

MARVELS

In framing Raymond's failure as a husband as his failure correctly to respond to his supernatural wife, *Mélusine* trades on a third romance trope: the knight's encounter with the marvelous. On all counts in *Mélusine*, Raymond is an exemplar of chivalric masculinity: he is handsome and courteous, and possessed of great prowess. When he sees Mélusine in her fairy form, however, the challenge he faces is not physical, nor one requiring conformance to well-established codes of aristocratic behavior. Mélusine's hybrid body instead poses a cognitive and ethical challenge. What is she? Is she good or evil? And, in response to a serpent-tailed fairy, what should a virtuous knight do? Because romance knights must regularly ponder such questions, the marvelous operates as an organizing principle for masculine adventure and subjectivity. And, as the spectacle of Mélusine bathing makes clear, knights encounter the marvelous, while female figures embody it.

In considering marvels, I begin by defining terms: what, in medieval romance, constitutes a marvel? In this context, the marvelous is determined not by the ontological status of a thing itself but the phenomenological experience of encounter: as Tara Williams puts it, "a marvel is something that makes one marvel" (Williams 2021: 108). Caroline Walker Bynum similarly observes that marvels are "deeply perspectival" in that they generate "a recognition of the singularity and significance of the thing encountered. Only that which is really different from the knower can trigger wonder" (1997: 3). The "singularity" that inspires wonder means that wondrous objects frequently defy the taxonomical categories through which a particular individual makes sense of the world. "Wonder," continues Bynum, "was ... associated with paradox, coincidence of opposites; one finds *mira* (wondrous) again and again in the texts alongside *mixta* (mixed or composite things)" (7). While a knight is required to respond virtuously to both mundane and marvelous challenges, the "complex wonder-reactions" invoked by the latter render correct ethical action more difficult to determine, and therefore more meaningful in establishing the knight's virtue (19).

In light of Bynum's commentary, the gendering of marvels in medieval romance makes sense: as "perspectival" phenomena, marvels materialize in relation to the perspective that a narrative follows. Because masculine subjectivity is the focus of romance, men are positioned to encounter marvels, while women are wonders to be encountered. Fairy mistresses and women transformed into serpents are examples of the female marvelous in romance, but so too are less supernatural women, especially if they happen to be beautiful. Feminine beauty is marvelous on account of degree—a woman whose beauty surpasses all others' is a wonder—and its ambivalence: as a property that marks both the best and worst of women, beauty inspires wonder because it is not immediately comprehensible. Moreover, if her outward beauty conceals inner vice, then the lady herself is, in Bynum's words a "paradox," a "mixed or composite thing."

We witness one such feminized marvel in *Le Bel Inconnu*, when our titular knight encounters a "huge and hideous" serpent (line 3136). The singularity of the serpent is repeatedly noted, both by the narrator—"No one ever saw such a serpent" (line 3133), he remarks— and the knight, who "marvelled greatly" at the creature, and "was so absorbed by looking at it / that he could not turn away" (lines 3181, 3183–4). The "complex wonder-reaction" the serpent evokes stems not so much from the danger the creature poses but from the taxonomical and therefore moral confusion it creates. The serpent may be "hideous," but its features call to mind aristocratic beauty: its tail contains "All the colors God created"; "its underbelly seemed to be golden" (3146, 3148); and its eyes shine "like two great carbuncles" (line 3140). This dazzling array of bright, shining colors, established through comparison to precious metals and gems, recollects romance descriptions of beautiful courtly ladies, as does the serpent's "mouth so red" (3182), which captures Guinglan's gaze. The human and the bestial, the beautiful and the hideous, all coalesce in this creature, to wondrous effect. It seems no accident that the serpent's wondrous hybridity recollects courtly femininity, both because, in reality, the serpent *is* a beautiful aristocratic woman, transformed through sorcery, and because femininity in medieval romance is itself a hybrid phenomenon, evoking worship and devotion, on the one hand, and bestial degradation, on the other. In the English *Lybeaus Desconus*, the creature's feminization is further compounded by the fact that this "worme," or dragon, bears "a womanes face" (lines 2067, 2068). This portrayal of the serpent seems not so much a departure from the earlier French romance than a literalization of the hybrid femininity that the creature metaphorically conveys.

In both the French and English romances, the creature's behavior defies expectations. In the French romance, which describes the encounter in detail, the serpent repeatedly bows and then kisses the knight. Terrified, the Fair Unknown reaches for his sword, but the creature's humility and "nobility of manner" dissuade him from striking (line 3194). In the shorter episode from the English romance, the hybrid serpent-woman immediately accosts the knight:

> And ere that Lybeous wiste,
> The worme with mouth him kyste
> And clypped about thee swyre.
>
> (And before Lybeous knew it,
> The dragon kissed him with her mouth
> And grasped him about the neck.)
>
> (lines 2082–4)

In both romances, this episode constitutes the "Fearsome Kiss" that the knight must withstand to complete his quest and break the spell that has transformed the lady. In both romances, too, the knight eschews martial performance—his means of addressing obstacles up to this point—to exercise restraint, explicitly so in the French *Bel Inconnu*, in which he stays his hand from attack, and implicitly in the English, where his uncharacteristic passivity in the face of threat might, as Williams notes, be read "as ... a further sign of Lybeaus's virtue" (2018: 54). The knight's success in this instance requires cognitive and ethical consideration. Borrowing Bynum's terms, this creature is, from the knight's perspective, singular and therefore significant: it demands contemplation of right action. By responding correctly to the serpent, the knight in turn establishes his own singularity as a pinnacle of chivalric masculinity. This point is underscored in both romances by the pairing of the revelation of the Fair Unknown's identity and lineage with his successful encounter with the marvelous: not only is Guinglan the son of Sir Gawain, one of the greatest of Arthur's knights but also *only* Gawain or one of his descendants could successfully face the Fearsome Kiss. Once again masculine virtue is both innate, deriving from Guinglan's lineage, and performative, established by his virtuous deed.

If the "Fearsome Kiss" episode establishes masculine virtue, it also raises questions about femininity: we can hardly ignore the fact that the challenge the knight confronts is an erotic encounter with a fearsome, feminized serpent. Due to associations between femininity, sexuality, and sin in medieval cultures, we might view these romances as adding a courtly veneer to a deeply misogynist tradition. For Eve Salisbury, the dragon-woman of the English *Lybeaus Desconus* exemplifies the "monstrous-feminine," a term she borrows from horror film studies to describe "any representation of a daunting mode of female sexuality eliciting fear in the men who encounter it" (2014: 67). The monstrous-feminine is "both dangerous and attractive," a pairing that renders it all the more threatening and results in various strategies of containment, including the "attempt to enfold the monstrous-feminine into more normative gender roles" (69). Thus, in the English *Lybeaus Desconus*, "the dragon-lady of Synadoun is transformed into a viable marriage partner," as also she is in

Le Bel Inconnu, although a partner whom Guinglan does not wish to accept (69). Nevertheless, in both romances the marvel of the dragon-lady facilitates normative structures of feudal marriage.

What disrupts this feudal marriage in the French *Bel Inconnu* is another marvel, one quite common to the romance genre: the fairy mistress. Guinglan does not want to be married to Blonde Esmeree because he remains devoted to his fairy lover, the Maiden of the White Hands. In the Middle Ages, belief in fairies was both widespread and sincerely held, as witnessed by the frequency with which church officials sought to stamp out such beliefs, or relegate fairies to the demons of Christian cosmology. While we might be tempted to attribute these beliefs "to some hypothetical primitive folk culture," Richard Firth Green notes that they permeated the aristocratic world and are reflected in its preeminent genre, the romance (2016: 44). Medieval formulations of fairies vary, but fairies are regularly associated with beauty, wealth, eroticism, prophecy, and supernatural powers. The first three attributes—beauty, wealth, and eroticism—also characterize courtliness; therefore, fairies might be thought of as an amplified version of aristocratic values. This is particularly true of the fairy mistress, a figure of masculine wish-fulfillment who, in taking a human knight as her lover, not only fulfills his erotic, *fin amor* fantasies but typically bestows wealth and power to boot. However, even as the fairy mistress is the apotheosis of courtly femininity, she exceeds those bounds, residing outside homosocial aristocratic societies. As James Wade notes, medieval fairies were "adoxic": they "existed in a 'state of exception' outside orthodoxy without also being strictly unorthodox. That is, they existed outside the established order of traditional customs, practices, and power relations ... without contradicting, or even directly opposing, such orthodoxies" (2011: 14). The fairy mistress's liaison with a knight does follow rules, but the rules are completely, often mysteriously, her own. Such rules frequently involve a prohibition, that the knight tell no one else of his fairy mistress, for example, or, as with the fairy Mélusine, that he eschew observing the fairy on specified occasions. The capriciousness and overt eroticism of the fairy mistress reinforce medieval antifeminist stereotypes, which frequently paint women as fickle and hypersexual, even as these negative traits are rendered marvelous, mysterious, and less condemnatory through their association with a supernatural figure. Residing within and beyond courtly traditions and anti-feminist stereotypes, the fairy mistress is a hybrid figure, a status that, coupled with her superlative beauty and supernatural powers, confirms her status as marvel.

The Maiden of the White Hands provides an apt example of the romance fairy. She resides outside the bounds of human society, both figuratively and literally; her home is the mysteriously named "Golden Isle." Upon her first appearance in *Le Bel Inconnu*, the Maiden seems like a typical romance lady. She is, of course, beautiful. She is also an object to be won—the man who successfully defends the bridge to the Golden Isle for seven years will be granted her hand in marriage—and consequently a figure around whom masculine identity is consolidated. En route to rescuing Blonde Esmeree, Guinglan arrives at the bridge and defeats its proprietor, a knight whom the Maiden despises. Yet Guinglan does not rescue the Maiden from an undesirable marriage, for we learn that she had no intention of *ever* marrying the knight, even had he completed the seven-year challenge. The Maiden's indifference to rules is underscored by her reaction to Guinglan; upon meeting the knight, she falls so deeply in love that she dispenses all together with the "custom" (Old French *usage* [2013]) of the bridge challenge and offers herself in marriage. Both the "custom" of the bridge and the customs that govern gender and sexuality more broadly do not apply to the Maiden, who is less an object to be won than a subject who acts on her own desires. As the romance progresses, the Maiden is revealed to possess additional fairy features, including incredible wealth, supernatural powers, particularly those of illusion and prophecy, and a frankly erotic investment in Guinglan.

The romance is nonetheless ambivalent about the Maiden's fairy status and makes concessions to the social systems that the Maiden otherwise seems to flout. For example, in her first intimate encounter with Guinglan, the Maiden's eroticism is curtailed by her mandate that the knight marry her before she fulfill his sexual desires; the Maiden refuses even a kiss from the knight (2450–3). In their second, equally premarital encounter, no such dictate limits the couple, as our narrator coyly reports:

> I do not know whether he made her his true love,
> for I was not there, and I saw nothing of it,
> but I know that the lady lost the name of maiden
> there at her love's side.
>
> (lines 4815–18)

The romance also signals ambivalence in its divergent accounts of the Maiden's supernatural powers. On the one hand, these powers mark her as fairy, an identity confirmed when Guinglan recollects his love affair with "la fee" ("the fairy," line 3699). The Maiden, however, provides an alternative account of her magic,

> My father was a very powerful king,
> a most intelligent and courtly man.
> I was his only heir,
> and he loved me so dearly
> that he had me study the Seven Liberal Arts
> until I had mastered them all.
> I learned a great deal about arithmetic and geometry,
> Necromancy and astronomy,
> and all the other arts as well.
>
> (lines 4933–41)

The Maiden's attribution of her powers to her mastery of the Seven Liberal Arts locates them within intellectual developments of the twelfth century, which similarly cast magic, particularly the "arts" of divination and illusion in which the Maiden specializes, as branches of knowledge acquired through diligent study. Skill in magic might be unusual, but it was no more supernatural than mastery of music or mathematics.[13] The attribution of the Maiden's powers to both her fairy nature and her Liberal Arts schooling may suggest some ambivalence about fairy femininity and its desirability as a characteristic of a romance hero's love interest. These are issues that the romance leaves notably unsettled, closing, as it does, with Guinglan's dilemma—will he—and, more importantly, should he—return to the Maiden and the fantastical realm of the Golden Isle, or remain with his wife, Blonde Esmeree, and serve as Arthur's vassal in Wales? In Bynum's terms, we might say that the Maiden's many paradoxes invoke a "complex wonder-reaction," from both Guinglan and the romance audience, and the ethical issues she raises are never fully resolved.

We encounter a different approach to fairies in Jean d'Arras's *Roman de Mélusine*. Mélusine is marvelous, as Jean frequently attests, but she is a marvel employed to mundane ends: she provides an origin myth for the House of Lusignan. As is typical of fairy mistresses, Mélusine is possessed of exceptional beauty; supernatural powers, including prophecy; and unsurpassed wealth, and she subjects her human lover to a seemingly arbitrary prohibition. Mélusine is unconventional, however, in that she is a fairy fully incorporated into human society. As a virtuous wife and mother, capable ruler, and self-proclaimed Christian, Mélusine sheds the "adoxic" morality of fairies such as the Maiden. Jean is keen to establish Mélusine's beauty and fertility, but he eschews erotic description of the fairy that might cast her morality in doubt. Despite Jean's efforts to anchor fairy glamor to Lusignan glory, his narrative frequently belies the hazards of tracing one's origins to a fairy mistress. That there is something indeed undesirable about Mélusine's fairy nature is indicated by her attempts to leave it behind and become fully human. When, at the beginning of the narrative, Mélusine's mother curses Mélusine for the imprisonment of her human father, she condemns Mélusine to retain her fairy status; otherwise, comments the mother, "the power of your father's seed would eventually have drawn you and your sisters toward his human nature, and you would soon have left behind the ways of nymphs and fairies forever" (D'Arras [c. 1392] 2012: 25). Frequent proofs and attestations of Mélusine's virtue counter her morally ambiguous status, but they at times come across as overly anxious, as if both the narrator and his protagonist protest too much. For example, when Raymond violates his wife's prohibition and she must depart from Lusignan, she addresses him as follows: "I want you to know who I am and who my father was, so that my children will not be stigmatized as the sons of a bad mother, a serpent, or a fairy. For I am the daughter of King Elinas of Scotland and Queen Presine, his wife" (194). Here Mélusine doubly denies her fairy status, both by claiming lineage through her human father and by designating her supernatural mother her father's "wife," a title that consigns her to human social conventions.

Mélusine's proclamation also addresses the concern that she might pass her problematic fairy nature on to her children. In romance, fairy offspring inspire both wonder and anxiety. In *Le Bel Inconnu*, for example, when Guinglan's lineage is revealed, his exceptionality is established not only through his father, the knight Sir Gawain, but also his mother, the fairy Blanchemal. This distinction, however, can cut two ways, pointing toward exceptional strength and prowess but also a demonic, evil nature, and it may be concern for the latter that accounts for the omission of Guinglan's fairy mother from the English *Lybeaus Desconus*.[14] Both forms of distinction mark the offspring of Raymond and Mélusine. Their sons are accomplished knights who defeat their enemies, rescue ladies, and expand Lusignan rule. However, they bear bizarre features—exceptionally large ears, a lion paw's birthmark on the cheek, a single eye—that mar their otherwise beautiful physiques. And, while the majority of sons behave virtuously, two do not. The aptly named "Horrible" is so "wicked and cruel" that in his infancy he kills two nurses (D'Arras [c. 1392] 2–12: 71). Another, Geoffrey Bigtooth, burns down a monastery and kills all the monks within, one of his brothers included. Enraged at the event, Raymond lashes out against his son and his wife as well: "By my faith in God, I believe that that woman is nothing but a phantom [Middle French *fantosme*], and that no fruit born of her womb can reach the perfection of goodness" (D'Arras [c. 1392] 2012: 189). These exceptions to the more virtuous rule of Mélusine's offspring not only call into question the fairy's virtue but also link her moral ambivalence to her sexuality, to her tainted "womb," and the equally tainted fruit her womb produces.

If Jean raises the specter that Mélusine's sexuality is problematic, he raises similar, oblique concerns regarding her femininity. All who encounter Mélusine extol her as the most virtuous of women. Notably, she establishes her virtue and promotes the Lusignan dynasty by exerting agency and performing tasks usually relegated to men: founding cities, building fortresses, and ruling wisely. The extent to which these are traditionally masculine activities is indicated through contrast to the many other women in *Mélusine* who perform traditional feminine roles. These women typically appear when Mélusine's sons travel abroad and their adventures require the rescue of a maiden heiress. Unlike Mélusine, these women are unable to rule independently or choose their husbands: while they are invariably happy to marry Mélusine's sons, these marriages are nonetheless arranged. The stark contrast between the fairy Mélusine and these mortal women underscores how exceptional Mélusine's fairy femininity is and the degree to which, even as she adheres to the socially sanctioned task of building her husband's kingdom, she nonetheless departs from standard expectations of noblewomen, both within and beyond the romance genre.

RAPE

The contrast between the exceptionally capable Mélusine and her more restrained daughters-in-law is one among many instances in medieval romance where female agency comes to the fore. Romance conveys femininity in terms of both helpless vulnerability and intimidating power. A woman's remarkable beauty, for example, can infatuate a knight and press him into her service, but it also renders her a desirable object to be fought over by men. This latter role brings me to the most radical form of female disempowerment in romance and to my final trope: the genre's portrayal of rape. On the one hand, in these idealized fictions of brave knights and beautiful ladies, rape appears nonexistent, operating only as an occasional threat from which the knight rescues the lady in the nick of time. And yet, as Kathryn Gravdal points out, "rape (either attempted rape or the defeat of a rapist) constitutes one of the episodic units used in the construction of romance" (1991: 43). In its rendering of rape as a literary motif, romance shifts the focus of rape from women to men; rape "becomes aestheticized and moralized" to consolidate masculine identity (14). For the knight, observes Gravdal, rape functions as a chivalric or ethical test, a test that requires he display his prowess or decide on the correct course of action. Rape, she continues, also "distinguishes the nobility from other classes: most ... would-be rapists are of inferior social origin, while ... female victims of assault or abduction are of noble birth." Additionally, rape "can be troped as an aesthetic marker of and testimony of physical beauty": a lady may, in other words, be so irresistibly beautiful that men seek to take her by force (44). As Gravdal demonstrates, these functions recast rape from a violent crime to "a moment of glory in the story of a knight's life" (76). Yet they also provide opportunities to explore the contradictions of a chivalric ideology that is itself based on violence and objectification of women (Figure 3.2).

An episode of *Le Bel Inconnu* illustrates several of the literary functions of rape delineated by Gravdal. En route to rescuing Blonde Esmeree, Guinglain encounters two giants, one of which is bent upon raping a maiden. This scenario presents Guinglain with an ethical test—should he disrupt his quest to rescue the maiden?—followed by a martial one. Up until this point in the romance, he has only fought other knights; fighting two giants is a more difficult challenge and one that will further augment his reputation should he succeed. As for the lady, the threat of rape is here marked by class distinctions. The maiden in need of rescue is the princess of Scotland, and the narrative implies that on account of her nobility rape would be a particularly horrible fate: the princess, we learn, "would not endure [rape] ... / She would rather have died" (lines 715–16). In suggesting that some women are so delicately refined that they cannot tolerate rape, the narrative divides women into two categories: those who are "rapable," presumably women from the lower classes, and those who are not—higher class women such as the princess. In rescuing the princess, Guinglan establishes both

FIGURE 3.2: Knight Coming to the Rescue of a Woman Threatened by Rape, from the Smithfield Decretals. BL Royal MS 10 EIV, fol. 74v. British Library, with permission.

her aristocratic worth—she is too good a woman to be raped—and his own—he possesses the ethical code and chivalric prowess to defeat the enemy.

While this episode clearly delineates between brutish rapists and virtuous knights, elsewhere in the romance such distinctions are murkier, as when Guinglan foists his presence upon the Maiden of the White Hands. This episode occurs after the lovelorn Guinglan returns to the Maiden to beg her forgiveness. The Maiden gives Guinglan a bedchamber adjoining her own but prohibits him from entering her chamber. Guinglan, stirred with longing for the Maiden, faces an ethical dilemma that plunges him into despair. Following Gravdal, at issue here is less the safety or autonomy of the lady than the internal processing of the knight, which is conveyed at length:

> My lady has forbidden me to go,
> and yet her face seemed to tell me
> that she was quite willing for me to do so.
> I fear that, if I stay,
> she will indeed think me faint-hearted.
> Dear God, if I only knew her wishes!
>
> (lines 4531–6)

What in the Maiden's "face" does Guinglan interpret as sexual willingness? We might guess that it is simply her beauty that "invites" violation: when first introduced in the romance, the Maiden is described as possessing "lips made for kissing / and arms for embracing" (lines 2239–40). This logic shifts agency from the knight to a depersonalized version of the lady: it is not her thoughts or intentions that signal her erotic "willingness" but her beautiful lips and arms. The violation of her command is in fact *necessary* to confirm the remarkable beauty that romance conventions require of her. By casting Guinglan as the helpless sufferer of *fin amor*, the narration further displaces his agency, and when he twice attempts to enter the Maiden's chamber, he is goaded to do so by "Amor," a feminized persona who acts as a double for the Maiden herself. Guinglan is thwarted, however, in his attempts by magical illusions that result in his humiliation and eventual remorse. On the one hand, this moment exposes *fin amor* as a courtly veneer, an ideology that, while ostensibly subordinating a knight to his lady's will, in actuality justifies its violation. On the other hand, the episode still frames the violation of the lady's will in terms of the knight's ethical development, development for which he is eventually rewarded with the prize he sought in the first place: entrance into the lady's chamber.

CONCLUSION

If, in providing a small sampling of the configurations of gender and sexuality to be found in medieval romance, this chapter demonstrates the complexity and ambivalence of medieval "fairy tales," then it has met its goal. Fantasies of brave knights and beautiful ladies are not indicative of a "child-like" culture, as has often been said of the Middle Ages, nor do they represent a clichéd calcification of gender and sexuality. In closing, I wish to suggest that this is just as true of more recent manifestations of "romance," by which I mean popular love stories, as it is of their medieval predecessors.

Popular romance is a frequently vilified genre, on counts that include its association with women readers, its focus on love, and its recycling of stock tropes such as the chivalrous knight and beautiful lady. In the film *Pretty Woman* (1990), for example, Vivien, a beautiful prostitute who captures the heart of the billionaire Edward, turns out to be a "lady" under the skin. Her beauty, as in medieval romance, serves as an outward marker of her inner virtue. As with romance ladies, too, Vivien's increasingly elegant clothing—iconic outfits including the brown and white polka dot "derby" dress and the red opera gown complete with a ruby and diamond necklace—proves key to her beauty and lovability. Vivien falls in love with Edward, but refuses to become his mistress, informing him, in one of the movie's most famous lines, "I want the fairy tale." A fantasy she recollects from childhood, Vivien's "fairy tale" is notably "medieval": she imagines herself as an imprisoned princess who is rescued by a knight, complete with white horse, "colors flying," and sword drawn. At the film's conclusion, Edward fulfills Vivien's fantasy, rolling up to her apartment building in a white limo and ascending her fire escape, calling out "Princess Vivien!" as he does so (Figure 3.3).

It is easy to mock this moment as pandering to sentimentality and reinforcing gender stereotypes, but we might better ask how and why such tropes continue

FIGURE 3.3: "Courtly" Beauty in *Pretty Woman* (dir. Garry Marshall, 1990). © Touchstone Studios, 1990. All rights reserved.

to circulate in our own culture, and why we are so quick to ridicule them. Elizabeth Scala observes that, like its medieval analogues, *Pretty Woman* is a self-conscious romance that trades on nostalgia; "the real danger of the film," she argues, "lies not in regression but in seeing it *only* as such" (1999: 42; emphasis in the original). While, for Scala, medieval romance and *Pretty Woman* are by no means identical, the former nonetheless provides a way to rethink our investments in the latter. Following Scala, my hope is that studying medieval romance conventions of gender and sexuality in all their complexity, intertexuality, and ambivalence not only helps us identify their continuation into modern-day fantasies but also sheds light on our cultural investments in such fantasies and their ongoing ramifications today.

CHAPTER FOUR

Humans and Non-Humans

Writing the Fairy, Reading Melusine

SARAH L. HIGLEY

A story motif circulated among writers in twelfth- and thirteenth-century western Europe about a beautiful, unknown woman in the woods—sometimes by a source of water—discovered by a nobleman who wanders there. Clearly, an unchaperoned noblewoman does not belong in the woods alone, but she fascinates the man sexually with her beauty, gentility, and availability. He agrees to marry her, sometimes on a strange condition she imposes to which he consents, and he acquires great prosperity in this miscegeny only to find, when he breaks her taboo or when she is shown the Host or made to hear Mass, that she reveals her hideous nature and flies away through the roof. Wherever and whenever she originated, she and her kind are the subject of this chapter. This mysterious woman straddles the human and the inhuman, the natural and the unnatural, the holy and the unholy, and meaning and the rupture of meaning. She is a well-known motif that I call "The Woman in the Wood" (Figure 4.1). Elsewhere she's known as the "fairy-wife."

FIGURE 4.1: The Woman in the Wood, Raymondin meets Melusine. Bibliothèque nationale de France, MS Francais 24383, fol. 5v (fifteenth century), Bibliothèque nationale de France, with permission.

The inhuman human in medieval Western European culture, particularly the figure of the fairy, has stayed with us for centuries. Throughout Europe, storytellers have been fascinated by an invisible people of a spiritual realm—what the Scottish author Robert Kirk called in his seventeenth-century book the "Secret Commonwealth" ([1692] 2008), or in Norway the *huldúfolk* (hidden people). They exhibit, as Thomas Shippey puts it, some quality of "strangeness which does not quite exclude humanity" (2005: 158), or vice versa: a humanity that is strange. There are similar creatures all over world literature and lore who, neither gods nor ghosts, emerge from the wild and assist humans magically.[1] But the European fairy is remarkably hard to define because the term has absorbed so many types and undergone so much evolution. Folklore studies of fairies that list their hierarchies, castes, names, and regions have gradually been replaced by studies of the overarching idea of the fairy itself and its contribution to literary, religious, and political thought. The medieval fairy examined here is para-human: it looks human, it exists on the margins of human society, and it intrudes upon human beings' social and salvific status as Christians—frightening, fascinating, erotic, and unknowable.

The fairy lives not merely in the oral tales about it but also in written texts whose authors manipulated it, argued over it, and fashioned it to their agendas. This chapter addresses that literary quandary, along with the disputed origins of what we now call "fairies." It explores the fairies' relationship to nature and the unnatural, examines their status in Christendom as both theologians and writers attempted to shape them, and gives some background on early contributions to the trope of the "woman in the wood" and her association with supernatural queenship. It ends with a discussion of *The Tale of Melusine*—the famous matriarch of Lusignan who is both a dragon and a woman—irresistible and damaging to the mortal who marries her. Melusine emerges full-blown in two long fourteenth-century French texts that together reveal complex political and personal controversies. *La noble histoire de Lusignan* was written by Jean d'Arras in 1393 for the Duc de Berry, who laid claim to Poitou after bitter fighting with the English, and *Le Roman de Parthenay* (c. 1399)[2] by Coudrette, which supported Guillaume de L'Archeveque's descent from the rulers of Parthenay, a citadel in Lusignan, and commissioned to prevent the demise of his own dynasty (Colwell 2011: 215–29). *The Tale of Melusine* is the quintessential "woman in the wood" story, about a fairy who longs in vain to achieve Christian salvation. She creates the Royal House of Lusignan in the wilderness of Poitou, and with the help of her authors pulls it apart historically and narratively. Part romance, part tragedy, part falsified history, this story epitomizes the category crises surrounding the fairy itself.

PINNING DOWN THE FAIRY

A fundamental uncertainty accompanies defining the fairy. Most likely, fairies are the ungodded versions of old, local gods—desacralized by Christianity but not erased. Michael Ostling's introduction to his anthology *Fairies, Demons, and Nature Spirits* focuses on the absorption of "small gods" into mainstream religion (2018: 1–53). For Kirk they were "subterranean habitants" of "a middle nature betwixt man and angel" with "bodies of congealed air" ([1692] 2008: 47). They comprise, he wrote, the "elves," "fauns," "fairies," "brownies," and "siths" (a variation of Old Irish *síd*, the mound or rath of the magical *Tuatha Dé Danann*, which became a term for its denizens: the *sidhe*). They live in fairy hills and other wild retreats, glimpsed only by those with "second sight." Medieval fairies are not so hidden or incorporeal: they are fully embodied, richly dressed, and can engender and bear children. They emerge from lakes and woods, seen singly in companies on their wild rides or "fairy rades." They can be mistaken for one of our own in the way an ordinary monster cannot: a chimera or a unicorn cannot be a fairy. Nor can a ghost or a ghoul. Fairies aren't dead, though they can be "apparitions." They appear to humans, help them, deceive them, seduce them, marry them, kidnap them, torment their babies or steal them, leaving "changelings" in their place. But they often gift one with poetic and prophetic talents and great wealth. They inspired taboo terms much the way the Greek Furies (*Erenyes*) were called the *Eumenides*—"the Gracious

Ones." The *tylwyth teg* (the fair folk) in Welsh, the Scottish *sleagh maith* (good people), or "the good women" reveal the need to "prevent the dint of their ill-attempts" (Kirk [1692] 2008: 47).

Their origins are difficult to line up: generally speaking, the medieval European fairy merges classical mythology with Germanic, and Continental and Insular Celtic mythology about supernatural humanoids whose names announce their provenance—"nymphs," "sylvans," and "fauns" being terms taken from Greek and Roman myth. Their dwelling places cannot be reached except by invitation and are often located in inhospitable areas: a region under a lake or a mountain, in a deep wood, on a mysterious island, or inside a pre-Celtic earthwork. Going there does something peculiar to human visitors, turning them strange ("awa' wi' the fairies") or warping space and time: the host in Chaucer's *Canterbury Tales* remarks that the narrator himself "semeth elvish by his countenance," because he is shy and unsociable.[3] In the eighth-century *Voyage of Bran*, the Irish king is approached by a mysterious woman who beckons him over sea to an Edenic island where he finds a people who live without sin and speak of Christ's coming. But returning from *Tír na mBan* (Land of Women) neither he nor his men can touch ground without dissolving into dust; hundreds of years have passed and he is only a legend (Meyer 1895).

In his important book *Fairies in Medieval Romance*, James Wade provides us with a useful term: the "ambiguous supernatural" (2011: 30–1), that which straddles the boundary between human and inhuman worlds. In efforts to pin the creature down, he limits the criteria for his "true fairy" to medieval Romance, excluding Morgan le Fay of Arthurian tradition from fairyhood since she is a sorceress. A fairy doesn't study magic, it *is* magic. A fairy has exceptional beauty and immortality, extraordinary power, origins from outside the known pale, and motivations that are often incomprehensible (12–16, 7). A fairy's response to cultural norms are often peculiar, such as the fairy-wife in the Welsh folkore tale *Llyn y Fan Fach* ("Lake of the Small Hill") who cries at a wedding and laughs at a funeral (MacLeod 2012: 129–30). Nor are fairies necessarily excluded from Christendom, writes Wade; rather, they are "adoxic"—freed from the moral practices (*doxa*) that govern human logic and religion, existing "in a state of exception" (2011: 15). Over the centuries "fairies" lost their extravagant bodies, sprouted insect wings, and traded beauty and terror for the "cute." C. S. Lewis rejected the term in *The Discarded Image*, declaring it "tarnished by pantomime and bad children's books" that encouraged us "to read the old texts in the light of it" ([1964] 2012: 123). He proposed instead the term *longaevi*, "longlivers." But "fairy" is too entrenched to be replaced.

The word derives from Latin *fata*, plural of *fatum*, "destiny": the three Fates or *Parcae* are the Roman version of the *Morai*, or "Lots" in Greek—Clotho, Lychesis, and Atropos—the daughters of the goddess Nyx, "Night," who spun, stretched out, and cut the threads of a mortal's life. Gervase of

Tilbury, writing his *Otia Imperialia* in Arles (*c.* 1200 CE), may have brought the word into scholarly use from Provencal *fada* (Green 2016: 79). The French had their own word for a fairy, *luiton*, from *nuiton* (a "neptune," nymph), but adopted the Provencal one, *faée/fée*, which gave English its "fay" and "fae." *Faery*, the region of the *fées*, became the word in English for the being itself. In Middle English it was used in tandem with "elf," derived from Old English *ælf/ ylf*, cognate with Germanic *alp* and Old Norse *álfr*, an invisible and spiritual being whose name may derive from an old word for "white." *Ælf* was both an honorific prefix in Old English names (Ælfred, Ælfric, Ælfwine: "elf-counsel," "elf-realm," "elf-lord") and creators of disease in the charms and medical remedies (*wið ælfsiden*, "against elf-magic"). *Beowulf's* Grendel is in a league with Cain and his monstrous spawn: *eotenas*, *ylfas*, and *orcneas* (line 112), but the term *ælfscine*, "elf-beautiful" in Old English, suggests an association of elves with the remarkable beauty seen in Romance depictions (Hall 2007: 25). J. R. R. Tolkien's elves clearly draw from this concept—immortal, aristocratic, hidden, and vanishing from civilization.

THE NATURAL AND THE UNNATURAL

Fairies are associated with natural or wilderness settings, many of them "unnaturally" shaped. The impressive illustrations in Brian Froud and Allen Lee's *Fairies* (1978)[4] attempt to make older versions of the fairy visible to us today by depicting its various peoples in lively motion—gnomes, pwcas, pixies, goblins, leprechauns, fairy rades, the *Gwragedd Annwn*,[5] and so forth. What impressed me was how they oppose the anodyne versions of children's fairy tales, painting some disturbing pictures of nude, distorted bodies, grotesquely slanted eyes, and sallow skin colors reminiscent of another race. Some of their changelings exhibit what looks like Downs Syndrome, pulling uncomfortably close to protected categories in the projection of difference and disability on imaginary beings. Many of their fairies are animalistic—the exaggerated muzzle, a snail crawling across a naked breast—and of course the pointed ears that come, actually, from earlier drawings of goatish satyrs. The background, everywhere in the book, is a natural setting: drawings and paintings of leaves, twigs, tangled woods, and wild flowers.

This is a complex nexus. What the medievals considered a "natural" setting is yet another crux on which the tale of the fairy rests uncertainly. In its long development the fairy is a type of nature deity and assumed in some traditions to care for the fertile world, even to bless births and weddings, as Shakespeare's fairies do in *A Midsummer Night's Dream*. But nature, an enormous topic in the long Middle Ages, was not always "nature" as admired by the Romantic movement and threatened by industry. In Latin literature, "Natura" was God's servant hammering out the teleology of the world and its things, visible and invisible. It is what established one's "kind" (an early word for "nature").

Wilderness was a result of the Fall, no longer the sheltered world of Eden. Certainly, medieval writers celebrated the inhabited outdoors, especially in their *reverdies*,[6] but every uninhabited valley and mountain was potentially dangerous and the haunt of wolves, outlaws, and the ambiguous supernatural. Women who strayed into the woods, as in *Sir Degaré*, might meet inhuman ravishers. For men, the wilderness was a signifier of madness or grief: the *Man* in the Wood—such as Nebuchadnezzar, Merlin, Lancelot, King Orfeo, and Raymondin—retreated there when they abandoned reason and civility. In Old English and Icelandic tradition it was a place of banishment. Outside the protection and recognition of society, outlaws were no longer valid persons and could be killed with impunity. In its human instantiations, the fairy, come from the wilderness, is often not a valid person. It is a fake, a poseur, an inhuman human that often "passes" for human, like the woman in the wood, while paradoxically being part of the invisible world of God.

The facsimile of a human is scary; not knowing whether one's loved one is an actual person or a diabolical, illusory, or mechanical copy of one still haunts our science-fiction and horror stories. Melusine, who is half-human (her father was mortal) carries the burden of her fairy nature but presents herself as human and Christian. Encountered in the woods by Raymondin, she longs to be lifted of the curse that keeps her in a hybrid state between mortal and immortal, woman and serpent-woman. "A woman who can die a Catholic death," writes Matilda Bruckner, "is natural; a fairy who suffers penance until the day of Judgment ... is not. In this view there are necessary exclusions: Melusine is natural only if limited to her identity as a woman" (2016: 23). She is only able to occupy a city when regarded as naturally marriageable, and even then she fashions it herself using mysterious workers, wandering into the domain of masculine making. Her manifestation as half-snake one day of the week stems from an ancient association of female water-deities hiding serpent or fish-tails under water, which in turn uncovers a long-standing association of woman's nature as duplicitous, aqueous, and evil.[7] However just and pious, Melusine gives birth to the violent, godless, and deformed Geoffroy *á la Grand Dent* who destroys Raymondin's faith in her. When her condition is revealed by her husband in Coudrette's poem, Melusine accuses him of consigning her to torment, when she might have had "le cours naturel comme la femme naturale" ("a natural heart like a natural woman") and been given the final sacrament and Christian burial (d'Arras 2003: 694; my translation).

CHRISTIAN, NON-CHRISTIAN, OR "THIRD SORT OF WIGHTS"

This raises an important question: how did authors reconcile treatment of a being that for whatever political and philosophical purposes is *theologically* as well as supernaturally ambiguous? In *Elf Queens and Holy Friars* (2016)

Richard Firth Green addresses the topic of "belief" in the fairy and efforts by the Church to quash it. The fairy's relationship to Christendom has a fraught history beginning with the early debates over *De Deo Socratis*, by the Numidian author Apuleius (*c.* 125–170 CE) and the status of the *daemon* (Ger. *daimon*). Apuleius enlarges on Plato's theory of the gods, wherein different intelligent beings are assigned to three regions: the celestial gods in the highest region are removed from human souls on Earth, but in the middle, aerial beings "the Greeks call 'demons' (*daemonas nuncupant*)" function as "ambassadors and goodwill messengers for both" (Apuleius 2017: 359–61). Apuleius tells us that just as the air itself is changeable, so too are the daemons susceptible to human emotional disturbances (367–73). In his fifth-century book *The City of God Against the Pagans*, Augustine opposes Plato's view along with Apuleius's endorsement of it that the daemons are entirely good and virtuous (2018: IX.1–3, 8: 250–1, 256–7). Could there be both good and bad daemons? Augustine denied it, and the demon acquired evil connotations as Christianity overtook it, sharing characteristics with the *incubus*, the spirit that "lies upon" a mortal woman in lust: "Many have verified by their own experience," writes Augustine, "that sylvans and fauns, who are commonly called incubi, had often made wicked assaults upon women ... and that certain devils called Duses (*Dusii*) by the Gauls, are constantly attempting and effecting this impurity is so generally affirmed, that it were impudent to deny it" (XV.23, 461).[8]

Ecclesiastical writers such as Burchard of Worms in the early eleventh century and William of Auvergne in the thirteenth worked hard to stamp out the spark among Christians who believed in fairies side by side with Jesus and the saints (Green 2016: 23). Green cites the "corrections" Burchard administered in his Penitential: "Have you believed what some are accustomed to believe that there are rural women (*agrestes feminae*) whom they call sylvans (*sylvaticas*)?" (15). The extraordinary beauty and benignity of fairies, as conceived by common people and reflected in the romances, along with their sexual allure, fecundity, and the fact that they could die in some traditions (unlike demons) made it difficult, writes Green, "to find ways [for their condemners] to rationalize them" (57).

A persistent Christian explanation for the phenomenon of fairies assigned them to the angels of tepid allegiance who fell with Satan, neither assisting nor opposing his rebellion (Green 2016: 21). The same debate arose: could there be both good and bad fallen angels? People seemed resistant to assigning such creatures entirely to evil. A number of medieval writers, including ecclesiasts, argued in favor of the benevolent fallen angel. The thirteenth-century German monk Caesarius of Heisterbach stands out in his sympathy for such creatures, and in his *Dialogus Miraculorum* he tells of a knight's faithful servant who is faultless in his beauty, fidelity, and reliability. He saves the knight supernaturally on several occasions, which sparks the knight's suspicion. When asked who he is, the servant admits to being one of the demons who fell with Lucifer. "It is the greatest consolation for me to be among the sons of men," he explains

(Newman 2018: 103–4). The knight dismisses him with an offer of payment, but the servant refuses and asks him to buy a bell to hang in a destitute church. Certainly there are fairies who are mortal, even Christian: the Fairy King Oberon in *Huon of Bordeaux* bequeaths the hero his kingdom at his death. Muldumarec in *Yonec* by Marie de France visits his lover in the form of a bird, is killed by her jealous husband and avenged by his son. Bertilak, a nobleman in his avatar as Green Knight or a fairy in his avatar as Bertilak, observes Mass in *Sir Gawain and the Green Knight*. Leslie Ellen Jones remarks that the Old Irish bird deities, a shape taken by the Irish "fairies," appear in one of the early Latin versions of *The Voyage of Saint Brendan* (*c.* 900 CE)—strangely similar to *The Voyage of Bran* (Jones 2002: 129). As described by Coree Newman, one of them tells the saint that they are the neutral angels cast out with the rebels and enjoy a liminal existence without pain: "Here we can see God's presence. But God has separated us from sharing the lot of the others who were faithful" (Newman 2018: 107). Later Norwegian folktales assigned fairies to the unwashed children of Eve who hid them from God out of embarrassment (Shippey 2005: 167). In early modern writings, advocates for a "neutral" spirit suggested "a third sort of wights," a term Richard Baxtor proposed in 1691 drawing from centuries of speculation that positioned fairies as outside Christian purview altogether (quoted in Briggs 1959: 171).[9] And yet not: Wade discusses at length the arbitrary conflation of faerie and damnation in the thirteenth-century tale *Thomas of Erceldoune*, where Thomas is abducted by the elf-queen to the typical otherworld of beautiful courts and ladies that must nevertheless pay a tithe to the Devil. And yet it is described as being separate from either heaven or hell (Wade 2011: 83–6)—hence the idea of the "Middle Kingdom." The fairy-queen was often identified as Proserpina, bride to Hades, directly in Chaucer's "Merchant's Tale" and indirectly in the English Breton Lai "Sir Orfeo," whose wife is abducted by a Fairy King to his land of the dead.

Perhaps due to the polysemous nature of Fairyland, "writing the fairy" provided medieval authors with a useful framework for invention or *poeisis* in what Wade calls "internal folklore" or "subcreation" (2011: 12–16, 7). Writers reshaped the fairy figure to their own narrative agendas, in hopes, too, of establishing their relationship as an author to a patron, or as an authority providing proof and patrolling falsehoods. The anonymous author of the ninth-century *Liber Monstrorum* satirizes the "impious" (and by implication "effeminate") writings that propagate stories about marvelous creatures (Orchard 1995: 257). He takes literary control over orally transmitted *rumor* (the monstrous goddess described by Vergil), which like the female body threatens to escape masculine moral authority, and glibly compares his book about them to painting "a little picture of a sea-girl or siren, which if it has a head of reason is followed by all kinds of shaggy and scaly tales" (257). Even in denying belief in them, authors were refashioning them and exhibiting them enthusiastically.

ELF-FASHIONING AND THE WOMAN IN THE WOOD

My inspiration for "writing the fairy" derives in part from the term "elf-fashioning," used by James Woodcock in his study of Edmund Spenser's *The Faerie Queene* (2004: 5). So having brought up this matter of controlling the female body, I turn now to the trope of the "woman in the wood," which outrightly associates the fairy-wife with the demon, but also with queens. Echoing the title of Stephen Greenblatt's book, *Renaissance Self-Fashioning: From More to Shakespeare* (1980), Woodcock shows how Spenser's use of "fairy" (i.e., "Fairyland") engaged him "both in writing about Elizabeth, and writing about the process of writing about Elizabeth": "Spenser persistently draws attention to his own role as poet and mythmaker throughout *The Faerie Queene*; this authorial self-fashioning is an integral part of his programme of 'elf-fashioning'—of representing Elizabeth as the fairy queen" (2004: 6). However, Spenser wrote in an age when the word "fairy" no longer raised an alarm among the literati. "The Good Women" were the stuff of Old Wives' Tales, even if Spenser took pains to change the name of his Fairy Queen from Proserpina (queen of the dead) to Gloriana.

Woodcock's analysis of "fairy" in *The Faerie Queene* (1590–6) is directed at a specific era, author, religion (Protestantism), and monarch, which draws allegorically from an idealized Welsh fairy culture representing the Tudors. Nevertheless, a similar analysis regarding authorship, patronage, and the use of a Celtic myth might be applied to *The Tale of Melusine*. Woodcock asks why Spenser needed "fairy" as a mythology for the reign of Elizabeth (2004: 2–3). In both England and France, a fascination centered on the supernatural nature of queenship. "Writing the Fairy," then, involves reining in and refashioning the wayward and all-too-powerful queen. *Melusine* is sprinkled with the same weird fairy dust emitted by a much earlier English queen given a "fairy-wife" story. Henry II's French wife, Eleanor of Aquitaine, held her "salon" of troubadours and poets in Poitou when she was escaping her English husband. It is obliquely told in the anonymous thirteenth-century text *Richard Coer de Lyon*: Richard's father, Henry II, asks his courtiers to find him a wife. They encounter the King of Antioch's daughter, Cassodorion, not in the woods but in an otherworldly boat. During the marriage ceremony, she faints at the sight of the Host during Mass, crying "for i am thus ishent; / i dar nevere se no sacrement!" ("For I am thus destroyed; / I dare never see the sacrament" [Larkin 2015: lines 193–4]). After bearing him children, including Richard and John, Henry exposes her fairy nature by making her look at the Host, and, screaming, she takes flight through the roof, disappearing with his daughter but dropping Richard to the ground (line 210–34). In his *Chroniques rimées* (c. 1240), author Philippe Mouskès likewise tells a story about how Eleanor's beautiful mother, lingering in the wood near a fountain, seduces the Conte d'Aquitaine, who has become separated from both the hunt and his dogs. He marries her, she gives him seven children, and when discovered to be a demon leaps through the church roof (Mouskès 1838: lines 18,696–809, 244–8). Even Gerald of Wales, a contemporary of Walter's and another Welsh Marcher (and no lover of the Plantagenets), tells in his *Liber de Principis instructione* (*c*. 1193) how Richard the Lionheart boasted that his family was descended from the demonic Countess of Anjou, in which we find all the familiar paraphernalia: the Count of Anjou meets her in a foreign land and marries her before he knows her heritage. When forced to observe the consecration of the Host, she flies away through a window (Gerald of Wales 1891: 301–2).

The all-too-real Eleanor and Elizabeth were brilliant and headstrong monarchs, but Eleanor was foreign and a queen consort, and her reputation for misbehavior (and beauty and charisma) was rewarded with a demonic heritage. She threatened the masculine authority of her husband, who put her on house arrest, so it's fitting that she or her French mother skyrocket through the ceiling.[10] Eleanor's own great-granddaughter to the eighth degree was Elizabeth Woodville, grandmother to Elizabeth I, said to have seduced Edward IV under an oak tree by sorcery. Spenser's allegory, rather, projects the shape-shifting Woman in the Wood upon Duessa, the fake human, the allegory of the monstrous feminine, and the ultimate abject whose exposed nether parts are far more repulsive than Melusine's rather beautiful snake tail. Spenser also tempts us to decode his poem, writes Woodcock, "with the promise that the most vigilant readers might 'find' fairyland through 'certein signes here sett in sondrie place'" (2004: 2; *The Faerie Queene* [hereafter FQ] II.Proem.4), again drawing further attention to the authorial process of recreating Elizabeth who had already recreated herself by assuming two bodies as woman and "prince": the "body natural" becomes "an inherently artificial construction, subsumed within the image or sign of the queen's political body or body politic" (Woodcock 2004: 39). Spenser tempts us to interpret not just his poem but his queen.

THE MELUSINE MYTH

Jean and Coudrette likewise rein in bad rumor about queens. Melusine assumes three bodies, all of which are troubled: her fairy body is deformed; her body politic is fraught with grisly battles, parricide, fratricide, homicide, and infanticide; and in her instantiation as human she is an actor, behaving *like* a generous, pious, and motherly lady. How Jean tempts us to interpret his fairy is more speculative, but all these elements were put in a romance that celebrated a family history while remaining faithful to a nightmarish fairy tale. Jean gives assurance to his patron that he has consulted the best sources for the authenticity of his story, calling upon among other texts Gervase of Tilbury's *Otia Imperialia* (*c*. 1215) as a major source for the adventure of Raimundus and his encounter with the iconic woman in the wood (Gervais of Tilbury 2002).

Gervase tells two stories related to the Melusine myth. The one is called "The Lady of the Castle of L'Éparvier," the usual story set in the Kingdom of Arles where she flies away with a demon, taking part of the chapel with her (Gervais of Tilbury 2002: III.57, 665). In *Melusine*, "Sparrow Hawk Castle" is a site of punishment for Melusine's sister Melior. Jean directly references the other story: Raimundus, lord of Rousset in Aix, meets a beautiful woman in a forest, who tells him he will have great material prosperity if he agrees to marry her on one condition: that he never attempt to see her naked. He rises in fortune, and she bears him beautiful children whose descendants still survive; but one day he wants to see her in her bath: she turns into a snake, plunging her head under the water, disappears, and the man's prosperity plummets (III.57: 88–91). It is more likely that Jean drew upon Pierre Bersuire who in his *Reductorium morale* (c. 1325) describes a legend in his Poitou homeland which draws closer to the plot of Melusine. An unnamed nobleman marries a fairy who is the founder of Lusignan and ancestor to kings in Jerusalem and Cyprus. She transforms into a snake when discovered naked, but returns, as does Melusine, whenever the House changes ownership (bk. XIV.Prologue).[11] In his *De nugis curialium* (c. 1190) Walter Map tells a darker, more misogynistic version: Henno finds a girl alone near the shore of Normandy who tells him that she survived a tempest on a ship that bore her unwillingly to wed the king of France. He agrees to marry that "brilliant pestilence" (*nobilam illam pestilenciam*) and the woman bears him beautiful children. Observing that she won't take Mass, his mother spies on her through a chink in the bathroom door and sees her bathing as a dragon, her maid attending her, until she resumes her human form. Sprinkled with holy water, the brilliant pestilence and her maidservant leap through the roof with loud shrieks (Walter Map 2002: IV.9, 344–9). Robert L. Chapman thinks Walter intended this story to satirize Eleanor of Aquitaine, but he misses mentioning its similarity to Gervase and *Melusine* (1955: 393–6). He hints at the caché attached to monarchs and popular heroes with inhuman parents and quotes Caesar of Heisterbach: "Even the kings now ruling in Britain, which we call England, are said to be descended from a phantom mother" (396).[12] Given Eleanor's connections with both Aquitaine and Poitou, it seems likely that a legend peculiar to southwestern France generated both stories: a diabolical French queen and mother of English kings who claimed that territory, and a fairy noblewoman and mother of French crusaders and conquerors who also claimed it. Both Jean and Coudrette may have banked on their respective patrons' desire to have an illustrious supernatural for an ancestor in Lusignan who matched Eleanor of Aquitaine in conduct, power, and progeny. Or the reverse: Henry's medieval court acquired the prestige (and curse) of a Melusine.

This may be why she wasn't allowed to leave more than a footprint in Renaissance England. Misty Urban exposes the strange lack of interest shown in her by early modern English readers and writers. Aside from two anonymous translations made at the end of the fifteenth century—one of Jean's prose story and another of Coudrette's poem—"Melusine spawns no imitations or adaptations of her story [in England] as do the legends of Arthur and Charlemagne, Jason and Alexander ... nor does she acquire an intertextual life as parable or literary icon as do other mythical women like Dido or Iseult" (Urban 2010: 43–4).[13] There seems, she suggests, a distaste in early modern England for stories of monstrous, shape-shifting heroines, coupled with the fact that after the Hundred Years War and the bitter fight over Poitou, the English were disinclined to promote her (50–1). Melusine seems to have been dismissed in favor of lighter fare; Renaissance England's premiere writers on fairies dropped their association with the doomed. In *A Midsummer Night's Dream* Oberon declares in response to Puck's references to damned spirits of the night "but we are fairies of another sort" (Act III, scene ii, line 1445), putting the quietus on the religious drama central to Melusine. The sixteenth-century Swiss physician and alchemist Paracelsus submits Melusine to a scientific reanalysis. In his chapter "On Nymphs, Sylphs, Pigmies, Salamanders and on Other Spirits," he conducts an examination of the "four kinds of spirit men" inhabiting the four natural elements, purified, in chemical terms, of evil (Paracelsus 1941).[14] Above the animals intellectually and below humans spiritually, they appear to us when God wants them to. The nymphs, or water-people (like Melusine), seek marriage with men to acquire souls, and it is wrong to condemn her kind by succumbing to *superstitiones*, a fault of the "Roman Church" (Paracelsus 1941: 245–6). On the continent, though, Melusine's urgent need for Christian salvation made her both admirable and tragic. Melissa Ridley Elmes proposes in "The Alchemical Transformation of Melusine" that Paracelsus's scientific critique was more influential on nineteenth-century interest in her as a fairy figure than the romances (Elmes 2017a: 95–105). Both authors succeeded, however (especially Coudrette's poetic version), in producing a beloved female figure in France whose sad story attracted fifteenth-century translators in Spain, Germany, the Netherlands, Iceland, and two in England.[15]

PASSING FOR CHRISTIAN: *MELUSINE* AND THE LUSIGNAN DYNASTY

Unlike Spenser's poem, *Melusine* is a pseudo-genealogy that not only takes the existence of fairies seriously but also uses the myth of a supernatural ancestor to bolster the prestige of Poitou for their writers' patrons. The site of Melusine's origin is Lusignan, its castle built in the eleventh century by a powerful family from Poitiers whose descendants conquered and controlled kingdoms in Jerusalem and Cyprus during the crusades. The legend of its fairy architect and matriarch offers a counterpart to the Matter of Britain at a time when France was fighting the Hundred Years War with England. It closely follows the paradigm of the "woman in the wood": for cruel treatment of her mortal father, Melusine suffers a curse laid upon her by her fairy mother. She becomes a hybrid snake-woman every Saturday. If she can find a mortal husband who will respect the taboo she imposes, never to seek her out on that day, she will become mortal and receive last rites at her death. Eventually, Raymondin is tempted by jealousy and, at the urgings of his brother, he finds her chamber and spies on her, whereupon he sees her, a woman from the waist up splashing her enormous snake tail in the bath (Figure 4.2). He says nothing of it, distraught more about his betrayal of her trust than her fairy-nature. But when their son Geoffroy in a fit of temper burns down a monastery with his brother in it, Raymondin denounces her as a demon and she takes wing as a dragon and flies from the window, howling with grief. She returns for three nights every time Lusignan acquires a new sovereign.

Reception of her then and now is sympathetic. Chera A. Cole makes a relevant point about Melusine and racial miscegeny, arguing that the fairy in this text is treated like a subrace whose genetic makeup deprives her of the privilege of salvation (Cole 2019: 240–58). Her doom is fore-ordained because of her hybrid blood, even though her marriage bed is blessed by a bishop, and she "performs" as human in all Catholic rites. Cole's essay brings to mind the racialized imagery in Froud and Lee's *Fairies*, along with Paracelsus's claim that fairies are elevated animals, beneath humans spiritually, and Cole laments

FIGURE 4.2: Melusine in her bath. Bibliothèque nationale de France, MS Francais 24383, fol. 19 (fifteenth century). Bibliothèque nationale de France, with permission.

that it is Geoffroy and Raymondin who in being human can achieve salvation: "for all of fairy's beauty and allure, humanity is the privileged race in this paradigm" (258). In "The Elves as a Category Problem," Shippey explores the matter of the fairy as racial and religious conundrum, addressing the degree of "humanness" the *huldufólk* and other semi-supernatural creatures of Scandinavian origin exhibit, much of it in post-medieval literature and folklore, where the elves "seem to be effectively parallel and similar to humans" in needs and lifestyle (2005: 166–7), almost as though pagans have taken to the woods and cross paths, occasionally, with Christians. He recites the story of the elderly Scotsman reading his Bible who is approached by an elf-girl. She asks him if it mentions salvation of her kind, and she kills herself in despair when he insists that reward belongs solely to the sons of Adam (165–6). The Franciscan author Louis Marie Sinistrari opposes that implacable opinion in his *Daemonalitas*, citing John 10:16: "Alias ova habeo, quae non sunt de hac ovuli" ("I have other sheep who are not of this fold") "in support," writes Shippey, "of there being a divine mission for non-humans: There seem to have been widespread but disconnected traditions both of disagreement about the possibility of salvation for non-humans, and of a search for Bible texts which might answer the Scottish fairy-woman's question more favorably" (2005: 166).[16]

A divine mission for non-humans is vividly described by St. Jerome in his *Life of Paulus the First Hermit* (c. 375 CE). Both Gervase and Walter reference it. Saint Antony goes into the desert to find the first hermit, Paul. He asks a centaur for directions. "The creature, gnashing out some kind of garbled speech, attempts a courteous reply," and points. Antony proceeds and meets "a tiny little man ... his brow knobbly with horns, and his body terminating at the other end in goats' hooves." When asked who he is, the creature replies that he is a mortal worshipped by heathens such as fauns, satyrs, and incubi: "I bear a message from my flock: we beg you to pray for us to your God and our God. We know that salvation once came into the world, and its sound has gone out to all the earth." Antony condemns the ignorance of Alexandria, "you who worship prodigies[17] instead of God! .... The very beasts speak of Christ" (Gervase of Tilbury 2002: I.18, 98–101). The "beasts" seem to be less fairy and more pagan. Walter's version is predictably cynical, losing the story when he gets to the little horned man who told him he was "of the angels who were cast out with Lucifer, and were scattered throughout the world, each one according to the deserts of his pride" (Walter Map 2002: II.15, 162–5).

These two accounts, creatures humble and blessed and creatures proud and cursed, underscore the paradox Jean d'Arras addresses. He begins his preface to *The Noble History of Lusignan* by quoting obliquely from Aristotle's *Metaphysics* 5.16, about the progress of the soul toward perfection impeded by vice. The reference is double-edged as it expresses his own need to perfect a tale about a fairy who aims to perfect herself but is cursed by her circumstances. Her project is fragile because it depends on the loyalty of an imperfect human being and not God's mercy. But God's plan for fairies should not be questioned, Jean declares, quoting biblical evidence of His divine mission for the invisible as well as the visible: "The prophet David says that the judgments and punishments of God are like a boundless, bottomless abyss …. And I believe that the marvels which occur on earth and throughout all creation are eminently true, including those things that are said to be the work of fairies or enchantments [*les choses dictes faees*] …. Thus we mortals should not, through outrageous presumption [*par oultrageuse presumption*], strive to fathom the judgments and works of God with our human understanding" (d'Arras [*c.* 1392] 2012: 19–20; 2003: 113).[18]

The rest of his prologue acknowledges the legends surrounding the "woman in the wood," giving prominence to Gervase's account of Raimundus, and evidence of fairy activity by his people:

> Things some call *lutins*, others fairies, and others the "good women" who go about at night. Of these, says a certain Gervase, the lutins enter houses at night without battering down or even opening the doors, and snatch infants from their cradles and contort their limbs or burn them. Yet when they depart they leave them as healthy as they were before, and to some of them they even grant good fortune in the world.
>
> (d'Arras [*c.* 1392] 2012: 20)

Already, Jean is knee-deep in conflicting data. What point is served in linking his beautiful, tragic fairy-wife with Gervase's account of sadistic violence against children by *lamiae*, female monsters depicted in the Middle Ages as infanticidal serpents with women's heads?[19] Whereas Coudrette saves Melusine's fairy history until the discovery of her father's tomb, Jean begins by announcing Melusine's monstrous situation. His female fairy characters are driven by *gessa*, or taboos laid upon them: her mother, the fairy Presine, provides the illogical quotient in the first of three woman in the wood stories.

A king of Scotland and newly widowed, Elinas goes hunting a stag in the forest and is drawn to a fountain where he hears a woman, Presine, singing. Enchanted by her beauty, he agrees to marry her on condition that he never undertake to see her in childbed, obscurely echoing the injunction in Gervase not to see her naked. When she bears three daughters, his son by his previous marriage urges his father to behold them, and his wife vanishes. Presine takes her children—Melusine, Melior, and Palestine—to Avalon where they view Scotland, the land they would have inherited from Elinas, were it not for his betrayal; for the seed of their father (*la vertu de germe de ton pere*) would have drawn human nature to them and liberated them from the condition of nymphs and fairies (*des meurs nimphes et faee*; d'Arras [*c.* 1392] 2012: 25; 2003: 135). Melusine convinces her sisters to use their powers to enclose Elinas under the mountain Brumblerio in Northumberland, apparently assuming that this vengeance would please their mother. For this cruel act, Presine curses her daughters, shutting up Melior and Palestine, but imposing the harshest "gift" upon her eldest because it bears with it bodily humiliation and pins all hope on a fallible mortal. In this way, Jean rescues her condition from being native, but doesn't entirely erase her proximity to the legends of the lamia. Every Saturday Melusine transforms into a snake from the waist down. She can remain in human form the rest of the week and acquire her father's humanity only if her husband agrees not to seek her out on that day.

The story then proceeds to mirror this scene a second and a third time: a nobleman quarrels with the nephew of the King of Brittany and slays him. He flees to the forested mountains near the Rhone, approaches a fountain and a beautiful woman tells him his life's story. They marry, building fortresses in that wilderness that they name Forez ("forest"). After a quarrel the wife leaves the Count of Forez, and he marries the sister of Aimery, the Count of Poitiers, with whom he has a son Raymondin. Aimery adopts him, and on a boar hunt he and Raymondin get separated from the chase. Aimery is an astrologist and reads in the stars a curious prophecy: he who kills his lord this night will prosper. The boar charges out of the woods at them, and Raymondin strikes it with his sword, which glances off the boar's back and kills his uncle by accident. After slaying the boar and weeping over Aimery, he flees the scene, having neither buried his uncle nor called for help. He then trades perjury for honesty, because while he is lamenting his terrible mistake he encounters three women at a fountain in the woods. The noblest one hails him by name and to his astonishment knows his predicament and the prophecy. Perceiving his suspicion that she is a fairy, Melusine recites the Creed, assuring him she is a practicing Catholic and that it's safe to marry her. She gives him legal advice that will rescue him ("besides God Himself, it is I who can best advance your cause in this mortal world"; d'Arras [*c*. 1392] 2012: 33).[20] He is to join the search party and act as though he lost his uncle during the hunt, and mourn with the others for Aimery's death by the boar. Melusine then counsels him how to deceive Bertrand, Aimery's son and the new Count of Poitiers: have the count grant him as much land in Poitou that the hide of a deer covers. He cuts a thin, continuous thread from the hide that her servants attach to stakes planted around the fountain and the valley, surrounding a sizeable territory to everyone's amazement. His cousin is suspicious because Raymondin has consented to marry a woman of unknown heritage. When the wedding party arrives, they find a castle where none was before, and a chapel so lavishly decorated no one can doubt that Raymondin is marrying a noblewoman, although the work has been done so quickly it astounds them.

At this point, a reader might question the integrity of killing one's uncle, leaving him unburied and lying about it, sins that Raymondin represses in the enchanted life that follows. One may ask the same of Melusine's role in encouraging his deceit. Seen outside the usual fairy ostentation, the unnatural construction of the chapel borders on the sacrilegious. In a non-Christian context, Melusine provocatively merges the demon fairy and the Sovereignty Figure of Irish tradition wherein a shape-shifting matriarch assists the young king in legal matters. In the eleventh-century tale "The Adventures of the Sons of Eochaid Mugmedon," for instance, Níall is rewarded for having sexual intercourse with the hideously ugly lady his brothers refuse, and in return she not only transforms into a beautiful woman (declaring herself the symbol of his kingdom—lovely when it is peaceful and ugly when it is at war) but she also teaches him how to get the fealty of his brothers and declare himself king (Carey 1997: 192–7). Meanwhile, Jean does something clever that no other source does: he makes it impossible for Raymondin to refuse the woman in the wood if he wants to live, refining the incautiousness of his predecessors by stepping up the psychological nuances. Both he and Melusine depend on each other for something they need and cannot confess, both of them encumbered by patricide and connected in this matter of the boar, the fulcrum that brings the two together in disaster. Melusine bears Raymondin ten sons, eight of whom have a facial blemish, three of them marred by animal totems that call to mind the bestial nature of fairy lineage: Antoine's lion paw growing from his cheek; Fromont's mole skin on the tip of his nose; and Geoffroy, who kills his brother deliberately, has a tooth the size of a boar's. The eighth son, "Horrible," has three eyes, sharp teeth, and kills his nurses when suckling them.

Geoffrey, especially, plays a paradoxical role in this story. Sylvie Roblin begins her seminal essay "Le Sanglier et la serpente" by noting that the early sixteenth-century Lyonnais printer Francois Fradin designed an escutcheon for the Lusignan family that put Melusine, depicted as a siren, on the right side of the coat of arms and Geoffroy "Grand Dent" in his armor on the left—not Melusine and Raymondin (Roblin 1985: 247). What gets sublimated, here, she argues, is a conflict, not an alliance: the boar versus the serpent. What is also sublimated, I propose, is the historical figure of Geoffroy II of Lusignan (1198–1247) whose real deeds did not flatter the Duke and his claims on both Berry and Lusignan, contested as well by the L'Archeveque family and its English sympathies. The demise of Melusine leans upon Raymondin's betrayal of her secret when he learns of the fictional Geoffroy's deed—his tusk a reminder of his betrayal of his uncle during a boar hunt. Violent on the battlefield, Geoffroy II was notorious for both atheism and brutalizing the Abbey of Maillezais in Poitou for seven years, demanding that he take charge of it as protectorate since he had inherited it. When it wasn't handed over he burned it along with its monks, for which he was excommunicated. Pope Gregory IV absolved him after he did penance and rebuilt the abbey (Nolan 1974: 83–6). Jean gives none of this background, but instead has Geoffroy object to his brother Fromont's decision to throw away his inheritance and join a monastery rather than the military, over which he is so enraged he incinerates him along with his fellow "lecherous" monks (*ces lecheours moynes*; d'Arras [*c*. 1392] 2012: 187; 2003: 680). No justification is given for the "lechery" or Fromont's involvement in it. Coudrette in his poetic version attempts to rationalize it: when Fromont asks permission to join a monastery, Raimons suggests one of prestige and reputation: the monks at Maillezais, he says, are *testus*, "obstinate," of dubious Christian behavior (Coudrette 1982: 204, line 2873). Fromont insists, and Geoffroy trembles and swells up like a boar (*pors*, the vulgar term for *sanglier*), accusing those "lecherous monks" of enchanting his brother (225, line 3520). Geoffroy's action is still an incommensurate response to an unclear misdemeanor. So the boar, like the repressed, returns, inspiring Raymond's rage and his betrayal of Melusine as a mother of monsters.

Scholars have debated whether the facial blemishes of Melusine's children are the *envies de mères* or "mother marks" of a demonic woman or whether they represent the weakness of her husband's false shot at that boar.[21] Except for one campaign in Brittany encouraged by Melusine, Raymondin does nothing else of note in the story except spy on her and out her as a demon. Everything has been provided for him by magic: a wife, a court and castles, material wealth, name, prestige, sons whose military exploits bring the family fame, and a reprieve from punishment for his crime. It is Melusine, an architect par excellence, who designs the city. It is she who sends her sons off to the Crusades with advice for Christian conduct and courage, not their father, wherein Jean upgrades her wisdom from Sovereignty Figure to Mirror for Princes.[22] It is she who gives them magic rings that will ensure their success on the battlefield if they are virtuous. Raymondin believes his brother's suggestion that he has been "enchanted" by his wife, who on Saturday is either committing adultery or visiting the place where fairies go. Raymondin peeps at her, but her curse is postponed until Geoffroy's incendiary act. "The boar (*sanglier*)," Roblin declares, is the moral perception (*conscience*) of Lusignan (Roblin 1985: 248) because in opening Raymond's eyes, Geoffroy Big Tooth reveals and destroys Melusine's latent malignity, and diminishes her in her support of him as a rational and humane agent.

Observe her attempts to comfort her husband in his grief. She enters his chamber with an entourage of lords and ladies and reminds him bloodlessly of the futility of weeping so much, because it is useless and unseemly for a lord, and then supports Geoffroy's atrocity with an atrocious argument: Geoffroy has performed God's will against sinful monks who deserved it:

> My lord, it is very foolish that you, the wisest prince alive, should grieve this way over something that cannot now be changed. Do you wish to challenge the will of the Maker of all things, who also unmakes them when it pleases Him? Nowhere is there such a great sinner that God does not extend him even greater, more willing pardon if he repents and cries out to him for

mercy, sincerely and from the heart. If your son Geoffroy committed this outrage on account of his extraordinarily fierce temperament [*son courage merveilleux et fort*], you can be sure it happened because of the sinfulness of the monks, whose ways were so lax and dissolute [*qui estoient de mauvaise vie et desordonee*, "who led a bad and dissolute life"] that our Lord wanted [*voulu*] to punish them, however inconceivable that may seem to mortal beings [*humaine creature*]: for God's judgements are so secret that they surpass human understanding.

(d'Arras [*c.* 1392] 2012: 190–1; 2003: 692)

Here she repeats Jean's declaration in his preface that a mortal is not (through outrageous presumption) to judge God's mind, although a fairy presumably can do so better than any *humaine creature*. Jean has finally elevated her from clever adviser and counselor to a semi-divine figure of wisdom like Lady Philosophy who shows her distinction from humanity, the very state she craves, by a rejection of human compassion. Melusine even thanks God for their material wealth (provided by her own magic) that can rebuild and repopulate Maillezais with "more monks than before."

This matter of salvation, then, is curiously evaded when it comes to their own son Fromont. Raymondin counters this unnatural argument with the natural response that her monastic child, the best among her sons, deserved God's mercy too (d'Arras [*c.* 1392] 2012: 191; 2003: 692–4).[23] Cursing the fate that made him kill his uncle and seek refuge in a woman in the wood, he publicly accuses Melusine of polluting their sons with her fairy blood. In Jean's version, Melusine never acknowledges Fromont, whereas Coudrette has her remark: "If your son is dead along with them / Have no grief or pain for him," (1982: 241, lines 3974–5). Her argument in his version is even more incongruous: "God does not at all wish death / Upon a sinner," she says in the poem, meaning Geoffroy, and preposterously a few lines later she announces that God has summarily killed a hundred "lechers" and "false monks" by Geoffroy's hand: "know that it was for punishment / Inflicted by God upon the order" (241, lines 4017–18). In omitting any explanation of the monks' conduct, both Jean and Coudrette must work around a hole in their story that prevents proper closure. After a heart-rending farewell in both versions, Melusine turns into a dragon, leaving her footprint on the sill of the window as she flies away wailing (Figure 4.3). The rest of the story accounts for Geoffroy's visit to the pope, his penance, and the long-postponed confession of Raymondin who enters a hermitage.

Jean's dilemma in writing the fairy reveals what Jane H. M. Taylor calls "violations in narrative schemata," by which she means the expectations promoted for plot that are "blocked" or neutralized: the magic rings that are never mentioned again; the facial features of the sons that are blithely dealt with and dismissed such that no one thinks they mar the heroes' beauty (1996: 165–200). Taylor wonders if these apologia "indicate an authorial

FIGURE 4.3: Melusine flees Lusignan. Bibliothèque nationale de France, MS Francais 24383, fol. 30 (fifteenth century). Bibliothèque nationale de France, with permission.

embarrassment" at having to include from the sources that Jean consulted "potentially disgraceful marks" (174). There is no extant source for these blemishes and Jean may have invented them. His narrative, writes Marina S. Brownlee, is plagued with supernatural and literary "interference," where writing the fairy both sustains and undermines his project (1996: 226–40). Brownlee proposes that Jean was aware of the perils he took in producing an allegory of political and Christian strength that draws upon a demonic myth of deceit and violence. He is caught between having to "render credible the genealogical succession between Melusine and his patron" (hence the appeal to authorities at the beginning) and distancing himself from its contents by specious neutralizations (237). He focuses, therefore, on the folly of Raymondin to portray his patron's "consummately human—rather than mythological—lineage" (239). Far from being the befuddled storyteller embarrassed by his content, Jean urges us to view Raymondin's dilemma and that of his countrymen symbolically—as one cushioned by enchantment, what Stephen J. Nichols calls the "distorting perspective" of the demonic image from which Raymondin finally awakens: "He recognizes that for once he can look at his wife and children without her surrounding gloss" (1996: 142, 147). The story can get on, then, with the business of Raymondin's and Geoffroy's maturation as human patriarchs in place of the phantom matriarch.

CONCLUSION

None of the other medieval stories about the "woman in the wood" extend the human/inhuman paradox into the development of their characters so thoroughly as have Jean d'Arras and Coudrette in their treatment of the fairy wife. Melusine's cold-bloodedness in both versions is perhaps the hardest for us to understand, like the fairy who laughs at funerals. Her eerie lack of empathy in that conflict recollects the long development of the European fairy as a creature who is neither angelic nor demonic—and indifferent, despite its powers, to human psychology. It may be a fault of contemporary reading to miss the impact of Melusine's Boethian advice about kingly conduct especially juxtaposed to the human passions she does exhibit: desperation, love, grief, anger. But it's fundamentally strange behavior. There is yet another narrative reason for it: a justification of, if not ruthlessness, political practicality. It doesn't aid the political strength of the family for a son to seek holy orders in a poor monastery. So Jean neutralizes Geoffroy's fratricide. It doesn't protect the realm to let a vicious, destructive child live who would destroy it. So Jean neutralizes Melusine's infanticide. Throughout his account, Jean declares that three days alone should be devoted to mourning. Both blind infatuation and excessive grief mar a lord's judgment. In this sense, then, Melusine's double nature is appropriate: she is as gentle as a woman and as terrible as a serpent. Having done her duty exposing Raymondin's human flaws, though, she must return to the symbolic, whereas Geoffroy, the symbolic, grows into the human.

Melusine embodies most of the features Wade declares to be traits of his "true fairy": her origins from without, her seductive beauty, magic, immortality, but not inscrutability or religious neutrality. There is something unsettling about her screamed rage at coming so close to getting a tomb with a name on it and missing out. Behind the scenes she inherits the distrust of woman's hidden duplicity projected on nymphs, sirens, lamiae, fairy-wives, and head-strong queens whose dominance is "unnatural" and whose otherness (and ambition) leave her indifferent to human psychology. Her popularity derives from the pathos of this contradiction and sympathy for her betrayal as a woman. As a fairy, though, she is both too powerful and too fragile for this essentially realistic story, which does not allow her to be adoxic, or in "a state of exception." Since the duke's ancestors participated in a crusade against pagans, it is vital that neither the pagan myth nor its fairy wife be fully assimilated. However much we want to find answers to our questions—can a fairy be saved, can it live with humans, can it deliver Christian wisdom, can lineage be rewritten—the woods Raymondin wanders in reflects Jean's predicament as a writer writing the ambiguous genealogy for an ambitious Christian patron.

ACKNOWLEDGMENTS

I wish to thank Lydia Zeldenrust and Melissa Ridley Elmes for their help with the source for Paracelsus's chapter. Whatever else I've left out is due to my own error.

CHAPTER FIVE

Monsters and the Monstrous

Tracking Medieval Monsters into Fairy-Tale Worlds

CHRISTINE M. NEUFELD

One key reason why fairy tales are associated with the medieval in the popular imagination is because of a long-standing association of the Middle Ages with monsters and the monstrous. Even for those who recognize the aesthetic confections of Romantic medievalism in the fairy tale's ubiquitous pastoral setting, dotted by quaint villages, a many-turreted castle, and endless forbidding forests, the monsters that inevitably also inhabit these landscapes still strike us as the atavistic remnants of premodern cosmologies. As Umberto Eco famously pointed out, the Middle Ages are a space that we return to when we want to contemplate our origins and our potential for good or evil; thus we have made the period into an imaginative repository both of the most noble of human nature, selfless heroism, and the most abject, the monstrous nemesis (see Eco [1976] 1986: 61–85). In a sense, we imagine the Middle Ages in relation to modernity much like the fairy realm in medieval romances: it is a world adjacent to and occasionally intersecting with the human one, which contains beauty in its most exquisite form, as well as the most horrendous monstrosity, while sparing us the nuisances of our mundane lives. Like the fairy tale, it is a psychological space of wish fulfillment, as in the "brief shining moment" of Alan Jay Lerner and Frederick Loewe's musical *Camelot* (1962), or of nightmare, as an age synonymous with grotesque barbarism and superstition. If the fairy tale has been one narrative vessel that transmitted such a template of the medieval to future generations, then we might consider that while we have seen what is good, beautiful, or noble shift somewhat according to sociohistorical circumstances, our monsters seem to slip across these boundaries unattended, as shadow-walkers are wont to do.

The Middle Ages are indeed striking for their interest in monsters. They appear where the modern, conventionally Protestant, imagination hardly expects them, cavorting in the margins of prestigious manuscripts and peering down from the stonework of magnificent Romanesque and Gothic cathedrals. Teratology, the study of monsters, begins in this period, as medieval intellectuals sought to make sense of the scientific and literary legacy left to them by classical authors, to reconcile folk traditions with learned Judeo-Christian paradigms, and to create their own taxonomies of the world. Whereas monsters now are, along with fairy tales, among the childish things one is expected leave behind as one matures—or, at the very least, are firmly associated with secular, popular entertainment—the monster occupied the greatest minds of the Middle Ages. Consequently, before we explore the monsters of the medieval analogues to the fairy-tale genre, we must first consider how medieval texts defined the monster. Once we understand what the monster is in the Middle Ages, we can move on to what monsters do, the kind of cultural messages they convey, particularly in the narratives that, like so many streams, feed into the fairy-tale collections of later periods.

DEFINING THE MONSTER IN THE MIDDLE AGES

The etymological history of the word "monster" provides insight into the roles monsters played in medieval art and philosophy (OED Online 2019). The word "monster," a French loanword (*monstre*) that entered the English vocabulary in the late fourteenth century, derives from the Latin term *monstrum*, which stems from the root *monere*, meaning "to show or warn." Like the Greek term *teras* (as in the term "teratology"), *monstrum* refers to a prodigy or portent. An abnormality that captures one's attention, the monster is a revelation but also a phenomenon that requires interpretation. Linked to the concept of admonition (*monitus*) monsters are signals or symbols. The medieval Benedictine author Pierre Bersuire summarizes this understanding in his massive reference work for preachers, the *Repertorium morale* (1330–40 CE):

> Monsters are creatures from outside, beyond, or contrary to nature, just as if a man were to be born with a cow's head, or with two heads, or the feet of

a lion ... Such things therefore are called *monstra*, from *monstrando* either because they show or signify some future event or because they exemplify some moral or spiritual flaw.

(quoted in Friedman [1981] 2000: 116)

As David Gilmore observes, "from the beginning of recorded time, monsters have been part of a semiotic culture of divination, metaphors, messages, indications of deeper meaning or inspiration" (2003: 9). To the medieval mind, the nonsensical nature of monsters is precisely what makes them meaningful.

According to medieval scholars, one needs to understand the monster to comprehend the world. All the great encyclopedias inspired by the emerging scholastic culture of the twelfth and thirteenth centuries addressed monstrous marvels.[1] There were three major reference points for theories about monsters in this medieval intellectual tradition: Pliny, Augustine, and Isidore of Seville. Each of these authorities grappled with ancient Greek accounts of extraordinary beings living just beyond the boundaries of the known world produced by figures such as Ctesias, a physician at the Persian court (early fifth century BCE), and Megasthenes, ambassador to the Mauryan emperor Chandragupta (fourth century BCE). Tales of these exotic marvels found their way into the medieval imagination by way of the Roman naturalist Pliny the Elder and his immense encyclopedic work, the *Naturalis Historia* (77 CE). Incorporating anecdotes from numerous literary and scientific works, Pliny elaborates on the fabulous beings his Hellenic travel narrative sources located far to the east of the Mediterranean world, in and around lands variously (and interchangeably) referred to as India and Ethiopia. Among these "Plinian races" we encounter the famous Blemmyes first referenced by Herodotus, a headless race with faces in their chests, as well as the Cyclopes, the one-eyed giants of the *Odyssey* and *Aeneid* (Figure 5.1). The fantastical creatures that appear in the adventures attributed to Alexander the Great are also included, such as Amazons and giants, not to mention the Cynocephali, a dog-headed people living in caves. Along with peoples noted for their unusual physical qualities—horned or hairy peoples, for instance, or the Panotii, whose immense ears reach to their feet— there are also those notable only for their exotic customs, such as the Bragminni (naked wise men who live in caves), the raw meat eater race, and, of course, the Anthropophagi, cannibals who drink from and wear human skulls. To the classical mind the unusual appearances and customs of these remote peoples made them monsters, excluded from humanity—of which Greco-Roman culture was, of course, considered the epitome. This ethnocentric vision is reinforced in the literary realm by the many tales of Alexander the Great's march eastward battling human armies and myriad monsters, claiming and cataloging the Orient for the Western world, a tradition that provided a rich body of wonder lore that circulated widely in the Middle Ages.

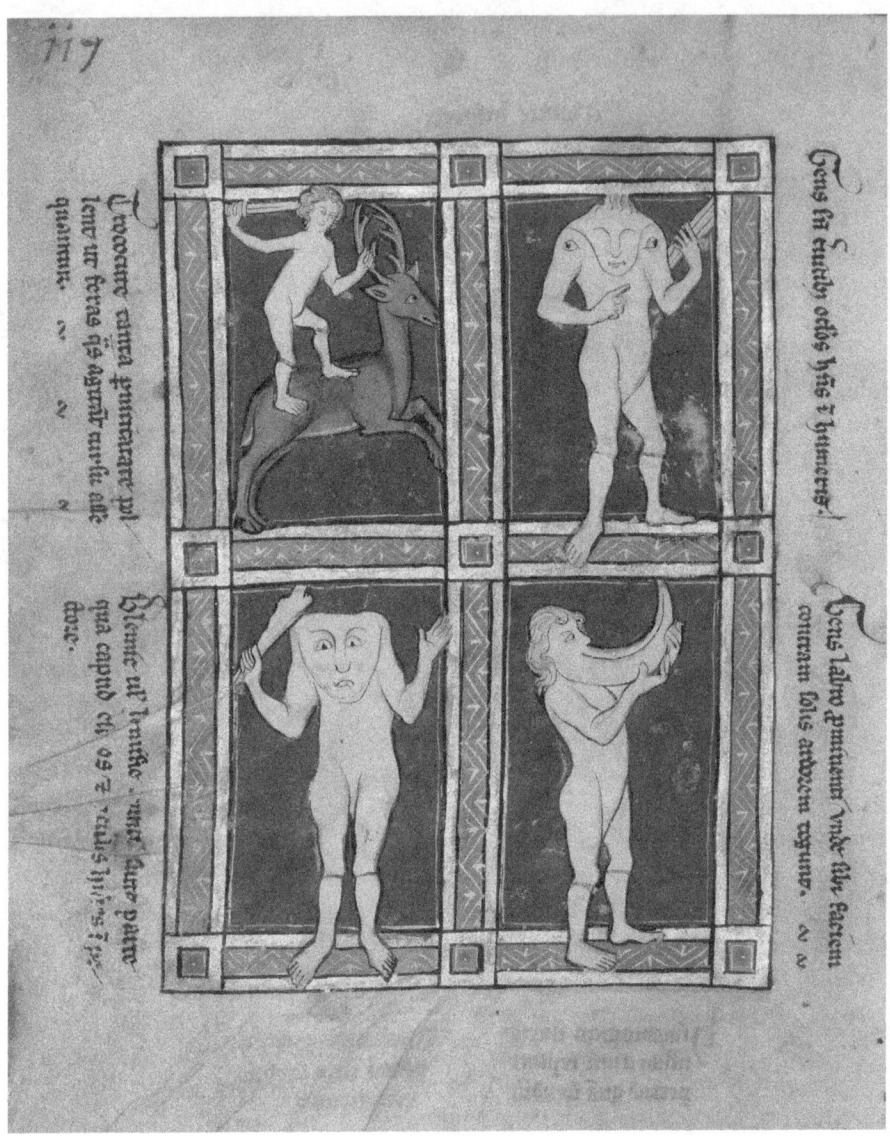

FIGURE 5.1: Plinian races. Getty Library MS Ludwig XV 4 (83.MR.174) (1277 or after). Courtesy of Getty.

For medieval Christians seeking to reconcile their classical intellectual heritage with a worldview shaped by Judeo-Christian theology, monstrous beings raised significant questions. Were the outlandish creatures of pagan antiquity deceptive fictions? The *Liber monstrorum de diversis generibus* (Book of Monsters of Various Kinds), an early medieval catalog of approximately 120 human, animal, and reptilian monstrosities, grapples with this issue. Acknowledging the arcane nature of pagan sources and the geographic remoteness typically attributed to monsters, the author sets out to distinguish truth from the "gilded speech of marvelous report" (quoted in Orchard [1985] 1995: 88). Those beings that do merit credence still elicit questions about how they fit into the Christian schema of the natural world order. If the great patristic authority, St. Augustine, defines the human as a rational mortal creature, what does one make of a being that mixes animal and human traits, for example? While Augustine deals with this topic relatively hypothetically, he does place the monsters of pagan tradition in a new theological light. In the *City of God* (fifth century CE) he proposes that such beings exist to illustrate the nature of God: "nothing that happens by the will of God can be 'contrary to nature.' The 'nature' of the particular created thing is precisely what the supreme Creator of the thing willed it be. Hence a portent is merely contrary to nature as known, not to nature as it is" (Augustine [5th c.] 1954: 21.8). Isidore of Seville (*c.* 560–636 CE) picks up this Augustinian notion in his enormously influential encyclopedia, the *Etymologiae*, arguing that monsters are manifestations of the divine plan: "they are not contrary to nature, because they are created by divine will, since the nature of everything is the will of the Creator" ([*c.* 560–636] 2006: 11.3.1). In other words, monsters may contradict our limited understanding but not the natural laws of the universe from the divine perspective.

Isidore follows Augustine in conjoining the individual monstrous birth with the monstrous races at the earth's extremities and directing the Christian to consider the religious messages communicated by such prodigies. In his efforts to shore up human understanding, Isidore's taxonomic exercises established detailed categories delineating monstrosity, categories that David Williams asserts remain pertinent to conceptualizations of the monstrous long after the Middle Ages: variations in overall size or the size of a particular body part; the superfluous presence of or the absence of a body part; a repositioning or merging of parts; the failure of one or more parts to grow; a mixture of any of the above categories, including the mixture of sexes (1996: 107).[2] For Augustine, the deformities that elicit fear or revulsion in viewers attuned to the harmonious nature of the good mean that monsters should dialectically call to mind the state of perfection that humanity may attain after the resurrection. Isidore's encyclopedic classifications of various prodigies, reading both the human and the animal as part of the Book of Nature, expanded the range of religious morals attributed to monsters, providing medieval preachers with engaging matter to deploy in their spiritual instruction. According to Lisa Verner, once Isidore's text became incorporated in medieval bestiaries (treatises cataloguing real and mythical animals according to their physical and symbolic characteristics) the meanings that were assigned to monsters expanded beyond religious truths to also include what she defines as "secular morality" (Verner 2014). The end effect is, as Jeffrey J. Cohen observes, a radical transformation of the monster in the medieval intellectual tradition: "The monster's real presence, indicated clearly by a variety of cultural and textual maps and attested to by reliable witnesses, was no longer important; monsters exist for these ecclesiastical authors as signifiers first and material beings only afterwards" (1998: 48).

If medieval intellectuals were clear on *why* monsters existed in God's creation, the question of *how* they had come to be was also compelling. Whereas antique authors gave little thought to the histories of barbarous peoples, Christian thinkers needed to account for the monster as a part of the divine plan that began with the creation of Adam and Eve. The Old Testament offered evidence of specific individual monsters, such as the Leviathan and Behemoth, or the giant Goliath. However, given the absence of monstrous races in scripture, when and how had God introduced such beings into the world? Several theories existed. One was that some female descendants of Adam, in an act mirroring Eve's original offense, disregarded a warning not to eat certain herbs. The *Vienna Genesis* describes the progeny that result from this disobedience:

> Some had heads like those of dogs; some had their mouths on their breasts, their eyes on their shoulders; they had to make do without a head. Some had such large ears that they covered themselves with them. One had a single foot, very large; with it he ran quickly as the animals in the forest. Some bore children which went on all fours like cattle. Some completely lost their beautiful coloring; they became black and disgusting, and unlike any people. Their eyes shone, their teeth glittered. Whenever they displayed them, they made the devil terrified. The descendants displayed on their bodies what the forebears had earned by their misdeeds. As the fathers had been inwardly, so the children were outwardly.
>
> (quoted in Friedman [1981] 2000: 93)

This historical explanation for the monstrous races introduces a moral reading alongside the ethnocentric tendencies of classical texts. Physical difference here is an incarnation of spiritual corruption. The most widespread and well-known theory of how monsters came into being, the legend of Cain's punishment and exile, shares this identification of the monstrous races with moral degeneration, treating monstrosity, furthermore, as a divine punishment. Both Jewish and Christian texts in the Middle Ages imagined Cain, cursed to wander the earth in Genesis 4:11-12, as physically manifesting his evil nature.[3] Rabbinic midrashim went so far as to suggest Cain was in fact the offspring of Satan and Eve whose appearance revealed his diabolic parentage even before he committed fratricide. The "mark of Cain" that is God's punishment for the first murder frequently becomes in the medieval Christian imagination—again following Jewish tradition—a set of horns, anticipating the deformities of his progeny, who like him are exiled from the rest of humanity.

The "kin of Cain" was a rubric that easily incorporated not only the monstrous races of the classical imagination but also more local monsters, folk remnants of the pagan past. We see evidence of this, for instance, in the way a Middle Irish recension of the "Six Ages of the World" brings classical, biblical, and local folk legends together in its account of the Second Age. The historical treatise follows other authors who treat Noah's curse on Ham for laughing at him (Gen. 9:20-27) as an extension of Cain's curse, even after the Flood should have wiped out the monsters of the First Age:[4]

> His famous father cursed the son called Ham so that he—he excelled in perversity—is the Cain of the people after the Flood. From him with valour sprung horse-heads and giants, the line of maritime leprechauns, and every unshapely person; those of the two-heads—it was a crime—and the two bodies in union, the dun-coloured one-footed folk, and the merry blue-beaked people. Every person in the east without a head, going from glen to glen, and his white mouth protruding from his breast, he is of the posterity of Ham.
>
> (Carney 1955: 109–10)

This Christian interpretation elaborates the classical conception of the monstrous as culturally inferior and far from the center of civilization into a more distinctly moral geography in which the exiled being may also bear an archetypal antagonism against its unmarked, righteous cousins. Moreover, the concept of exile applies here not only to persons from "the east" but also to creatures closer to home. Distance from the human reference point could be marked in terms of time, such as the giants the Irish would have identified as the Fomorians of their own mythological past, or of element, as in water sprites referred to as "maritime leprechauns."[5]

The concept of the monster as a kind of problematic legacy, linked to a pagan past and embedded in the landscape, passes into medieval storytelling by way of the clerics who first recorded the poetry of local communities alongside the imported classical, biblical, and patristic sources they were preserving in manuscripts. There is no better example of this phenomenon than the Old English epic *Beowulf*, which has drawn the attention of many teratologists not only for its stirring renditions of the hero's battles with monsters but also because the poem is part of the Nowell Codex, which is clearly thematically interested in the monstrous.[6] In addition to *Beowulf*, the codex contains: two texts featuring the fantastical monsters of Greco-Roman tradition, *Wonders of the East* (with illustrations of the Plinian races) and *Alexander's Letter to Aristotle*; the legend of a dog-headed giant saint, the *Passion of Saint Christopher*; and *Judith*, a poem based on the deuterocanonical story of an Israelite widow who slays the Assyrian general, Holofernes—a story that has fascinated many an artist with its subversion of gender conventions.[7] In *Beowulf* itself we see the intertwining of pagan and Christian paradigms clearly in Grendel, a monster who attacks the great hall of the Danish king Hrothgar, wreaking havoc for twelve years before the Geatish hero Beowulf arrives to save the day. A creature with eyes that glow like fire (line 727) and steely nails (line 985) that let him slit open his victims to drink their blood and gobble their flesh (lines 741–5), Grendel's nature has its source in his ancestry:

> This grim spirit was called Grendel.
> Mighty stalker of the marches, who held
> the moors and fens; this miserable man
> lived for a time in the land of giants,
> after the Creator had condemned him
> among Cain's race—when he killed Abel
> the eternal Lord avenged that death.
> No joy in that feud—the Maker forced him
> far from mankind for his foul crime.
> From thence arose all misbegotten things,
> trolls and elves and the living dead,
> and also the giants who strove against God
> for a long while.
>
> (lines 102–14)[8]

Even as he is described as a "fiend from hell" (line 101) and as Cain's misbegotten offspring, Grendel is also referred to as *eoten* and *þyrs*, both Old English terms for "giant" that etymologically call to mind the monsters of Germanic mythology.[9] As J. R. R. Tolkien explains in his influential essay "*Beowulf*: The Monsters and the Critics," the poem brilliantly summons the ancient Germanic *fifelcyn*, monster-race, with gripping physical detail to then interpellate this pagan cosmology into the soteriological vision of Christianity, shaping the subjectivity of his Christian audience as they perceive the irony of their benighted ancestors praying to pagan idols, which is to say begging the Devil himself for protection from Cain's kin (see lines 175–88).

Interestingly, when Tolkien wrote "The Monsters and the Critics" as an intervention in Old English scholarship to argue that *Beowulf* was worthy of being studied for its poetic artistry rather than merely as a historical document or linguistic artifact, he did so on the basis of its monsters. He claims that because the monsters were brought in from the margins to the center of the poem critics had dismissed the poem as a "wild folk-tale" focused on a trivial topic, "as if Milton had recounted the story of Jack and the Beanstock in noble verse" (Tolkien [1936] 1964: 16, 17). Tolkien's insistence that *Beowulf*'s monsters provide the structure for the poem's thematic agenda shaped not only the critical reception of this canonical medieval poem but also scholarly perceptions

FIGURE 5.2: Hell mouth. Getty Library MS 30 (87.MN.141.17), fol. 17 (1475). Courtesy of Getty.

of the monstrous in medieval literature more generally. Scholarship over the past few decades in particular has explicated the importance of monsters in a variety of medieval contexts, which might surprise the contemporary reader. For instance, critics have observed that the medieval conception of the monster as a morphological oddity, as a hybrid that disrupts natural categories, makes it a useful figure for conceptualizing not just the foreign but also the supernatural. Hell itself is increasingly represented in the visual and plastic arts from the twelfth century onward as a ravenous monstrous mouth stretched wide to consume sinners destined for an eternity of torture at the hands of hybrid bestial demons (Figure 5.2) (see Pluskowski 2003).

In addition to the association of monstrosity with the forces of evil in Christian thought there are also depictions of God as a three- or two-headed being to illustrate the mystery of the Trinity, and of the incarnation, where spirit becomes matter when god becomes man (see Mills 2003). David Williams's study of monsters in the negative theology of Christian Neoplatonism argues that the unintelligibility of the monster functioned as a critique of rational discourse, highlighting the limitations of intellectual concepts of the divine in relation to its ontological reality. In other words, for these theologians and mystics, the monster as an embodied paradox illustrated the unknowability and ineffability of the divine. The oddity of some medieval monstrous iconography for contemporary audiences, whether it be a bicephalic Christ or a Blemmyae, highlights that even as the monstrous operates in accordance with some principles that appear universal—a human fascination with category disruptions, for instance—monsters are also bound to the intellectual, cultural, and generic contexts that created them. Even those creatures who cross the boundaries of time and culture require our careful attention as their meanings can shift even when their shapes do not.

MEDIEVAL MONSTERS AND THE WONDER TALE

Obviously, not every medieval monster migrated into what became the fairy-tale tradition. The virtuosic monstrosities of Dante's *Inferno*, though the stuff of nightmares in a renowned poem, do not find their way into fairy tales, for instance.[10] This has to do with the types of medieval narrative material that contributed to the development of the wonder tale as it emerged as a recognizable literary form in the early modern period through authors such as Giovanni Francesco Straparola and Giambattista Basile. Given the multimodal nature of medieval society, the monsters that inspired later fairy-tale authors would have been transmitted by both oral and written means, with little respect paid to the neat distinctions or alignments critics have often made between oral and literate, secular and sacred, popular or learned.[11] In the Middle Ages the folkloric motifs that are the *jongleur*'s stock in trade find their way into the urbane romances written for aristocratic courts, just as classical learning became fodder for sermons addressed to uneducated audiences of all social strata. However, while we may not be able to identify a specific medieval precursor to the fairy tale as a genre, and the medieval narrative corpus hardly resolves debates between folklorists and fairy-tale scholars about the primacy of the oral or the literary mode in the history of the *Märchen*, we can identify medieval genres responsible for spawning the monsters that came to populate the fairy-tale tradition at its apex in the great nineteenth-century collections.[12]

The medieval monsters that entered the fairy-tale tradition stem from sources ranging from heroic narratives to the historical chronicles, hagiography, and sermons of ecclesiastical culture. Particular plots, themes, and motifs from these texts helped to shape those folktales most likely to feature monsters, what folklorists since Stith Thompson have called magic or wonder tales. The basic elements of such *Zaubermärchen* indicate an obvious relationship to medieval heroic genres like the epic and romance: "(1) the structure is episodic and constructed primarily on motifs; (2) the genre is unabashedly fictional, the setting indefinite, and the mode of reality in which the characters move is supernatural or fantastic; and (3) protagonists overcome obstacles to advance to rewards and a new level of existence (achieving wealth, power, marriage, and/or social status)" (Haase 2016: 321). Clearly, the ancient myth of the dragon-slayer hero who contends with a preternatural obstacle to save a community and win fame can be traced from the medieval epic, romance, and legendary saga (*fornaldarsögur*) to the wonder tale.

The Breton *lai*, a related short genre especially focused on the supernatural and full of folkloric motifs, is also an obvious source for later fairy tales, as evidenced by the attention paid by *ancien régime* fairy-tale authors, such as Marie-Catherine d'Aulnoy and Charles Perrault, to the twelfth-century Anglo-Norman poems of Marie de France. The twelfth century also offers additional folkloric repertoire in Latin texts, such as *Otia Imperialia* by Gervaise of Tilbury, Walter Map's *De nugis curialium*, and Petrus Alfonsi's *Disciplina Clericalis*, works whose clerical authors actively pursued the inclusion of local anecdotes and folktales in their writing (Ziolkowski 2009: 42). Perhaps surprising for those who associate the fairy tale with secular art is the degree to which the medieval religious imagination contributed to the thematic conceptualization of both the hero and the monster. Pitted against snake-breathing giants (St. Honorat) and consumed by bearded dragons (St. Margaret), the saints of medieval hagiography battle monsters for metaphysical stakes in adventures that rival, as Huw Grange observes, the modern comic book (2017: 1–2). Finally, ecclesiastical authors transmitted local legends as well as classical themes and motifs (the tale of Cupid and Psyche, for example) through their moralizing commentaries on Ovid and Apuleius, along with tale collections, such as the popular *Gesta Romanorum*, that provided homiletic material for preachers and inspired medieval literary luminaries like Giovanni Boccaccio and Geoffrey Chaucer.

We must also consider that, just as not every medieval monster appears in wonder tales, not every medieval monster that *does* appear actually functions as a monster according to the genre. While the Aristotelian definition of the monster in the *Generation of Animals* is anything that strays from "generic type" (1963: 401), not every deviation registers as monstrous in the context of the wonder tale. The fact that supernatural creatures such as the dwarf, the mermaid, or the selkie, while meeting Isidore's criteria for monstrosity, do not come to mind when one thinks of fairy-tale monsters suggests that an unusual physiognomy is insufficient in itself. The monster's nature seems clearly bound to the role it plays as the protagonist's nemesis or as a universal threat; in other words, it functions as a "villain" according to Vladimir Propp's morphology. And yet, not every villain is a monster either. Focused on the functions played by a tale's *dramatis personae*, Propp avers, "the dragon may be replaced by Koščéj, a whirlwind, a devil, a falcon, or a sorcerer" ([1928] 1968: 12–13). The fact that grandmother-devouring wolves and scheming stepmothers, while evil, do not qualify as monsters per se, while the amiable ogres of Basile's novellas arguably do, confirms Asa Mittman's assertion that "the monster is known though its *effect*, its impact" (2013: 6; emphasis in the original).[13] This is to say that whether or not it is a physical menace, the threat posed by the monster is above all a psychic one.

The fact that the monster is notoriously hard to define and yet we "know one when we see one," indicates that the monster is a product of specific sociocultural conditions.[14] In *No Go the Bogeyman*, a cultural study of fear focused especially on the frightening bogeys of fairy tales, Marina Warner characterizes monster stories as dramatizing "ways of confronting the foundations of the sense of identity and the self and of the self's historical and social place" (1998: 10). I would propose, then, that the question of which medieval monster makes its way into the fairy tale has to do not just with source studies but also with which monstrous effects proved most narratively compelling for storytellers. To identify those effects more precisely, we can turn to Jeffrey J. Cohen's groundbreaking theses on the cultural work that monsters do. In his introduction to *Monster Theory: Reading Culture* (1996), Cohen offers a series of postulates (to be applied individually or in concert), which help us understand the effects a monster generates in a particular text. These theses, I argue, have much to offer cultural historians of the fairy tale, and can help to suggest the roles medieval monsters may play as they enter the fairy-tale tradition.

Cohen's first thesis aligns neatly with Warner's observations above. Employing the medieval insight that the monster always "signifies something other than itself," Cohen observes that monsters embody the fear, desire, and anxiety of a particular cultural moment (1996: 4). His second thesis is borne out by the "irresistibility," to borrow a phrase from Jack Zipes ([2012] 2013), of the fairy-tale tradition itself—where no matter how many times the witch is pushed into the oven, she emerges again to fatten up another child for her supper. Cohen claims that because they are both corporeal and incorporeal, no matter how often we slay monsters in our stories, they return to us, for they are protean enough to bear our latest fears (1996: 5). Thirdly, he draws our attention to a crucial lesson from medieval teratology: monsters are "harbingers of category crisis" (6). If, as Warner claims, monsters are "abominations against society, civilization and family" (1998: 11), this is due in no small part to the fact that the monster's hybrid nature refuses classification, disrupting our epistemological systems and demanding what Cohen calls "a radical rethinking of boundary and normality" (1996: 6). The concept of the taboo evoked by Warner's use of the term "abomination" is important here for, as Cohen's fourth thesis explains, as "difference made flesh," the monstrous body tends to manifest forms of alterity—cultural, political, racial, economic or sexual difference—that threaten the social body (7). Thus, Cohen's fifth and sixth theses will be familiar terrain to both psychoanalytic and cultural historians studying the socially formative role played by fairy tales. Monsters are "vehicles of prohibition," policing what is possible, warning against the exploration of uncertain domains, be they geographic, social, or intellectual (15). And because they are "linked to forbidden practices," they are also attractive as spaces of escapist fantasy and rebellion against social constraints (16; see also Warner 1998; Zipes [1983] 1991). Through the effects they produce, Cohen concludes, monsters have much to teach us about ourselves (Cohen 1996: 20).

"HERE BE DRAGONS": THE CULTURAL WORK OF A MEDIEVAL MONSTER

The second half of this chapter uses these criteria to delineate the various lessons taught by the dragon, medieval literature's most notable contribution to the fairy tale's menagerie of monsters. While the dragon may seem easily interpretable as the ultimate primordial threat, I argue its medieval incarnations suggest a more complex legacy for fairy-tale scholars to consider. Although there is no actual medieval map bearing the proverbial expression "Here be dragons," medieval and early modern cartographic depictions of monsters in uncharted territories established the popular association of the dragon as a guardian of boundaries, the gatekeeper one must overcome to obtain that which is forbidden, be it knowledge or treasure.[15] Representing boundaries that should not be crossed, the dragon is by definition a hybrid, a mixture of taxonomies. Archetypally associated with bodies of water or, in its serpent form, with chthonic depths, it nevertheless breathes fire and sprouts wings in the Middle Ages, exhibiting the qualities of both cold- and hot-blooded creatures. In fact, as Paul Acker observes, between 900 and 1450 CE the Northern European dragon was an even more composite creature than we currently imagine: "It has the scaly body of a

FIGURE 5.3: Perceval flies a hybrid dragon. Bibliothèque nationale de France, MS Français 112, fol. 23 (1470). Bibliothèque nationale de France, with permission.

serpent, devolving into a mass of coils, the feathery wings of a bird, the head, ears, and teeth of a predator (often a wolf), and two front legs of a mammal or bird of prey" (2013: 53; see Figure 5.3).

Even though dragons were typically narratively situated in faraway or secret places, the image of the dragon was ubiquitous in medieval European art and culture. Dragons appeared in manuscript illuminations and marginalia, in ecclesiastical and civic statuary, as battle standards and ship's ornaments, and as decorations on armor or weaponry. Elaborate maneuverable dragons were built to be carried in medieval Rogation processions on days of prayer and fasting in the Catholic liturgical calendar. Dragons also inspired place-names throughout Western Europe. Reflecting on whether or not medieval people believed dragons to be real, J. S. Tatlock wryly observes:

> Reports of dragons are constantly retailed by English chroniclers. They are heard of as battling each other in the sky, as seen passing over on their own errands, as ominous, and rarely as arriving and spreading ravage .... Dragons were the kind of phenomenon which might be seen last year or next year, were common in the next county and not unknown in the next province.
>
> (1933: 223)

Certainly, some people had their doubts. Albertus Magnus, for instance, questioned the aerodynamic capacities of an enormous winged serpent and suggested that perhaps people reporting a dragon sighting had, in fact, witnessed a comet (Tuczay 2006: 173). Regardless, the dragon remains an iconic element of the Middle Ages because of the important role it played in medieval thought.

Discursively, the dragon appears in three different domains: scientific, theological, and fictional. In the encyclopedias the dragon is a real animal found in exotic realms such as India or Ethiopia, often guarding something valuable, much like the classical dragon Ladon. The *De proprietas rerum* of Bartholomaeus Anglicus is typical in its physical characterization of the dragon as a big serpent that can fly, which is at perpetual enmity with the elephant, and whose most dangerous feature is its tail.[16] Theological considerations of the dragon, on the other hand, inherited the Near Eastern monsters of ancient Judaic scripture and their early Christian adaptations in the Bible. Marc Epstein's account of the dragon mythos in Jewish art reveals a distinctly different animal from the classical large serpent: "The balance of the Pentateuch, the Prophets and the Writings, paint a composite picture of the *taninim* as huge 'fiery' or poisonous animals with the capacity to swallow a human being .... The *tannin* frequently and fiercely conflicts with God, rising up from the Deep, to attack the very throne of God" (1996: 358). The prominence of the dragon as an archetype of evil, usurpation, and tyranny in Rabbinic literature finds its early Christian parallel in St. Michael's battle with the seven-headed dragon in St.

John's Apocalypse, where the dragon is explicitly identified as the source of evil from the beginning of human history: "And that great dragon was cast out, that old serpent, who is called the devil and Satan, who seduceth the whole world; and he was cast unto the earth, and his angels were thrown down with him" (Rev. 12:9).[17] This diabolical ambiance enhances the melodrama of secular heroic and courtly northwestern medieval literature where the native Germanic *ormr*, a poison-spewing worm, may gradually grow legs with talons and sprout leathery wings, but obviously still bears a clear relation to the Indo-European dragon-slayer myth in which, according to theorists such as Georges Dumézil, Mircea Eliade, and Jan de Vries, the hero's initiation involves a primordial battle to establish cosmic order against the forces of chaos and death in the form of an enormous sea serpent.[18]

Even as the evolutions of these three types of medieval dragons can be individually tracked, true to the dragon's nature, the boundaries can become blurred as the traditions mutually influence one another. Travel narratives, such as the popular, late medieval *Book of Sir John Mandeville*, mapped sacred history onto geographical terrain, placing dragons in the Arabian desert in the wasteland surrounding the Tower of Babel, recalling an archetypal moment of divine prohibition in the face of human presumption. According to Louise Lippincott: "In this manner, reliable eyewitness accounts confirmed the equation between deserts, dragons, and godlessness made in the Bible, and the biblical boundaries between godly (Christian) territories and ungodly (dragon-infested) outer deserts could be seen in the concrete terms of the earth's political geography" (1981: 4). Even more fantastical journeys, for instance the *Voyage of St. Brendan* (early tenth century), in which the Irish saint sets out to find Paradise, feature dragons and fire-breathing serpents that threaten the heroic company's progress. In fact, on one *mappa mundi*, dragons guard the very gates of hell (Honegger 2017: 528). Given their infernal associations, dragons inevitably also appear in visions of purgatorial punishments in the otherworld, such as *St. Patrick's Purgatory* and the *Vision of Tundale*. According to Jacques Le Goff, by the Gothic period dragons come to materialize the devouring, fiery mouth of hell itself (1980: 178; see also Lippincott 1981: 13). This diabolical association makes its way into secular heroic literature as well. Chrétien de Troyes, for instance, invokes the allegorical mode of the bestiary when, in a definitive moment that shapes the identity of his knightly hero, Yvain chooses to intervene in a battle between a lion and a fire-breathing serpent: "When he considered which of the two he would help, he decided to go to the aid of the lion, because a serpent with its venom and treachery deserved nothing but harm" (Chrétien de Troyes [c. 1180] 1990: 297).

What will likely strike the reader of medieval dragon-slayer stories is how frequently the hero is not a chivalric knight but a saint. Certainly, the military association of the dragon as a battle standard existed in the West since Roman times. This association clearly inspires Geoffrey of Monmouth's attribution of the Pendragon designation to medieval literature's most renowned champion (despite the fact that King Arthur encounters dragons primarily as portents in dreams).[19] Nevertheless, the "combative saints" of medieval hagiography were also influential heirs of classical dragon-slayers such as Hercules, Perseus, or Jason (Riches 2003: 127). According to David Patterson, more than fifty medieval saints appear to be associated, either by story or iconography, with a dragon-fight, including female saints such as Saint Margaret and Saint Martha (Patterson 2013: 15). Observing the trajectory of saintly dragon-slayers helps us to discern the different boundaries medieval dragons could represent. Some of the earliest accounts, as in the sixth-century *Life of Marcellus*, actually place the dragon in the very heart of human society (in cities such as Paris, Metz, and Rome) spreading disease or destruction, until a bishop-saint subdues the beast. If classical dragon-slaying is linked to the foundation of a city, these accounts, typically set during the period of conversion, cast the bishop-saint as a civilizing hero, where the dragon plays the role of the *genius loci* that must be banished, a polluting agent that must be removed to allow for an improved Christian civic order to emerge. A more gendered concept of this pollution is evident when a virgin martyr saint like Margaret confronts a dragon while defending herself against the advances of a pagan captor; her successful defense of her chastity represents the inviolability of the church militant (Figure 5.4).

While the bishop-saints and women saints typically subdue their dragons by means of sacred words, gestures, or objects, the Carolingian period focused on St. Michael's military battle to defend cosmic order (Rev. 12:1-8). "In Revelation, Michael's conquest of the dragon ended the reign of Satan and cleared the way for the Resurrection and creation of paradise on earth. To medieval interpreters of the Bible, Michael became the ideal type of the Christian soldier or crusader seeking to fulfill God's orders through military conquest" (Lippincott 1981: 4). The associations of dragons with hostile un-belief reach their apex in the figure of St. George, a martyr whose legend circulated from the fifth century onward, but who only becomes a dragon-slayer in the eleventh century in the context of the Crusades. Byzantium's preoccupations with military threats from both Slavs and Muslims transform George from an exemplary proselytizing martyr to a warrior saint who rescues a heroine from a dragon and then forcibly converts a heathen city with it. This legend is picked up by Western Christian crusaders, inspiring accounts of the saint appearing to support crusaders at the Siege of Jerusalem in 1099 and other military encounters. Fascinatingly, as Oya Pancaroğlu (2004) documents, dragon-slayer saints also moved across the fluid cultural boundaries between Christian and Muslim society in medieval Anatolia, where cross-cultural contact in border territories saw Byzantine equestrian dragon-slayers get picked up in Turco-Islamic tradition during the twelfth to fourteenth centuries. Pancaroğlu's insightful identification of the dragon-slaying

FIGURE 5.4: Saint Margaret and the Dragon. Getty Library MS 37 (89.ML.35), fol. 49v (1469). Courtesy Getty.

saint as a "frontier legend" (2004: 157) highlights how the dragon ultimately comes to be identified not just as a diabolical test for holy men but also as a symbol for the religious other who must be overcome, a conflict between East and West that is still evident in the folk rituals related to St. George in contemporary England and Spain.

If dragon-slaying becomes part of a heroic career for medieval romance heroes such as Gawain, Guy of Warwick, and Tristan, as well as the intrepid fairy-tale heroes that follow in their footsteps, this may stem as much from medieval saints as from the influence of epic heroes, since often it is the romance hero's Christian virtue rather than his physical prowess that enables the victory. Sir Bevis, for example, calls on St. George (line 2817), and prays to Christ, God, and the Virgin Mary (lines 2860–70) before successfully defeating a dragon, who flees upon hearing the prayer. In contrast to such combats, however physically onerous, the battles fought between dragons and epic heroes are more complicated. By the time the epic tales of dragon-slayers such as Sigurd/Siegfried and Beowulf were recorded by Christian scribes the great venomous serpents of the pagan North were taking on some Latin characteristics like wings and fire, potentially also due to contact with saints' lives (Acker 2013: 55). Like their Mediterranean analogues, these creatures are chthonic guardians of treasure, and in the case of Fafnir a source of occult knowledge. However, while in each case the beast is vanquished, the success of the hero is qualified. In *Þiðreks saga* Sigurd is sent to fight Fafnir in part because he himself is difficult to control; he digs a pit to gut the dragon as it passes over him, a strategy more cunning than courageous; and he discovers he will die as a result of gaining the treasure. Beowulf, too, dies in the process of killing the dragon, a battle in which the elderly hero requires assistance from the young Wiglaf only to acquire a treasure that is in fact cursed. Much scholarly ink has been spilled debating whether this death is to be celebrated as a heroic sacrifice or tragic mistake due to overweening pride.

The association of pride with dragons can be found in Judeo-Christian tradition, where it is associated repeatedly with the glorification of the self over God (Kiessling 1970: 171–2). However, if, as Dumézil has established, the heroic tradition of Indo-European myth has always expressed an ambivalence toward the hero as a possible threat to the very stability he is meant to maintain, then this ambivalence extends beyond a specifically Christian reading to address a more general boundary between social and antisocial behaviors.[20] Implicit in this critique of the heroic ethos is the suspicion that the hero is not, as is the case with the saints, the antithesis of the dragon; rather, through his violence and his solitary quest for glory, he potentially participates in the monstrous himself. This possibility becomes most apparent in those cases where the dragon is, in fact, a metamorphosed person, as in the case of Fafnir, the son of the dwarf-king Hreidmar, who became a dragon after killing his father to possess the cursed gold of Andvari. The symbolic dimensions of such epic monster encounters may have specific implications for how we read fairy-tale versions of ATU 300 "The Dragon-Slayer," especially those in which the hero is (figuratively speaking) no saint, but rather a cunning trickster, for instance Miuccio in Basile's tale "The Dragon."[21] Rather than cleansing or ordering the world, the trick combat—often linked in later folktales with lower-class heroes—echoes an ancient epic melody, which, in its refusal to align victory with virtue, questions the boundaries of civil society itself.

Finally, the shape-shifting dragon plays another important role in the medieval imagination as a monster manifesting anxieties around sexual difference, an iteration with a surprising connection to another central fairy-tale monster: the witch. In addition to women dragon-slayers, medieval romances offer numerous examples of the dragon-woman, a figure that also appears in Central and Northern European serpent-maiden tales, such as the Grimms' *Das Schlangenmädchen* (The Snake Girl) and the Child Ballad 34, "Kemp Owyne."[22] The ancient association of serpents with fertility, and female sexuality in particular, is apparent in the classical monster Echidna (She-Viper). Through her congress with Typhon, the half-beautiful-maiden and half-snake becomes the "mother of all monsters," producing offspring such as Cerberus, the Sphinx, the Chimera, the Hydra, and the dragon Ladon. However it is another hybrid serpentine monster, the Lamia, that truly captures the medieval imagination. A female monster granted shape-shifting abilities by Zeus and associated with serpents in various traditions, the Lamia began in antiquity as a child-devourer, transforming into a seductress of young men by the first century CE (Ogden 2013). These qualities lingered in the Christian Middle Ages, where she is imagined as a "voracious, poisonous, predatory, sexually ambivalent, infant-killing and theriomorphic" (part-woman, part-animal) being (Resnick and Kitchell Jr. 2007: 89).

St. Jerome's Latin Bible brings Greek and Jewish mythology together for his Christian readers when he translates the Hebrew reference to Lilith, a Talmudic winged demon with a woman's face who is also a nocturnal seductress and threat to children, as "lamia" in Isaiah 34:14. The juxtaposition of Lilith and Eve in Jewish legend, however, draws attention to a key distinction between the classical lamia and the medieval dragon-woman. Whereas medieval monastic authors considered lamia reproductive spirits that threaten celibacy or marriage, Lilith represents the figure of the wife herself as threat. The eighth-century mystical Jewish text, the *Aleph-Bet of Ben Sirah*, portrays Lilith as Adam's first wife who, when she refuses to be sexually subordinate to her husband, is banished to the Red Sea, where she becomes the mother of demons. The thirteenth-century *Zohar* of Rabbi Moises De Leon casts Lilith as a testing figure, the feminine counterpart to Satan/Samael, the Accuser:

> She stands at the entrance to roads and paths, in order to seduce men. She seizes the fool who approaches her, kisses him and fills him with a wine whose dregs contain snake venom .... Those fools who come to her and drink this wine, commit fornication with her. And what does she do then? She leaves the fool alone, sleeping in his bed, and ascends to Heaven. There, she gives a bad report of him.
>
> (III, 19a, quoted in Fredrick 2016: 63)

The seductive woman as a dangerous test for the virtuous man is also central to medieval Christian commentary and art, a theme that frequently invokes ophidian imagery. For instance, medieval Christian accounts of Genesis, with their emphasis on Eve's affinity for the serpent, her seduction and seductiveness, often depict a temptation scene in which the serpent is in fact a hybrid with a beautiful woman's face.

While the Adam of Jewish legend receives a dutiful helpmate in his second wife, Christian conceptions of Eve continue to contemplate the threat she poses, her sexuality in particular raising questions about the monstrous potential inherent in the daughters of Eve. Medieval medical treatises such as *De secretis mulierum* (On the Secrets of Women) by Pseudo-Albertus Magnus make this idea explicit, with one commentator elaborating on Aristotelian medical theory to claim: "woman is not human, but a monster in nature" (Lemay 1992: 106). The threat posed by women takes on the familiar monstrous dimensions of poison and pollution: "women are so full of venom in the time of their menstruation that they poison animals by their glance; they infect children in the cradle; they spot the cleanest mirror; and when men have sexual intercourse with them they are made leprous and sometimes cancerous" (60).[23] This underlying assumption that womankind is constitutionally a threat to small children and sexual partners promulgated by such popular thirteenth-century medical treatises contributes, Helen R. Lemay argues, to late medieval claims in inquisitorial treatises such as the *Malleus Maleficarum* that women are predisposed to witchcraft (49–58). Thus, one unexpected legacy of these medieval theories for the fairy-tale tradition is the character of the witch, a figure that becomes fully realized in the minds of early modern witch hunters and is dramatically elaborated by Renaissance artists captivated by her menace.

As a monster, the witch no longer meets the medieval morphological criteria for monstrosity, but her psychic impact requires evaluation. While the witch has ancient roots in the lamia and striga of antiquity, the medieval dragon-woman also contributes to what the witch represents in fairy tales. Medieval romances featuring the shape-shifting dragon-woman, most famously those of *Mélusine* and the *Bel Inconnu* (Fair Unknown) cycle, again shift how we view the relationship between hero and monster. In place of the ancient motif of the hero as dragon-slayer—as in the case of the Babylonian Marduk who slays the goddess Tiamat in the form of a sea dragon—here the motif of the supernatural or animal bride (ATU 402) places him in an ambivalent relation of both desire and loathing to the dragon. Indeed, the legend of Mélusine suggests that a bond with the monstrous can, in fact, be a boon. In Jean d'Arras's *Roman de Mélusine*, for instance, the marriage is disrupted not when the mortal husband initially breaks his oath and discovers his wife's hybrid form, but later when his horror at a son's offense provokes him to reveal her nature to the world. While he then exclaims, "Ah! you deceitful serpent, by God, you and your deeds are nothing but phantoms, nor will any heir you have borne ever come to a good end," he regrets his words upon his wife's departure in the form of a dragon (d'Arras [c. 1392] 2012: "Betrayal, Fratricide"). Moreover, even as Mélusine's fictional offspring all bear deforming birthmarks that announce their occult parentage, her blood paradoxically became a mark of distinction for those historical noble houses—Lusignon, Luxembourg, and Plantagenet— which claimed her as a legendary ancestor.

This desire and fear is also apparent in the motif of the *fier baiser*, "the daring kiss" with which a hero rescues a princess trapped in ophidian form, thereby obtaining her hand and her fortune. As the popular story of Hippocrates' daughter (the Lady of Lango) transformed into a dragon by Diana illustrates, the challenge the hero faces here is of an erotic rather than martial nature, though no less dangerous. In one version of the fourteenth-century *Book of Sir John Mandeville*, for example, a knight of Rhodes turns to flee when he sees the "hundred foot long" beast, whereupon the dragon takes him in its teeth and casts him into the sea (line 305). This threat is not diminished in the romances of the Fair Unknown, in which the dragon's hybrid appearance suggests its marvelous nature and potential. In the Middle English *Lybeaus Desconus* the hero's heart nearly bursts from fear (lines 2079–80) at the sight of the Lady of Synadon as a winged dragon with a woman's face. Luckily for him this dragon-damsel takes the initiative, grasping him by the neck and kissing him before he can react (lines 2082–4), thus essentially freeing herself from the enchantment and granting the knight knowledge of his paternity, along with her lands and riches, so that he may take his rightful place at Arthur's court. In fact, the agency the lady displays by engaging the hero erotically contributes to her monstrosity, a disruption of gender categories highlighted by a beautiful female torso bearing a powerful phallic tail.

As a markedly composite figure, the dragon-woman symbolizes, in the words of Kevin Brownlee, the "problematic relations between the female body and power," an anxiety that extends to all women in their relationships to men (1994: 19). Her visual hybridity, particularly emphasized by illustrations of Mélusine, sets her apart from other shape-shifters, such as the hapless medieval werewolves Bisclavret or Gorlagon, whose animality, however frightening, pales in comparison to the monstrous treachery of their perfectly human wives. Eve Salisbury links the threat posed by the medieval dragon-women to Barbara

Creed's concept of "the monstrous feminine": "female monsters take on many forms and assume many guises; some have more to do with reproduction and motherhood—the archaic mother, woman as monstrous womb, woman as witch, for instance—while others address sexual desire—the *femme castatrice* and the *vagina dentata*" (2014: 67; see Miller 2010). Yet, when it comes to the fairy-tale witch, conventionally imagined as a postmenopausal hag, she frequently is neither reproductive nor seductive. Certainly, in the form of a child-devourer she is a kind of anti-mother.

What do we make, then, of the fact that in the European context the fairy-tale witches most easily called to mind are those who pursue a plucky young heroine rather than an eligible bachelor? The rupture of epistemic categories such as human/animal, predator/victim, rescuer/rescued in the dragon-woman of late medieval romance show us that in such instances the threat embodied by the witch is not just one of sexual difference but of the inadequacy of gender distinctions: she is the woman who both threatens and appeals because she acts in her own interests (see Oswald 2004). As the outer limit of the fairy-tale heroine's own independent orbit, the witch's agency is both tempting and terrifying, a medieval theme that features prominently in contemporary feminist rewritings of fairy tales, as in Emma Donaghue's aptly named *Kissing the Witch: Old Tales in New Skins* (1997). That such a figure continues to frighten and compel in our own time is evidence that these close encounters with our monsters continue to teach us about ourselves because their transformations mirror our own.

As the quintessential fairy-tale monsters, the dragon and the witch serve to remind us that as fairy tales continue to metamorphose in response to the new cultural environments that host them, the monster endures through its ability to shape-shift. Tracking monsters across the medieval terrain of scientific encyclopedias, travel writing, biblical exegesis, saints' legends, folk customs, and heroic narratives into later fairy-tale worlds illustrates their adaptability, a quality related to, indeed perhaps even resulting from, their innate hybridity. Monsters have always been creatures commingling past and present, entangling the familiar with the foreign, embodying both taboo and boon. Fittingly, if the quest for the monster takes the fairy-tale heroine or hero to the edge of the world and the fairy-tale reader to limits of the imagination, medieval teratology teaches us that the source of a monster's power is found much closer to home, both in our fears and in our capacity for wonder.

CHAPTER SIX

Space

Place, Non-Place, and Identity in the Medieval Fairy World

HELEN FULTON

Where was the medieval fairy world imagined to be? Whatever spaces we assign to fairy peoples in legendary and fantasy literature are products of our own ways of dividing up the world according to particular political and spatial norms. The "Fairy Land" of Shakespeare and Spenser, located deep within an English countryside aesthetic, was the precursor to an emergent nation-state ideology in which separate peoples—including fairies—were defined by the land or nation that they occupied. The popular conceit of "fairies at the bottom of the garden" (immortalized in a 1917 poem by Rose Fyleman) responded to the growth of suburban England and the cultivation of the cottage garden. Medieval writers, on the other hand, located their fairy protagonists in kingdoms ruled by fairy monarchs, often in regions characterized by distinctive topographic features with no clearly defined borders. These were the spatial locations that medieval writers and readers of Europe internalized as part of their own experience of the physical world, where they lived under the jurisdiction of kings or lords and belonged to specific chorographic regions that provided their core communal identity. To put it another way, an imagined fairy world, as much as the real world, exemplifies "the organization of space as a social product" (Soja 1980: 209), where lived-in spaces produced social meanings—political, economic, cultural—articulated through relations between individuals and the larger social order.

The social construction of space has been further theorized in recent times as part of a "spatial turn" in the humanities, which considers the significance of space, whether physical, geographical, or imagined, in the process of meaning-making. While medieval fairies might be interpreted as representing alterity in terms of cultural and ethnic identities (Huot 2008: 238), the places where fairies live can similarly be interpreted as representing alternative social spaces. One idea that seems particularly fruitful in relation to fairy worlds is that of the "non-place." Just as "place" exists as "a culture localized in time and space" (Augé 1995: 34) so there are "non-places," detached from specific histories and events, which offer the "experience of solitary individuality and non-human mediation between the individual and the collectivity" (Benko 1997: 26). Such modern theories of place as those of Augé and Benko arise from postmodern anxieties about globalization, the privatization of public space, and the construction of the individual as consumer rather than citizen; their examples of "non-places" include the casino, airport lounge, and shopping mall. Yet comparable concerns about the marked decline of "reference points for collective identification" (Augé 1995: 37) can be pre-glimpsed in medieval texts where tensions between the individual and the community order are frequently rehearsed, with varying outcomes. For medieval audiences, narratives of the supernatural world were "a form of cultural resistance" (Le Goff 1988: 32) expressed through non-places, where the absence of history and collective norms set them apart from the social and socializing spaces of the mortal world. The medieval fairy world was not so much a mirror image of the real world (though this is how fairy tales were and are often received) as a site of individual agency that challenged the cultural practices of medieval territories and their power relations, in which individuals were subordinated to a collective, and often rigidly applied, social order.

Thus the "non-place" of the fairy world, with its lack of history or points of reference for a collective identity, stands in an opposing polarity to the mortal world, presenting an alternative reality that seems better, brighter, and altogether richer than the human world—at least for a while. In this chapter, I want to explore the imagined spatial locations of medieval fairy worlds in a number of different linguistic traditions: Irish, Welsh, French, and English.[1] I begin with the spatial organization of the early Irish otherworld, imagined as physical subterranean places where mortals find themselves trapped, outside their own time and place, while the fairy people inhabit at will the mortal world with impunity. There are close similarities between the Irish otherworld and that of medieval Welsh legends, where the fairy world, ruled by avatars of human princes, is mapped explicitly on to political territories and natural topographies. More than in the Irish sagas, the Welsh prose tales contrast the collective decision-making of human princes with the seemingly random and motiveless actions of the supernatural characters.

French romances of the twelfth century focus on the conspicuous consumption apparent in the fairy world, a theme also found in Irish saga but now explicitly associated with the new wealth of Europe's burgeoning towns and cities. Mortal heroes are dazzled by the riches on display in the otherworld, which seem to offer a utopian vision of freedom, but once again the mortals are subject to fairy power and have to compromise some aspect of their social identity in exchange for access to this utopian world. The Middle English romances of the fourteenth and fifteenth centuries share this enthusiasm for commodification, exhibited now in supernatural contexts that tend to correspond not to cities but to the landed estates of the nobility, whose wealth was increasingly dependent on urban trade. Roaming unaware into these supernatural lands, knightly heroes are tested and often found wanting and, like the heroes of French romance, are forced to adjust their sense of a socially produced identity in the face of a resolutely individualist and ahistorical otherworld.

All these fairy worlds can be theorized spatially as "non-places," where mortal travelers find themselves removed from collective social action, from time and history, and enabled to pursue their own desires of material and sensual consumption. Yet, as for the modern consumers who occupy non-places, removed from time and meaningful social identification, the consequences of such apparently untrammelled agency can be baleful.

THE SPATIAL ORGANIZATION OF THE IRISH OTHERWORLD

Early Irish tradition recounts the prehistory of Ireland as a series of invasions, detailed in the prose text *Lebor Gabála Érenn*, "The Book of Invasions of Ireland" (Carey 2009; Macalister 1938–56).[2] The earliest waves of settlers were led by Cessair, a female leader, then Partholón, and Nemed, followed by the Fír Bolg, who settled in what had become a deserted land. The Fír Bolg were still in possession of the island when the Tuatha Dé Danann, "the People of the Goddess Danu," arrived and defeated the Fír Bolg before the two peoples reached a compromise and occupied the island together. With their magical powers, the Tuatha were able to fight off a group of long-term dissidents and troublemakers, the grotesque Fomorians, but not even the Tuatha, with their magic spells, could withstand the warrior skills of the Milesians, the sons of Míl Espáne (literally, the "Spanish soldier"), who were the last and final invaders of Ireland and the ancestors of the Gaels (Carey 2001: 11). Following two decisive battles, the Milesians came to an agreement with the defeated Tuatha: the land of Ireland was divided into two horizontally, with the Milesians occupying the above-ground spaces and the Tuatha living under the ground (Gantz 1981: 190; Rees and Rees 1961: 38).

The Tuatha were the original "fairy folk" of Ireland, and some of the leading Tuatha, such as Lugh and Manannán, clearly have a mythological function as pagan gods reconstituted into supernatural warriors (Mac Cana 1970: 57–73; Ní Bhrolcháin 2009: 26). From the beginning, the Tuatha were, like the mortal inhabitants of Ireland, a people ruled by kings, a term that applied to territories ranging from the lands of a single *tuath* (a kinship group, the basic unit of social organization) to the whole of a province such as Connacht or Ulster (Byrne 1973: 41). Among the Tuatha Dé Danaan, the unit of social organization was a spatial one, the *síd* (pl. *síde*), the name for a fairy habitat. There were fairy kings of the whole of the Tuatha, such as the Dagdae (the "good god") and Manannán mac Lir, once a god of the sea, who distributes ten *síde* among the noblemen of the Tuatha; and also lesser kings who ruled over individual *síde*. In the eighth-century tale *Aislinge Óenguso*, "The Dream of Óengus," the hero's father, the Dagdae, is called "king of the *síde* of Ériu," that is, of all the individual fairy places of Ireland, while his ally Bodb is called "king of the *síde* of Mumu" (Gantz 1981: 109), that is, of all the *síde* in the province of Munster.

Thus there are two spaces within Ériu, above ground and below ground, each divided into territories and each led by its own hierarchy of kings. In the ninth-century tale, *Tochmarc Étaíne* ("The Wooing of Étaín") the mortal king Echu Airem is described as the king of Ériu, to whom the five provinces of Ireland submit (Gantz 1981: 49), and he competes with Mider, fairy king of the *síde* of Ériu, for possession of Étaín, the wife of Echu. Inevitably Mider, with his greater resources of magic, wins Étain in a series of encounters in the mortal world. But, as in many medieval fairy tales, the boundaries between the mortal world above ground and the fairy world below it are elusive or nonexistent. At one point Echu tries to dig into Mider's *síd*, as if it were a mine, to find his wife:

> Echu and his people went north and began to dig up Mider's *síd*; they were at it for a year and three months, and whatever they dug up one day would be filled back in the next.
>
> (Gantz 1981: 57)

The fairy world is thus physical, made of earth, and at the same time hidden away, possessed of supernatural powers that impose themselves on the real world, defying its logic and materiality. Moreover, the traffic between the two worlds is largely one-way. While the fairy people move around the mortal world at will, entry to the fairy world is controlled by the Tuatha themselves; mortals cannot walk in at any time, only when they are summoned there or drawn to otherworldly places by forces beyond their control, such as Bran son of Febal, enticed by a fairy woman into the sea kingdom of Manannán mac Lir (Mac Mathúna 1985). Only the Tuatha can attack a *síd*, as in *Aislinge Óenguso* ("The Vision of Óengus") when the Dagdae, assisted by the men of the mortal king Ailill, destroys the fairy territory of Ethal Anbúail to take his daughter for Óengus, the Dagdae's son (Gantz 1981: 111). Again in this tale, most of the action happens in the mortal world, partly in Connacht where Ailill is king, and the people of the Tuatha move without difficulty between their world and the mortal world.

The spaces occupied by the Tuatha vary from one tale to another but share a subterranean or hidden aspect, including the insides of hills, areas beneath lakes or wells, islands in a lake or sea, and large houses or meeting places that appear at night or during a storm (Carey 1987: 2). Burial mounds, many of them prehistoric, were particularly favored as fairy locations (Sims-Williams 2011: 57), such as the one at Crúachu, seat of the kings of Connacht, where the supernatural Morrígan, a goddess of war, dwells in the "cave of Cruachain," described in the twelfth-century prose *Dindshenchas* as "Ireland's gate of Hell" (Waddell 1983: 22). Many of the key sites of the land-based *síde* are sacred places associated with burial rites and royal cemeteries, suggesting the quasi-divine status given to Irish kings, while the water-based locations are associated more with the earthly paradise of Christian tradition—though they are often more dystopian than paradisal.

The materiality of the fairy kingdoms is represented in terms of their specific topographies. In *Immram Brain mac Febail* ("The Voyage of Bran son of Febal"; late seventh or early eighth century), Bran's sea voyage takes him to two strange islands, the Island of Joy and the Land of Women. Cormac mac Airt, an early king of Ireland, goes through a cloud of mist to the Land of Promise in search of his queen who has been taken away from him by a fairy lord; the magical land is set out much like an Irish noble settlement, with a fortress and houses on a plain, surrounded by palisades, and a king and queen in residence who hold a great feast for their guests (Hull 1949: 878–82).[3] Sometimes the border of the otherworld is marked by a specific feature such as the stone where Cú Chulainn sleeps before encountering the sinister fairy women who beat him nearly to death and take his charioteer, Lóeg, with them to their island home (Gantz 1981: 159). The locations of the fairy world are mapped on to the real geography of Ireland, with its five provinces of Connacht, Ulster, Munster, Leinster, and Meath, emphasizing the seductive duplication of the fairy world beneath the ground of the mortal world above them. Thus Síd ar Femuin (modern Slievenamon in the province of Munster) is the home of Bodb, king of the *síde* of Mumu (Munster), while the Dagdae is said to live at Uisnech Mide, the exact center of Ériu (40). The place-name Dublind Froích in Connacht is explained as the place where the hero Fróech emerged from his battle with the water-monster in *Táin Bó Fraích* ("The Cattle-Raid of Fróech") (Gantz 1981: 121; Meid [1967] 1994: 9) (Figure 6.1).

The fairy people move freely about the mortal world and interact easily with kings and warriors, but when mortals visit the realms of the Tuatha they often

FIGURE 6.1: Sea Voyage. Heidelberg, Cod. Pal. germ. 60, fol. 179v (1460). Public domain.

find themselves unable to leave, trapped in a time warp where endless feasting and consumption of fine things is provided and time does not pass until they try to return to their own world. When Bran and his warriors visit the Land of Women, they are treated to food that never runs out in a timeless present:

> In praind do-breth for cech méis ni(r)-airchiú[ir] diib. Ba blédin don-árfas-sa dóib boith and. Ecmaing bátir ilblédni.
>
> (The food that was put on every tray did not run out on them. It seemed to them a year that they were there. In fact, it was many years.)
>
> (Mac Mathúna 1985)

On their return to Ireland from their voyage, Bran and his men discover that they have been away for hundreds of years, and will turn to ash if they set foot on the land, condemning Bran to eternal wanderings in the fairy world.[4] The Christian tradition of the paradisal afterlife has here been pasted over a pagan theme of a timelessness that might be more threatening than consolatory. In another tale demonstrating a more positive Christian appropriation of pagan tradition, *Echtrae Chonnlai* ("The Adventure of Connla"; eighth or ninth century), the mortal hero falls in love with a fairy woman and ends up abandoning his much-loved people and joining her in the eternal otherworld, called here *tír inna mbéo*, "the land of the living" (McCone 2000), from where he never returns.[5]

The "non-place" of the fairy world thus has no perceptible linear time or history but is a space of pure consumption, removed from the real world, like a modern casino or shopping mall, and can be just as dystopian. When Fróech, the mortal son of an otherworld woman, visits his mother's sister in her *síd* (in the eighth-century *Táin Bó Fraích*, "The Cattle-Raid of Fróech"), he returns with fifty of every valuable commodity, including textiles, jeweled weapons, horses, and hounds (Gantz 1981: 115), conjuring up the wonder of the *síd* as a place of limitless resource. But the experience of the Connacht hero Nera, in the eighth-century *Echtra Nerai* ("The Adventure of Nera") is frightening. When the royal court at Cruachu is burned to the ground by Tuatha warriors, Nera follows them through the sinister cave of Cruachu into the *síd* where he marries a fairy woman. Although he returns briefly to Ailill's court—where no time has passsed since he left—in the end he must remain in the shadowy *síd* "until Doom" (Rees and Rees 1961: 300).

There are a number of ways in which the spatial organization of the early Irish otherworld provides something of a blueprint for the fairy worlds of later medieval cultures. Firstly, there is the division into two worlds, above and below ground, with the otherworld accessible via hills, caves, water, plains, and other topographical features. Fairies operate, not so much in a liminal space, as Spyra argues (2020: 41), as in a space that is distinctively their own. In both worlds, the political organization of a hierarchy of kingdoms of different sizes is broadly similar, with each territory of Ireland having its counterpart in the subterranean world, duplications that sometimes offer a distorted version of the above-ground world. Secondly, the fairy realms are material—visible in the topography and place-names of the land—and yet inaccessible, with elusive boundaries that are not always obvious to mortals. Moreover, the fairy people can walk at will in the mortal world, but the opposite is not the case: mortals seldom choose to visit the otherworld but are drawn there by force or compulsion and, once there, find it hard or impossible to return. Finally, the realms of the Tuatha are "non-places," detached from linear time and thus from history, characterized by self-motivated individuals whose relationships with each other are minimal and consumerist.

FAIRY WORLDS IN WELSH LITERATURE

Our understanding of the Welsh "otherworld" comes from the group of eleven tales first published together under the umbrella title of "Mabinogion" by Lady Charlotte Guest between 1838 and 1849 (Davies 2008: ix). The earliest of the eleven tales, *Culhwch ac Olwen* ("Culhwch and Olwen") is dated to about 1100, with all the others likely to have taken literary shape in the twelfth and thirteenth centuries (Luft 2019: 73–4). All of them contain an element of fantasy; supernatural events are common, magic is practiced, and men and women from the otherworld affect the lives of mortals for better or worse.

There is only one name recorded for the Welsh otherworld, and that is Annwfn (or Annwn), a term variously explained as meaning "the depths" or "non-world" or "under-world" (Sims-Williams 2011: 57–8). The name is found in a number of the prose tales and also in some of the early poetry, notably "Preiddeu Annwfn," or "The Spoils of Annwfn." In this eighth- or ninth-century poem, narrated by the legendary poet Taliesin, Arthur sails off in his ship Prydwen with a band of men to seize supernatural spoils, including the cauldron of the Ruler of Annwfn (Haycock 2007: 433–51; Koch and Carey 1995: 290). Strikingly, one of the strongholds visited by Arthur is called Caer Siddi, a name borrowed from the Irish *síd*, and in the context of the poem this name clearly conveys a sense of magical otherness even if the original Irish concept was not perceptible to Welsh audiences (Sims-Williams 2011: 68–9).

The world of Annwfn takes on its most distinctive form in the First Branch of the Mabinogi, *Pwyll Pendeuic Dyuet* ("Pwyll Prince of Dyfed") where the first half of the narrative describes the adventures of Pwyll, the prince of Dyfed in south Wales, in the fairy kingdom of Annwfn. Following an encounter in the forest while out hunting, Pwyll is led through forest land into Annwfn by one of its kings, Arawn, who asks Pwyll to act in his place to kill his rival, Hafgan. Arawn and Pwyll exchange places for one year, with Pwyll taking on Arawn's appearance and ruling in his fairy kingdom, while Arawn takes on Pwyll's appearance and rules in Dyfed. At the end of the year, Pwyll has succeeded in removing Hafgan from Annwfn and Arawn is able to return as the sole king of the territory. Pwyll returns to his own kingdom, and finds that Arawn has been an exemplary ruler in his place, cementing a long friendship between the mortal and fairy kings.

While Annwfn is sometimes regarded as a single realm common to Wales, and therefore different in nature from the independent *síde* of Irish tradition (Sims-Williams 2011: 58), Annwfn is only one of the Welsh otherworlds, and is thus a regional rather than national space. In the Four Branches, it corresponds to the territory of Dyfed, just as the *síd* of Mumu, for example, in the Irish tradition, corresponds to the political province of Munster. Like the historical Welsh provinces—Deheubarth in the south and west (of which Dyfed is a subdivision), Powys in central and eastern Wales, and Gwynedd in the north west—Annwfn is divided into at least two sub-kingdoms, ruled by Arawn and Hafgan respectively. Arawn's strategem of using Pwyll, the prince of Dyfed, to help him defeat his rival and appropriate his territory (a strategem not at all unknown to the historical princes of Wales) enables Arawn to create a single kingdom of Annwfn as the "non-place" of the territory of Dyfed (Figure 6.2).

In the Fourth Branch of the Mabinogi, *Math vab Mathonwy* ("Math son of Mathonwy"), the action takes place entirely in a magical otherworld, which is mapped directly on to the political province of Gwynedd in northwest Wales. Math is said to be the lord of Gwynedd while Pryderi, the son of Pwyll, is lord of Deheubarth in the south, thus setting the otherworld of Gwynedd in apposition to the mortal world of Deheubarth. Math and his nephews, Gwydion and Gilfaethwy, the sons of Math's sister Dôn, have magical skills and attributes that they use to trick Pryderi, the mortal king of Deheubarth, into battle where Pryderi, unable to compete with Gwydion's supernatural power, loses his life. In the otherworld of Gwynedd, Aranrhod, sister of Gwydion and Gilfaethwy, gives birth to a boy, Lleu Llaw Gyffes, literally "the fair-haired one with the skillful hand," whose wife Blodeuedd, meaning "flowers," is conjured up for him by Math and Gwydion out of wildflowers. But Blodeuedd falls in love with a mortal, Gronw Pebr, who seizes Lleu's land, joining it to his own kingdom. Lleu has the power to shape-shift, turning himself into an eagle to escape from Gronw, while Gwydion punishes Blodeuedd by turning her into an owl, changing her name to Blodeuwedd or "flower-face." Lleu finally gets his revenge on Gronw by killing him with a spear, thrown with such strength that it passes straight through the stone that the mortal Gronw uses to protect himself.

Taking the eleven tales of the *Mabinogion* together, the name of Annwfn is used relatively infrequently compared to the number of times supernatural settings are invoked in different places, so it is clearly not the only otherworld known to the Welsh but is specific to south Wales. A range of topographic markers are used throughout the tales to signify entry-places to various otherworlds, including hills, mounds, and plains, as in the Irish tradition, but also forests and streams, perhaps indicating the specific topographical features

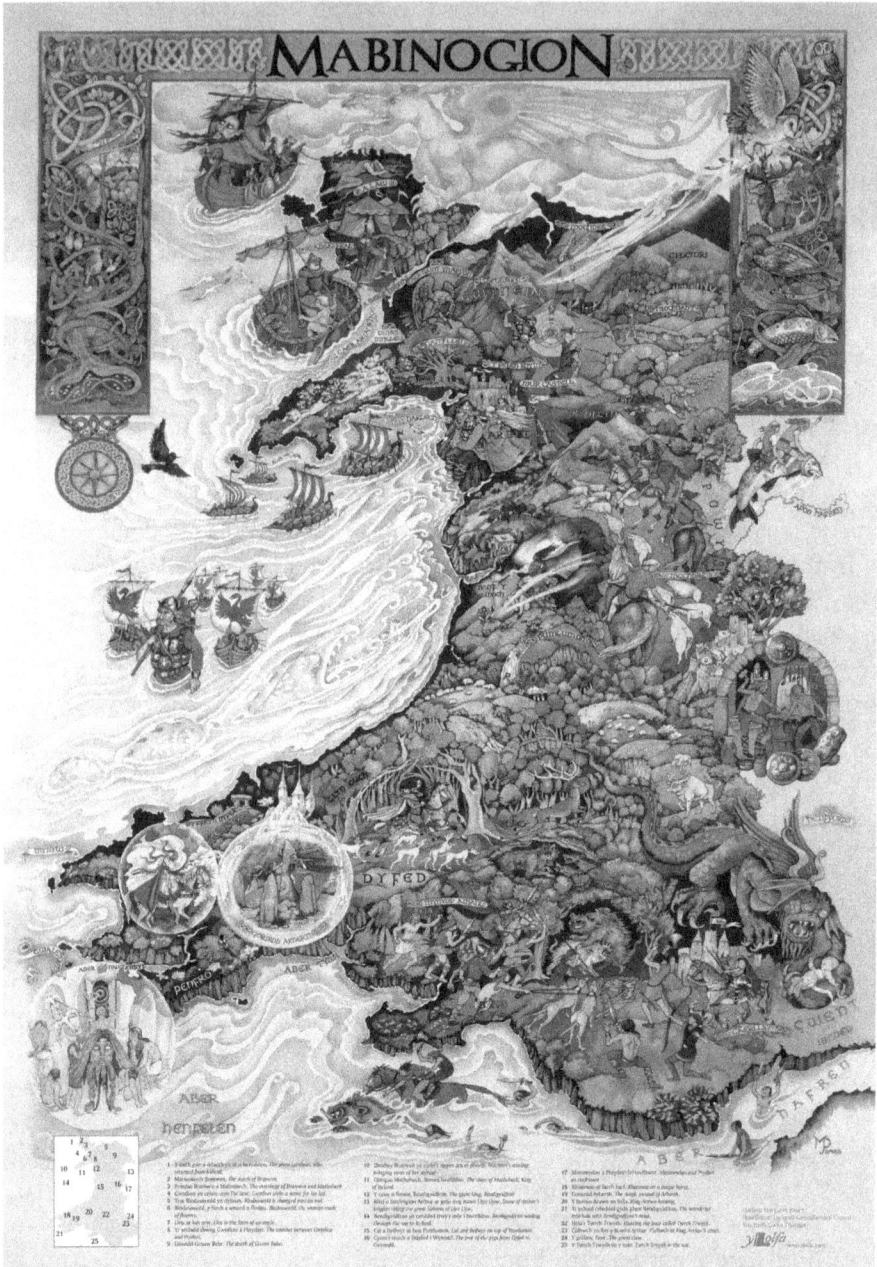

FIGURE 6.2: The Otherworlds of the *Mabinogion*. © Margaret Jones and Y Lolfa, reproduced with permission.

of the Welsh environment. *Culhwch ac Olwen* ("Culhwch and Olwen"), is a conglomeration of a number of folktale tropes, including that of the mortal man who marries a fairy woman, as in the Irish *Echtrae Chonnlai* ("The Adventure of Connla"). The human world of Arthur is a fantastical landscape inhabited by both mortals (including Arthur and his nephew Culhwch) and fairy people in Arthur's retinue, such as Cai, who has supernatural abilities, and Menw son of Teirgwaedd, who can cast spells of invisibility. Ysbaddaden Bencawr (literally, Ysbaddaden, "chief giant") is an otherworldly lord, like the regional kings of Irish *síde*, whose fortified court is approached by Arthur's men across a magical plain:

> They travelled until they came to a great plain, and they could see a fort, the largest fort in the world. They walk that day until evening. When they thought they were close to the fort, they were no closer than in the morning.[6]
> (Davies 2008: 190)

This spatial dislocation also occurs in the First Branch of the Mabinogi when Pwyll first sees Rhiannon, the fairy woman who becomes his wife; no matter how hard he rides after her, he cannot catch up with her and yet her horse seems to amble along at an easy pace. In *Culhwch*, a further signal that Arthur's men are crossing into a fairy realm is the fact that Custennin, the giant's brother, is tending sheep "on top of a mound" (*ar ben gorsetua*), using an older variant of the more common *gorsedd* (mound), which is a common topographical indicator of a point of merger between the mortal and fairy worlds. Moreover, Ysbaddaden's court is not the only "otherworld" in the tale; on their quest to achieve the impossible tasks imposed on Culhwch, Arthur's men enter the fortress of Wrnach Gawr, another giant in another region of the fairy world. It is only because Cai is himself from the otherworld that he is able to kill the giant and destroy the fort (Davies 2008: 202).

A frequently occurring boundary point in the First and Third Branches of the Mabinogi, the two tales set in the south of Wales, is Gorsedd Arberth, or the hill of Arberth (Narberth in its English form, a small town in Pembrokeshire). Arberth was the chief court of Dyfed, and it is on the hillside outside his court that Pwyll first sees Rhiannon, the fairy woman whom he later marries. In the next generation, when Pryderi, the son of Pwyll and Rhiannon, is ruling over Dyfed in the Third Branch, the hostile fairy enchantment that descends over the land, making it barren and deserted, is suddenly imposed when Pryderi and his family are sitting on Gorsedd Arberth (Davies 2008: 36). Later in the Third Branch, Manawydan succeeds in breaking the spell cast over Dyfed when he encounters a series of fairy people in disguise on Gorsedd Arberth. In the Second Branch, when the Irish king Matholwch tells the story of the magic cauldron, which restores the dead to life, he starts by saying he was hunting on top of a *gorsedd* in Ireland (Davies 2008: 26; Thomson 1976: 6, l. 157), overlooking a lake, both key indicators of otherworld manifestations.

The Welsh *gorsedd* is therefore similar to the hills and burial mounds that typically signify the presence of a *síd* in Irish sagas, and indeed the two terms are etymologically related as they both derive (independently) from the root **sed* (sit) (Sims-Williams 2011: 59). Such mounds, as raised points in the landscape, were often used as assembly places where lords could address their men, and *gorsedd* had the secondary meaning of "assembly" from at least the ninth century.[7] Burial mounds had the same function in early Irish society, as the location of the *oenach* or tribal assembly, but also as the site where mortals and fairies might come together (Carey 1987: 13). The association between mounds or hills and supernatural events is not exclusive to Irish or Welsh texts but is also found in other European literatures including Icelandic and German (Sims-Williams 2011: 62–3), and the common link seems to be the presence of the dead in what were usually burial mounds or barrows. Though the medieval fairy worlds were not commonly depicted as lands of the dead, "the wonders of Bronze Age megalithic tumuli" (63) throughout Europe may well have inspired perceptions of an uncanny otherness close at hand.

As in the Irish sagas, there are no obvious boundaries or barriers to prevent fairy people and mortals from mixing together, but it is nearly always on fairy terms—it is the fairy people who control access to themselves and their world, while mortals are unable to prevent fairy people from entering theirs, as when Gwydion and Gilfaethwy travel south to Pryderi's court, disguised as poets, to trick him into war. The otherworld of Gwynedd is strikingly imagined through its place-names and topography, marked by a number of features that attach the fairy world to its real-world location and thus create uncanny spaces that are not simply entry-points to the otherworld but rather physical signs of its immanence. When Gwydion and his men steal wondrous pigs from Pryderi—a gift to him from the king of Annwfn—and drive them northwards back to their land, the route of their journey is marked by place-names such as Mochdref ("town of pigs") and Mochnant ("valley of pigs"), reminders that fairy people went that way. When Gwydion creates a ship out of seaweed to help his nephew, Lleu Llaw Gyffes, his magic happens at a geographical place, Aber Menai, the estuary of the Menai Strait between north Wales and the island of Anglesey. The death of Gronw Pebr happens in a real place, on the banks of the River Cynfal in Ardudwy, at a spot marked by a stone with a hole through it called "Llech Gronw," "Gronw's stone," the one with which Gronw vainly tried to protect himself from Gwydion's fairy spear.[8]

The high incidence of onomastic anecdotes in the Fourth Branch draws attention to the status of Gwynedd as both the fairy kingdom of Math and the political kingdom of north Wales. In the human worlds of Gwynedd and Dyfed, their kings (Bendigeidfran in the Second Branch and Pwyll in the First Branch) are subject to the approval of their people and rule by consensus. Though Bendigeidfran has the status of the king of Britain, he nevertheless takes counsel with his advisors before invading Ireland, while in the First Branch Pwyll is similarly careful to listen to the advice of his counselors, even to the point of casting off his own wife. However fantastical the events of these branches, the lands of Gwynedd and Dyfed are places of lawful governance with socially agreed upon rules and boundaries. But in Math's world of magic, the protagonists are motivated only by individualistic needs and desires, detached from the collective politics of the mortal world and from any socialized responsibility. Math is strangely isolated—he has no counselors or men around him and takes no advice except occasionally from his nephew Gwydion, but he also has absolute power over his nephews, demonstrated when he turns them into a series of animals as a punishment for deception and rape. Actions and reactions are the consequences of individual agency and are delivered without reference to a system of social norms or laws. Compared to the kingdoms of Pwyll, Pryderi, and Bendigeidfran, the world of Math is a non-place dominated by the consumerism of magic, where identity has few reference points and where desire can be fulfilled without effort.[9]

WELSH AND FRENCH ROMANCE

Regional geographies shaped the settings of the fairy world in Welsh and French romances of the twelfth and thirteenth centuries, reflecting a political reality of Norman imperialism in Britain and much of northern France. The *lais* of Marie de France, composed in the second half of the twelfth century, move between Brittany, south Wales, and the north of England, and where there are overt references to an "otherworld," it often lies close to a territorial border between one country or jurisdiction and another. The fairy mistress of Lanval resides somewhere near the northern English city of Carlisle where King Arthur is defending his northern border against the Picts and the Scots (Burgess and Busby 1986: 73).[10] The Breton hero Guigemar is wounded by a supernatural deer on the edge of a waterway where a magical ship takes him away to another land (a plotline also found in the twelfth-century French romance *Partonopeus de Blois*).[11] The fairy knight Yonec comes in the shape of a hawk to visit his secret lover who lives in Caerwent in southeast Wales, close to the border with England. As in the Irish tradition, the worlds of the mortals and the fairies often overlap and operate simultaneously, but the borders between them are now marked by geopolitical circumstances rather than simply topographical features.

The same is true of the romance of *Yvain* (also known as *Le Chevalier au Lion*, "The Knight with the Lion"), composed by Chrétien de Troyes in about 1177 (Owen 1975: viii). Yvain sets out on his quest from "Carduel in Wales" (Comfort 1975: 180), which is likely to be Caerleon in southeast Wales,[12] and travels for days through forests, valleys, and mountains before he finds lodgings at a liminal point between Arthur's territory and the fairy world, marked by the presence of a monstrous giant, described by Calogrenant as "indescribably big and hideous" (183).[13] At this border point, Yvain finds the spring of water, as Calogrenant told him, and pours a basin of water on the stone to precipitate his entry into the otherworld of his beloved, Laudine. The story of Yvain is therefore a variant of the "fairy mistress" type (of which *Lanval* is another example) in which the hero is finally united with his beloved in her own land. What is striking about Laudine's world, mirrored also in the lay of *Guigemar*, is that this otherworld is primarily urban. Guigemar finds his beloved imprisoned in a fortress within the city ruled by her lord; Yvain finds Laudine within a fortified city of which he himself becomes the ruler. Already by the twelfth century, then, the growth of towns and cities as protected sites of commercial exchange provides a new kind of space for imagined otherworlds. The non-place of the fairy people is now located outside the court and landscape in a space whose overt function is commodification and consumption (Figure 6.3).

The consequent association of fairy worlds with urban wealth, rich commodities, and extravagant consumption becomes a feature of French romance and one that is carried over into Welsh and English romance. In the Welsh version of *Yvain*, the prose text *Owein, neu Chwedyl Iarlles y Ffynnawn* ("Owain, or the Lady of the Fountain"), the hero's journey also takes him to a fine city, which suggests, in the Welsh context, a Norman or English town since there were few native Welsh towns before the thirteenth century (Fulton 2012: 3).[14] While Yvain crosses from the mortal to the supernatural world at the place where he finds the spring, Owain has made a geographical journey from one country to another, from *pura Wallia*, native Wales, into the Welsh Marches and the territories of Norman lords, including their castles and towns. The conspicuous wealth of the French towns is romanticized in the gold and silk of Guigemar's magic ship, the endless resources of gold, silver, and precious fabrics held by Lanval's fairy mistress, and the rich commodities of food and clothing available in Laudine's city. Even Owain, in the Welsh story, is struck by the wealth of the city, where he is put to bed among "scarlet cloth and ermine and brocaded silk and sendal and fine linen [which were] fit for Arthur himself" (Davies 2008: 124). Such descriptions offer not only a new utopian version of fairyland, one based on riches beyond the dreams of avarice, but also an alternative vision of the fortunes that could be made, and the commodities that could be purchased, in the context of urbanization.

FAIRY SPACES IN MIDDLE ENGLISH ROMANCE

Highly influenced by medieval French romances and *chansons de geste*, Middle English romance, which began appearing from the middle of the thirteenth

FIGURE 6.3: "Urban Landscapes." Bibliothèque nationale de France, MS Français 111, fol. 1 (1480[?]). Bibliothèque nationale de France, with permission.

century and was still a popular genre into the sixteenth century (Cooper 2004: 29–31), retained the generic interest in fairies and the supernatural while moving further away from the "Celtic" motifs that characterize the Irish, Welsh, and French traditions. In imagining a spatial setting for the fairy world, English romance, perhaps because it was composed in a resurgent English language making its mark after the centuries of French elite usage in England, turned to its local folklore beliefs to create regional and topographical spaces for its fairyfolk, while an ambivalence about urban culture, which was fully established in England by the fourteenth century as the powerhouse of economic growth, tended to locate the "non-place" of the fairy people outside the towns and cities.

This difference is illustrated by the Middle English verse romance *Sir Launfal* (*c.* 1400), adapted from an earlier English text *Sir Landevale*, based on Marie de France's *Lanval* (Bliss 1960: 2). While *Lanval* features a poor knight whose fortune is made thanks to his fairy lover, and who spends his new money freely in the town, *Sir Launfal* has a more detailed plot that exposes the greediness of the townsfolk and the shallowness of urban values compared to the chivalric values of Sir Launfal, which are displayed in a long account of his single combats. Lanval meets his fairy mistress in a meadow by a stream just outside the city; Launfal, on the other hand, rides well away from the city of Caerleon to the west, that is, further into non-urbanized Wales, and is lying down in a forest under a tree when Tryamour's women come to fetch him. The "otherness" of the fairy is indicated in both texts by her extreme beauty and wealth, but these are even more exaggerated in *Sir Launfal* when twenty handmaidens (compared to four in *Lanval*) accompany Tryamour to Arthur's court, decked out in the most lavish clothes and accessories, while Tryamour herself wears a crown of gold and gemstones (not mentioned in *Lanval*) and other displays of wealth that clearly mark her out as someone who does not belong in a provincial border town. While *Lanval* ends with the knight and his fairy mistress disappearing to Avalon, never to be seen again, Sir Launfal and Tryamour ride off to an island, Olyroun (Oléron), her father's kingdom, where the knight may be seen once a year performing jousts. The otherworldly elements are therefore less developed in the English romance—Tryamour (who is given no name or parentage in *Lanval*) is less a fairy woman than a king's daughter, an embodiment of the dream of every under-resourced knight to marry a noblewoman of great wealth. The English story is at once more localized, along the Welsh border, and more materialistic than its earlier French counterpart, appealing to emerging audiences among the wealthy urban classes.[15]

The rejection of the urban milieu as a place too mundane for supernatural events, and the reinstatement of the otherworld in an idealized natural world, is particularly pronounced in the Middle English verse romance of *Sir Orfeo*. Dated to the late thirteenth or early fourteenth century and based on Ovid's tale of Orpheus and Eurydice, the poem claims to be a Breton lay and may well have been based on a lost French original (Laskaya and Salisbury 1995: 16). The topography of the fairyland to which Heurodis is taken against her will is first described by Heurodis as she recounts her dream to Orfeo:

[The fairy king] made me with him ride	
Opon a palfray* bi his side;	*palfrey (horse)
And brought me to his palays,	
Wele atird in ich ways*,	*adorned in every way
And schewed me castels and tours,	
Rivers, forestes, frith* with flours,	*woodland
And his riche stedes* ichon*.	*beautiful horses *each one

(Laskaya and Salisbury 1995: Sir Orfeo, lines 155–61)

Heurodis is then, as predicted, snatched away by the fairy king from beneath a tree in her own orchard, a frightening intrusion of the unknown into a domesticated setting. When Orfeo, self-exiled in the forest, determines to follow the fairy troop back to their home to find Heurodis, he has to enter through a cleft in a large rock, three miles (4.8 kilometers) wide, which marks the entrance to the otherworld. Once on the other side, he sees "a fair cuntray ... smothe and plain and al grene" (lines 351–3), on which is built a magnificent castle:

Riche and real* and wonder heighe.	*royal
Al the utmast* wal	*outermost
Was clere and schine as cristal;	
An hundred tours ther were about,	
Degiselich and bataild stout*.	*strange and strongly crenellated
The butras* com out of the diche*	*buttress *moat
Of rede gold y-arched riche*.	*richly arched with red gold

(lines 356–62)

The description continues with references to gold pillars, enameled surfaces, and jeweled rooms, so that the castle shone "as bright as doth at none the sonne" (line 372). To Orfeo, it seems as if he has entered "the proude court of Paradis" (line 376), but this is the home of the fairy king whose land, however beautiful, is also a place of horror because it is a land of the dead, where people lie just as they died, from war wounds or illness or drowning or burning. There are echoes here of the folktale motif of the "wild hunt," attested from classical times (Hutton 2014: 165), where monstrous huntsmen, often accompanied by the wretched dead, chase through woodland and forest.

The fairyland of Sir Orfeo is quite different from the beneficent world of Tryamour and projects an image of the "bad fairy" of folktale who brings good people to ruin or death.[16] The landscape setting draws on the ordered beauty of the manorial estate, in opposition to the built-up city, and the importance of the fortified castle as a symbol of noble privilege and authority. The description of the fairy king's shining castle belongs to a subgenre of descriptions of heavenly cities modeled ultimately on the revelation of St. John and his view of the heavenly Jerusalem (Rev. 21.x), a genre found in the fourteenth-century Middle English poem *Pearl* (lines 985–6) but exemplified much earlier in many of the French *chansons de geste*, such as the twelfth-century *Aymeri de Narbonne*, where Charlemagne covets the richly jeweled city for himself. In *Sir Orfeo*, the conventional description of urban wealth is transferred to the castle, occluding the town and its unromantic ordinariness and emphasizing instead the feudal ideal of the lord in his castle ruling over his territory.

It is significant that the land of the fairy king is not so far removed in type from that of Orfeo himself, who is also a king in his own land. Orfeo's kingdom is centered on the great classical city of Thrace (explained in the poem as the old name for Winchester) whose fortified "cite" is the equivalent of the fairy king's gilded castle. By representing the fairy world as a kingdom, the poem links it by analogy with the normative political model of independent kingdoms such as England, whose monarchs are engaged in competitive struggles for territory and sovereignty, often achieved through strategic marriages. But by locating the fairy kingdom in a distant and rural landscape, devoid of cities, the poem creates a fantasy of wealth and consumption existing in splendid isolation from the urban trade and commerce that supplied them.

This fantasy version of lordship receives its most powerful expression in the late fourteenth-century Middle English poem *Sir Gawain and the Green Knight*. Of all the medieval English romances, whether in prose or verse, this poem is the richest in locational description, creating a series of topographical, chorographical, and domestic settings that are realized through sensual imagery, particularly the visual, but also touch, sound, and the apprehension of heat and cold. The long sections of physical description depicting external and internal settings work to create a sense of anticipation, almost of dread, delaying the moment when we, like Gawain, are forced to realize that danger lurks not only in the wilderness but also in the luxurious and suffocating environment of Bertilak's otherworldly court.

As in the stories of Yvain/Owain and Orfeo, the route to the fairy world—not a kingdom but a lordship somewhere on the margins of Arthur's realm—is through a natural landscape of dramatic topography, emphasizing the separation between the mortal and fairy worlds. On his way to find the Green Chapel to keep his appointment with the Green Knight, Sir Gawain travels through north Wales and the Wirral (in northwest England) where he then enters strange and unknown lands marked by mountains, crags, rocks, streams, and forests, all symptomatic of untamed lands far beyond the civilized landscape of manorial estates and urban settlements. That the Green Knight can maintain an extremely well-stocked castle out in the middle of such a wilderness is an expression of its fairy nature, and the castle, as Gawain approaches it, appears like a mirage, standing in its own tended grounds like a facsimile of Arthur's Camelot, of which it is, indeed, a simulacrum.

The most distinctive feature of this otherworld castle is the richness of its furnished interiors, which are described in a striking wealth of ekphrastic detail. Welcomed by his genial host, Gawain is taken to a bedchamber fitted with silk curtains, embroidered coverlets, ermine trimmings, wall tapestries from Toulouse and Tars (Tharsia, in Asia) (Putter and Stokes 2014: 312–13, lines 852–81), recalling a similar reference to the rich hangings of Guinevere's throne in Arthur's court, which are also from Toulouse and Tars (line 77).[17] Gawain is given rich clothing to wear, of silk and fur, and the food and drink served to the company of noble men and women is of the best quality, followed by wine and spiced delicacies (lines 979–80). While the conspicuous consumption of Bertilak's court recalls that of Camelot, it also surpasses Camelot in its extravagance and opulence. Most importantly, the wealth of this supernatural realm seems all the more magical and powerful because it exists in the middle of a wilderness. Fabrics such as silk and fur, and commodities such as spices, were typical of the goods that came into Britain via the long-distance trade routes from Asia, and their distribution across the country depended on urban commerce. Camelot is introduced following a description of the gradual urbanization of Italy, which then spread to Britain (lines 11–22), setting Arthur's castle in a normative, if idealized, milieu of towns and castles in close proximity, where noble families could take advantage of urban trade to display their wealth while eschewing the more bourgeois aspects of urban life. Bertilak's court, several days' journey from any settlement of any kind, is a simulacrum of Camelot, filled with the richest consumer goods without any apparent effort or any obvious source. The court in the wilderness is the magical riposte to the attempts made by aristocratic landowners to tame nature, their distaste for urban culture, and the careful distances maintained between castle and town.

This utopian setting, based on unimaginable wealth, masks the dystopian underpinnings of Bertilak's engagement with Gawain. Though Gawain is eventually restored to his friends, with seemingly not much harm done, yet harm has been done to Gawain's sense of social identity and honor in a "non-place" outside historical time governed by its own rules of consumerist bargaining. While Sir Launfal's experience of the fairy world was positive and rewarding, leading to his final migration into that world, Sir Gawain's experience is more like that of Sir Orfeo, a disturbing experience made all the more disturbing by its apparently sumptuous and pleasurable setting. The fairy world "both resembles and surpasses the human world" (Saunders 2010: 179–80); as an exaggerated and distorted version of the mortal world, its appealing similarity to a hyped-up feudal experience masks the intrinsic dysfunction of a world based solely on individual agency and consumerist desire.

CONCLUSION

The space occupied by "fairyland" in medieval Western literature represents a political and social organization familiar to its audiences—that is, a kingdom or court ruled by a monarch or an aristocratic lord engaged in competitive struggles with rivals for territory and authority. The journey toward this space often has distinctive topographical and chorographical features, marked by hills or mountains, rivers and waterways, forests and wilderness, creating a borderland between the mortal and supernatural worlds that has its parallel in medieval travel from one jurisdiction to another, often through dangerous and unpoliced borderlands. In some of the "otherworld" texts, the interactions of the protagonists serve as a commentary, often a challenging one, on the cultural practices of the "real" world, as when clerical writers condemn the corruption of courtly life (an underlying theme of *Sir Gawain and the Green Knight*), or when "the removal of a narrative to an otherworld can enable engagement with the political realities of the historical world" (Byrne 2016: 116). Arthurian fairy tales, such as those by Chrétien de Troyes, function in part as a critique by the knightly class of arrogant or neglectful kingship.[18] The Welsh tale of Branwen fictionalizes the perceived lawlessness and barbarism of Irish culture (a theme also touched on in *Culhwch ac Olwen*), while the tale of Math points to the often counterproductive violence endemic in Welsh dynastic families in the twelfth and thirteenth centuries. In the Middle English tradition, both *Sir Orfeo* and *Sir Gawain and the Green Knight* dramatize the unhealthy competition between magnates for land, resources, and power.

It is limiting, however, to see the medieval fairy world simply as "an inverted mirror image of the real world" (Le Goff 1988: 32). Rather, it represents a simulacrum of the historical world that is superficially similar but whose practices and ontologies are very different. In these non-places, the dynamics are geared to individual consumption and the search for the fulfillment of individual desires, removed from the collective world of historical "place." Throughout the Western medieval tradition, the land of the fairy people is marked by its excessive consumption, of food, clothing, furnishings, jewelry, desire of all types, suggestive of the rise of urbanization and the commercial economy that presented both a threat and an opportunity to landowning authority. The fairy world is "where the acquisitive and utopian longings of their audiences found expression" (Rider 2000: 122), but the outcomes are not always benign. The fairy world is both utopian and dystopian, just as the non-places of modern consumerist society—the shopping malls and theme parks—are utopian in their visions of timeless wealth, leisure, and consumption, and yet dystopian in their failure to satiate the desires that have been invented for us. Fairy people operate as single individuals unrestrained by the reference points of conventional society, and their raison d'être is to enable, or force, mortals to do the same. The price to be paid is that of a coherent social identity, as Gawain found to his cost. Those few heroes who make an apparently unproblematic transfer to the fairy world as their permanent abode—men such as Connla, Lanval/Launfal, and Yvain (but not Owain)—have traded a flawed yet familiar "place" of collective identity for an otherworldly "non-place," never to be heard of again.

These journeys to obscurity, to a kind of social death, and the lure of utopian otherworlds anticipate later fairy-tale and fantasy traditions in which existential struggles and loss of identity have become central themes. In the nineteenth and twentieth centuries, identity is specifically related to class and gender, and the fairy world provides a space apart for change to happen. The miller's daughter who becomes a king's wife has to guess the name of Rumpelstiltskin to prevent this fairy creature from stealing her firstborn son, the heir to the kingdom; venturing into fairyland, she solves the mystery and saves her own position. Snow White grows up safely in an otherworld but is bereft of her social identity until she is restored to her rightful position. Hansel and Gretel are enticed into the witch's house by its sugar coating and gingerbread roof, but it is a house of horror and death. When they escape, they take the witch's jewels with them, which transform their economic and thus social position. Though the historical and social context of the later fairy tales is very different from the medieval tradition, the function of the otherworld as a "non-place," a place out of time in which identity can be lost, modified, or restored, can still be discerned.

CHAPTER SEVEN

Socialization

Renegotiation and Reconciliation

USHA VISHNUVAJJALA

Wete ye, his name es for to layne,
The whethir I wolde hafe weten fayne
What the childe highte.
Thus mekill gatt I of that knight:
His dame sonne, he said, he hight.

(Know that his name is hidden,
Although I would have known happily
what the child was called.
This much I got from that knight:
His mother's son, he said, he was called.)

(Braswell 1995)

In this passage from the fourteenth-century Middle English romance *Sir Perceval of Galles*, a character observes that, although the knight Perceval's name is hidden, even from Perceval himself, he calls himself his mother's son. This passage exemplifies a key feature of medieval romance: although the narrative trajectory of romance often involves self-discovery through quests and encounters with the unknown, the negotiation of community and social bonds is always central to that trajectory. In contrast to medieval writings of other genres, which may emphasize discovery through solitary meditation, dream visions, or divine encounters, romance—while it might contain passages depicting all of these—treats the development of the individual with, through, and at times against the community. Romances, like fairy tales, depict self-actualization as something that happens within a network of social relations.

Although romance is primarily considered a European tradition, initially called *romanz* to indicate a text in romance, or vernacular, language, it has close analogues with courtly texts from outside Europe, such as the Persian *Shahnameh* (*The Book of Kings*), an epic that includes passages about courtly culture, and the Japanese *Tale of Genji*. One common thread between the courtly elements of these traditions is their focus on the development of relationships within a community, whether that community takes the form of a family, a royal court, or a larger social group (see Kreuger 2000: 1). Unlike the epic, a primary genre of literature in the classical and early medieval periods which focuses mainly on the development of the hero, romance focuses on the negotiations between self and community that reflect the increase in urbanization, travel, geographic and social mobility, and the formation of different types of communities in the high and late Middle Ages (see Gaunt 2000: 47).

In this, the romance genre developed under similar conditions to those that, according to Ruth Bottigheimer, gave rise to the fairy tale in sixteenth-century Italy (that is, increased urbanization and shifts in socio-economic categories that led to changing forms of social interaction). Like fairy tales, medieval romances have been dismissed by critics of the period as well as modern scholars as frivolous because of their magical elements, broad appeal, and seemingly tidy happy endings (see Bottigheimer 2009: 1–26). But in their representation of the negotiation and reconciliation between self and community—as is the case of the early modern fairy tale—they represent far more than mere wish fulfillment. To work through societal concerns, romances are set at a safe distance in a magical or fantastic setting, but their happy endings are rarely the result of easy magical solutions. Rather, they depend on the understanding—and sometimes the renegotiation—of social codes and expectations. Redemption of the romance hero requires the reconciliation of existing and emerging community ideals and of competing social bonds, a very real concern for people during the period in which romance flowered (the twelfth to fifteenth centuries). Something similar can be said for analogous writings outside Europe, such as the *Tale of Genji*, written in the eleventh century by the Japanese aristocrat Murasaki Shikibu. In the introduction to his translation of the text, Dennis Washburn foregrounds the intricate connection between the *Tale of the Genji* and the realities of contemporary social life: "Written in the vernacular of court society, Murasaki Shikibu's vivid depiction of the world inhabited by her fictional hero, the Radiant Prince Genji, drew directly upon the realities of the lives of the aristocracy, providing the men and women who first read her tale with the shock of the familiar" (Shikibu 2015: x).

Just as romance blends familiar concerns with settings that might seem fantastic to many of its readers, it also blends narratives about privileged classes with concerns that would have been familiar to its wide audience. Helen Cooper describes the evolution of romance from its French roots into the most popular genre in late Middle English thus: "Romance emerges in the twelfth century in response to cultural pressures, and had changed from an elite- to a mass-culture form by the seventeenth century under new cultural pressures" (2004: vii). It can therefore be criticized—and in fact has been criticized—both for only representing the lives of the very privileged and for being accessible to a very broad audience, including those who might not have been considered traditionally literate or educated. In other words, although its subject matter was frequently the aristocracy, romance's audience quickly widened to include people of all classes, and by the early modern period it was frequently considered a form of mass entertainment rather than high art. Although the same tropes appear in romances across this period, Cooper argues, they often function—as do these same tropes in fairy tales, as Jack Zipes observes—like memes that come to represent different things as the material conditions that produce them change (see Zipes [2012] 2013). So even as romance retains a strong interest in social structures and social relations, the function of certain objects or characters in romances changes in relation to those social structures.

For example, a magic spring that requires any passing knight to fight a knight who protects it functions as the site of adventure and eventually character growth in Chrétien de Troyes's *Yvain, or the Knight with the Lion*. Three centuries later, in Thomas Malory's *Morte Darthur*, a similar custom—a point that no man can pass without fighting a knight who protects it—is labeled, in a moment of prescience, an "unhappy custom" by a knight who approaches it: he ends up fighting and killing his own brother (Field [1485] 2017: 71). These two iterations of what Cooper would call the same meme, which would have been recognizable to readers and listeners in the late Middle Ages and early modern period, have very different meanings. Chrétien de Troyes wrote in the twelfth century, a period of rapid expansion of courtly power, when the unknown represented an adventure and the potential for achievement. Malory adapted a variety of earlier material (much of which drew on Chrétien's work) to the concerns of the fifteenth century, when there were strong connections between courtly cultures across Europe and the Middle East; at the same time, this period in Western Europe was also characterized by interfamilial conflict, when brothers and cousins often fought against each other, which destabilized kingdoms such as Britain and France.[1]

Within the study of medieval English romance, scholarship on which is more fraught than that on its continental counterparts, scholars have disagreed about the central defining feature of the romance genre. Christopher Cannon argues that romance is a genre that is difficult to define, but that it becomes devalued, like a commodity, because of its surplus as it becomes the dominant form of Middle English literature—the sheer number of extant romances have the effect of devaluing the genre (2004: 173). Nicola McDonald, offering a different framework, situates the status of English romance within perceptions of its accessibility and prevalence: "Popular romance is the pulp fiction of medieval England, the 'principal of secular literature of entertainment' for an enormously diverse audience that endures for over two hundred and fifty years" (2004: 1). Both of these scholars locate the difficulty of defining romance partly in its breadth and the diversity of its narratives. But despite the large number of extant romances and the diverse range of narratives and themes within them, it is the genre's concern with material and social worlds that distinguishes it from epic, from dream visions, from didactic and spiritual writings, and from hagiography. The social worlds of medieval romance are both representative of social norms and material realities in the societies that produced them and, not unlike fantasy or science fiction today, also show us what material and social possibilities their authors and audiences wanted to imagine as possible. On the one hand, authors of romance critique certain types of social practices, such as the exclusion of individuals from courtly society or the spreading of malicious rumors. On the other, they imagine ways in which such damage can be repaired and how characters can be redeemed by acts of forgiveness or reconciliation, sometimes with the aid of magical or marvelous elements. As such, romances critique forms of behavior that marginalize individuals within society or destabilize social relations, and they provide examples for how one might be redeemed. Like fairy tales, then, romances carry out, to use Zipes's concept, "a civilizing mission" ([2012] 2013: xi).

Romance involves many different types of socialization and social bonds. I focus here on three main ones, all of which remain central in the later fairy-tale tradition: the development of relationships within the family, courtly communities, and marriage. As we will see, however, these categories not only necessarily overlap at times but also, more than occasionally, come into conflict with each other.

Although the subject of medieval romance was often the courtly classes, whose family relationships were usually more complex than those of the merchant class and the peasantry, these texts were widely read and circulated, and for the majority of the late medieval European society that comprised their audience, the nuclear family (defined by both blood kinship and cohabitation) was the "basic economic unit for working the land, producing and socializing the younger generation, and finally passing on wealth from one generation to another" (Hanawalt 1986: 3). This is not to suggest that every such family looked the same; as Barbara Hanawalt argues, the family "was able to maintain its basic structure" during cataclysmic times "because it was a remarkably flexible institution, permitting the pursuit of a variety of options while retaining the integrity of the unit" (3). So although the peasant and merchant families that formed much of the audience for medieval romances may not have typically had the experiences of living with extended family or sending sons to be raised at the courts of uncles, such practices would not have been entirely foreign to them either.

Romance often depicts events that threaten this basic unit of society, sometimes from the outside, but more often from the inside. Lies, jealousy, incest, and fratricide are frequent themes in medieval romance, which, unlike tragedy, usually includes some sort of resolution or reconciliation.[2] Sometimes the family unit is threatened by its own rigidity and its inability to allow its members to thrive in society outside of the family unit and eventually in new families of their own. In the twelfth-century *lais* or lays of Marie de France—often considered an early version of romance—disputes between spouses, overprotective parents, or lost children, and questions of paternity serve as plot points to raise larger questions about how families might either thrive or suffer. In one of Marie's lays, *Les Deuz Amanz* or *The Two Lovers*, the danger to the family comes from overprotectiveness: the lay tells the story of a widowed king who clings to his only child, a daughter, and sets an impossible standard for any man wishing to marry her: he must carry her in his arms up a high mountain without stopping to rest. The daughter falls in love with a young count who, determined to win the father's permission, attempts the climb fortified with a potion to increase his strength. Upon reaching the top, however, the young count collapses and dies, and the king's daughter dies of her distress. The mountain is named for the lovers, who are buried at its summit. Unlike many of Marie's lays, this lay has no happy ending and may be read more as a warning against those parents who cling too tightly to their children.

The fourteenth-century Middle English romance *Sir Degaré*, which may be based on a lost Breton lay, takes the dangers of corrupted parent-child relationships to its most extreme, telling the story of a young woman who is raped by a knight who turns out to be her father in disguise and gives birth to a baby she abandons, who later returns to fight his father/grandfather for his mother's hand in marriage. Marie's lay *Le Fresne* (*The Ash Tree*) tells the story of a woman who, upon hearing that her neighbor had given birth to twins, begins a rumor that this means the neighbor had been adulterous because she could only give birth to two babies at once if they had different fathers. When she herself gives birth to twin daughters, she resolves to have one baby killed to avoid becoming the subject of the kind of rumors she generated about her neighbor. Rather than kill one of the twins, her maid takes the baby and leaves her in the branches of an ash tree, from which the girl gets her name, Fresne. Brought up by the daughter of a porter at a nearby abbey, Fresne is eventually discovered by her repentant mother on the eve of her twin's marriage. The family is restabilized because the mother is able to admit her mistakes, the twins are reunited, and the family unit functions to allow both twins to marry and start new lives and families.

Other courtly texts narrate the search or longing for a family that has been lost due to death, distance, or estrangement, or even by the necessary relocation to court that is so often a part of courtly life. In her twelfth-century Japanese courtly memoir *As I Crossed a Bridge of Dreams*, Lady Sarashina writes of the tension between her fascination with the court, developed through reading courtly tales (including *The Tale of Genji*), and her despair at the necessity of living apart from her family, especially her father, when she remains in the capital and he is sent on embassies to distant places. Each time Lady Sarashina is chosen to go to court as a courtier, she finds the experience alienating, at one point writing, "Of course I had not expected that service at Court would suddenly lead to some brilliant improvement in my life; indeed there had been nothing very calculated about my decision to become a lady-in-waiting. The results fell even below my expectations" (1971: 79). Later in her life, Sarashina finds solace in solitude, family, and meditation, and is able to make her peace with her dissatisfying experience of courtly life through pilgrimages.

However, not all courtly texts depict healing from courtly life through spirituality. Although a period of solitary meditation or prayer occurs in many romances, social conflicts must often be resolved in the social world of the court or family that produced them, and sometimes reconciliation with lost family is possible. Chrétien de Troyes's twelfth-century French romance, *Le Conte du Graal* or the *Story of the Grail*, is the source text for most of the Arthurian romances—in all European languages—that follow it. The *Conte* draws on early stories of Arthur and adds the magical object that would eventually come to be known as the Holy Grail, as well as developing ideas about knighthood and adding a focus on familial drama. Chrétien is often credited with writing the first fully-fledged medieval romances (in addition to the *Conte*, he also wrote *Eric et Enide, Cligés, Yvain, ou le chevalier au lion*, and *Lancelot ou le Chevalier de la charette*) although he drew on earlier texts, and probably on oral sources that have been lost, as well as non-European sources.[3] In the *Conte*, the young Perceval, whose mother raised him alone in the woods after the death of her husband and two older sons, rides away to become a knight. Although his mother dies of grief as soon as he is out of sight, he does not know this, and spends the first half of the poem alternating between asking King Arthur to make him a knight and trying to find his way back to his mother, an endeavor that he can never fulfill. At the same time, the knight Gawain, who is not on any such quest but instead spends the second half of the poem riding around the country sometimes finding women in need of aid, and sometimes helping them, accidentally discovers a magical castle in which his own mother, grandmother, and half-sister, all of whom he believed to be lost, are living and waiting for him. This turn of events speaks to the uncertainty that nobles would have faced about their family members as they traveled for war and training, were sent by their parents to be raised at other courts, and formed affinities that meant that they, unlike peasant families, often lived away from their closest relatives and did not always know what befell their parents and siblings. In the fourteenth-century English adaptation of this romance, *Sir Perceval of Galles*, with which this chapter begins, Perceval's mother survives and is reunited with him at the end of the poem, in a change that might reflect a wish to mitigate this heightened uncertainty about family members in fourteenth-century England.

Not all medieval romances depict courtly life as alienating or threatening to the family, however. Many depict the court as the site of both pleasure and treachery, and in some cases, romance heroes' chosen families are the close friends they make at court. Although Chrétien de Troyes's *Conte* and Lady Sarashina's memoir depict life at court as a form of estrangement or separation from one's family, other texts begin at court, taking the background of courtly life as a natural starting point for the narrative, and a milieu that will be familiar to readers, even those who may have no experience with courtly culture. For example, another of Chrétien's romances, *Yvain ou le Chevalier au lion* (*The Knight with the Lion*) begins at King Arthur's court at Carlisle during the feast of Pentecost. The romance opens during a period of relative rest at court after Arthur has won a major military battle, and the celebrations and feasts form the backdrop for the narration of a very cozy scene in which several knights keep watch outside King Arthur's bedchamber and tell stories about their adventures. In this scene, outside the ceremonial strictures of the court but still within its larger social structure, the knight Calogrenant is telling a story about failing in battle when the queen, listening from inside the bedchamber, comes out to sit with the knights. Although they immediately stop speaking and Calogrenant jumps to his feet, the queen asks him to tell the story, starting again at the beginning. When the king comes out to join the conversation, the story is again interrupted and resumed, showing that the community of the king, queen, and knights is one that exists outside of the prescribed behavior of courtly culture and can extend to this intimate scene of camaraderie and companionship. This scene also serves as the catalyst for Yvain's own adventure, in which he tries to avenge the humiliation and defeat his cousin Calogrenant experienced. Yvain kills the knight who defeated Calogrenant and marries his widow, the lady Laudine. Although Yvain spends a good portion of the poem estranged from both the court and his new wife, it is his close social bonds with the court, especially Arthur and Gawain, that allow him to be welcomed back after a long absence.

While the court can be depicted as a home, toward the end of the Middle Ages, it is sometimes depicted as having become too totalizing, falling into the same bad patterns as the overprotective family and impeding the development of its knights and the new social structures (including families) they might want to create and take part in. Sometimes romances depict the impossibility of individuals satisfying the competing demands of courtly life, especially those to both be present at court and expand the kingdom by marriage. For example, in the second half of Chrétien de Troyes's *The Knight with the Lion*, after Yvain marries Laudine, Arthur and his knights appear at Yvain's new home and, after some celebrating, encourage him to ride away from his new wife and from the people and land he has promised to protect. Although his wife gives him a year to return to her, he fails to do so, and when she sends a messenger to tell him that she has renounced him, he consequently loses his sense of self and runs mad into the woods, where he spends a length of time in what seems like a dissociative state, living somewhat like an animal before finding a hermit with whom he wordlessly exchanges raw game for cooked meat and bread. As Yvain slowly resocializes himself in steps, first through exchanges with the hermit, then through meeting a maiden who revives his memory with an ointment, next by meeting the people of a nearby town, and finally by befriending a lion, he seems to do so almost from scratch, beginning with nonverbal encounters. Since Yvain's problems at court have stemmed from his attempt to adhere to strict social and behavioral expectations, including the two competing imperatives of knighthood (courtly love leading to marriage and adventures with the homosocial community of knights), his dissociation and need to relearn how to live in society can be read as the result of his oversocialization at court. We can see this especially in the way social expectations are repeatedly invoked by the narrator to suggest that Yvain is not free to express emotions such as shame, fear, and distress; his episode of madness can be read as the result of a string of attempts to suppress his own emotions in extreme situations to adhere to codes of knightly behavior. For example, when he realizes he has overstayed his time away from his wife, "With great difficulty he held back his tears, but shame forced him to repress them" (Chrétien de Troyes [*c*. 1180] 1991: 329). The friendships that Yvain forms or sustains once he is out of his strict adherence to social codes and freer to express emotions are more robust and more rewarding.

The court is also depicted as the site of oversocialization when its insularity and hubris make it impossible for its inhabitants to remember that there is a world outside of it. The action of the Middle English poem *Sir Gawain and the Green Knight* begins at Arthur's court at Christmas; here the court is named as the fully fictional Camelot, and the knights and ladies present are enjoying tournaments and a fifteen-day feast. Although this seems like a happy scene, the setting is one of excess and splendor, and that excess and splendor are part of the hubris that the eponymous Green Knight intends to critique. On the day the story begins, Arthur refuses to eat until he hears a tale of adventure or something marvelous or sees a joust between two of his knights (Borroff 2007: lines 90–9). This feast is interrupted by the entrance of a giant green (but humanlike) man riding a green horse, who rides into court to challenge Arthur. Arthur's nephew, Gawain, takes the challenge and cuts off the Green Knight's head, only to have him remain alive and request that Gawain find him and let him return the blow within a year. When, almost a year later, Gawain rides out of Camelot to find the Green Knight and rides through the wilderness on the English–Welsh border, he finds himself taking shelter at another court that is both like Arthur's and unlike it, and the lord of that castle, Sir Bertilak, turns out to be the Green Knight himself, sent by Arthur's own half-sister (and Gawain's aunt) Morgana to frighten Arthur and especially Guinevere, who she hopes to frighten to death (as revenge for Arthur's father killing her own father, which also motivates her behavior toward Arthur and Guinevere in other Middle English texts). When Gawain returns to court at Camelot, somewhat ashamed at having doubly failed his test by both concealing a secret girdle, given to him by Lady Bertilak, from the Green Knight and by flinching when the Green Knight swung an axe at his neck, the other knights make a joke of his failure and do not see that it reflects a failure of the values of Camelot by demonstrating that the bravest knight's courage will fail when confronted with the unknown. In this romance, unlike in *Yvain*, the court is revealed to be a place where the illusion of camaraderie and friendship disguises the failures of the court's espoused values to represent all of Britain, and one where Gawain's return leaves him feeling isolated rather than wholly welcomed home (Figure 7.1).

This type of critique of an oversocialized courtly culture does not always require that a romance take place at a physical court. The centrality of adventure or *aventure* (chance happenings) to romance means that, often, characters in romances discover important things about themselves and their courts or families in strange or marvelous places. For example, in the Middle English romance *The Awntyrs off Arthure* (The Adventures of Arthur), likely composed in the late fourteenth century, Arthur and his knights leave court (at Carlisle here) to hunt in the forest, accompanied by the queen. While Gaynor (Guinevere) and Gawain are waiting for Arthur, the figure of Guinevere's late mother appears to them. The figure is described as a ghost but is strangely corporeal, covered with dirt and with a toad on its head, and tells Guinevere that her sins during life have led to torment in the afterlife. The ghost warns Guinevere that she must not behave in the same way and criticizes the pride and covetousness of Arthur's court (Awntyrs of Arthur 1995: lines 239, 265). As in the case of *Sir Gawain and the Green Knight*, this critique comes from a woman related to the royal couple. Unlike Morgana in *Sir Gawain and the Green Knight*, however, Guinevere's mother here seeks to warn her own daughter, ostensibly out of love, while Morgana's attempts to sow disorder in Arthur's court are the result

FIGURE 7.1: The Green Knight entering Arthur's court. British Library, Cotton Nero A X, fol. 94v (c. 1375–1400). British Library, with permission.

of the dispute between their fathers. Guinevere's mother also approaches her directly, suggesting that the queen has the power to guide the court's behavior. These very different forms of social bonds within royal families ultimately serve a similar purpose: to critique courtly culture from the perspective of those who are part of its larger social structure.

Morgana's role in *Sir Gawain and the Green Knight* highlights another aspect of courtly life that can become toxic: jealousy, especially surrounding queen figures such as Guinevere (of whose queenship Morgana is jealous). The influence of queen figures such as Guinevere and Morgana is often a source of anxiety in romance texts. Sometimes, this anxiety is openly misogynist, as when Gawain, after his near-beheading, blames women's "wyles" (wiles) for the downfall of men throughout history, from Adam to himself (Borroff 2007: lines 2414–28). But romance's depiction of women's influence is complex, and Guinevere's influence in Arthur's court is not always presented in a misogynist context. Sometimes she is central to the community of knights, as in the storytelling passage from *Yvain* described above. She is also the catalyst for the action in the Stanzaic *Morte Darthur* (so called to differentiate it from the *Alliterative Morte Darthur*, more chronicle than romance, and Thomas Malory's prose *Morte Darthur*, which is a hybrid of genres but has many features of romance). The poem begins late in Arthur's reign, after the knights of the Round Table have sought the Grail, with the king and queen lying in bed talking. After discussing some of the adventures they've experienced and lamenting that the court has become empty of knights, the queen says to Arthur,

> Yif ye your honour holde shall,
> A tournament were best to bede,
> For-why that aunter shall begin
> And be spoke of on every side,
> That knightes shall there worship win
> To deed of armes for to ride.

> (If you are going to hold onto your honor,
> it would be best to announce a tournament,
> because that would begin adventures
> and be spoken of by everyone,
> that knights should win their honor
> by riding to deeds of arms.)
>
> (Stanzaic *Morte Darthur* 1995: lines 31–6)

While it brings together knights and briefly revives the renown of the court, the tournament also brings about a crisis in Guinevere's relationship with Lancelot by risking the revelation of their affair to the court and leading to the death of Lancelot's other would-be lover, the Maid of Ascolat. It also marks the eventual end of Arthur's reign through the social interactions that follow: growing suspicion that Guinevere is unfaithful to Arthur leads to suspicions of other kinds of treason. Meanwhile, deadly plots between the knights themselves lead to a knight's death after eating a poisoned apple. His death is blamed on Guinevere, forcing Arthur to hold a trial, and forcing knights to choose sides, weakening the courtly community's bonds in ways that lead to their disintegration. This downfall is due in part to the spread of gossip at court, including gossip about Guinevere, showing that the court can also be the location of social aggression, including ostracization.

Such social aggression toward women is also present in the *Tale of Genji*, a text that contains elements of both epic and romance. Genji's mother, a low-ranking but favorite concubine of the emperor, is shunned by other women at court, and Genji suffers from this same exclusion after her death. Genji's mother, "a woman of rather undistinguished lineage [who] captured the heart of the Emperor and enjoyed his favor above all the other imperial wives and concubines" attracted jealousy and gossip from those of both higher and lower social classes than her, leading her very presence "to provoke hostile reactions among her rivals," causing her to become ill from the "heavy burden" of gossip and hostility (Shikibu 2015: 3).

In medieval romance, the jealousy and gossip that characterize life at court mean that the genre depicts two very different ways romantic love interacts with larger social structures. Although there are plenty of happy endings that involve socially sanctioned marriages, there are also lots of secret lovers who try (and often fail) to escape the panoptic gaze of their courtly peers. The *Tale of Genji*, for example, details the many affairs and infidelities that can at times characterize courtly romance. One of the paradoxes of romance's representation of romantic relationships within the larger social fabric is that the courtly lover is often framed as admiring his (almost always his) lover from a distance. These texts typically deal with the problems with the consummation of romantic love, both in terms of the logistics of arranging extramarital affairs in a courtly setting where lovers are under scrutiny, and in terms of the questions of parentage and lineage that often result from such affairs.

In the *Tale*, Genji is at times described as finding these impediments a productive challenge. For example, in the episode "Sakaki," or "A Branch of Sacred Evergreen," Genji is excited by these challenges: "Her [Oborozu-kiyo's] older sister, the Kokiden Consort, happened to be staying in the main hall of the villa during this same period, and though her presence was intimidating, it served to heighten Genji's instinctive urge to pursue dangerous liaisons," which leads to long-term consequences for Genji when they are caught (Shikibu 2015: 247). In other texts of this period, the lengths to which lovers must go to hide their affairs or attempted affairs turn dangerous and even deadly. In Chrétien de Troyes's *Knight of the Cart*, Lancelot breaks through a window with heavy metal bars to reach Guinevere, after the two of them have agreed that she will remain lying in bed in case he is caught, to avoid implication:

> He grasped the iron bars, strained, and pulled until he had bent them all and was able to free them from their fittings. But the iron was so sharp that he cut the end of his little finger to the quick and severed the whole first joint of the next finger; yet his mind was so intent on other matters that he felt neither the wounds nor the blood dripping from them.
> (Chrétien de Troyes [c. 1180] 1991: 264)

As Lancelot leaves Guinevere's room shortly before dawn, "he left behind enough of his body that the sheets were stained and spotted by the blood that dripped from his fingers" and he does not notice his bleeding fingers until he is back in his own bed, having replaced the iron bars on Guinevere's window and crept back to his own room (Chrétien de Troyes [c. 1180] 1991: 265). When Meleagant, whose father King Bademagu is holding Guinevere prisoner, discovers the blood on her sheets and also on those of Arthur's seneschal Kay, who is recovering from a wound, he assumes that Guinevere and Kay have slept together, and Lancelot must go to great lengths as her champion to fight against the charge (266).

Sometimes the threat of physical danger to adulterous lovers who try to hide from their social world is not fully realized, but is no less frightening. In Marie de France's lay *Laüstic*, a knight falls in love with the wife of his friend and neighbor, who is also a knight. They talk to each other from their bedroom windows, and at night, when the lady's husband is asleep, often stand gazing at each other silently from their respective windows. When the lady's husband notices and asks why she always stands at the window, she responds that she is listening to the nightingale sing. Her husband has his servants trap the nightingale singing nearby, and presents it to her as a favor, saying that now her sleep will no longer be disturbed. When she asks if she may keep the nightingale, he kills it. Although the lay does not mention any explicit threat of physical danger to the lady or her lover, the knight's violence against the nightingale still serves to highlight the threat to lovers operating in a social world in which powerful men have the right and means of violence.

The physical dangers faced by secret lovers can also take darkly humorous forms, as in Marie's lay *Equitan*, which tells the story of the king Equitan who falls in love with his seneschal's wife and regularly meets her in secret. When his subjects become concerned that he is not married, his lover worries that he will leave her to marry someone else and conceives a plot to kill her husband so she can be with the king. She asks Equitan to ask her husband to take a bath with him, planning to fill her husband's tub with scalding hot water to kill him. But when he is delayed in coming to bathe, she and Equitan begin talking and then embrace, and when her husband enters, startling them, Equitan reacts by jumping into the tub intended for the husband, rather than the one intended for himself. He dies instantly and the seneschal, realizing what happened, throws his wife into the same scalding tub so that she is also killed.

The physical dangers the social world of romance poses to secret lovers is perhaps the starkest in another of Chrétien's romances, *Cligès*. The young lovers Cligès and Fenice must first hide their love from Cligès's uncle Alis and later attempt to escape from his court altogether. Fenice, the daughter of a German emperor, is going to be forced into marriage with Alis, who has seized the throne of Greece from his nephew Cligès after his brother Alexander's death, even though she and Cligès are in love. The scrutiny of the court means she must hide both her love and her distress:

> And these two concerns so troubled her that she grew pale and wan, so that it was clear to all from her loss of colour that she did not have everything she desired. She was less given to pleasure than before, laughed less, and was less carefree; but it anyone asked the reason for her change, she hid it well and denied everything.
>
> (Chrétien de Troyes [*c*. 1180] 1991: 159)

The necessity of suffering in secret, both because of her love for Cligès and because of her impending forced marriage to his uncle, the emperor Alis, reflects a frequent plot point in courtly romance: lovers, especially women, often suffer quietly, unable to act on their love. In this romance, her love is clearly reciprocated, but her lover is also not free to act. Because of their positions relative to the court, Cligès and Fenice are not free to run away together, so they must devise another way to escape together, with the help of Fenice's governess Thessala, who "was called Thessala because she had been born in Thessaly, where diabolical enchantments flourish and are taught. The women of this land practice magic spells and bewitchments" (Chrétien de Troyes [*c*. 1180] 1991: 159). While the use of magic is a central part of the romance genre, and is addressed much more comprehensively in other chapters in this volume, its role in romance's depiction of socialization and the navigation of the court's social world is also important here, where it is employed as a tool of liberating a woman from a forced marriage and helping a pair of young and endangered lovers escape the social gaze of the court. It is not without its dangers, though, and the physical injury and pain Fenice ultimately endures is considerably worse than Lancelot's. With help from a potion mixed by Thessala, she fakes her own illness and death, asking Cligès to ensure that her tomb is constructed in such a way that she will not suffocate when her unconscious body is placed there so that he may rescue her.

The potion meant to fake Fenice's death paralyzes her so that she appears dead, but does not dull her senses or render her unconscious: "She could not have moved foot or hand if they had flayed her alive; she did not budge or speak, though she could clearly hear the emperor's lamentations and the crying that filled the hall" (Chrétien de Troyes [c. 1180] 1991: 193). Three physicians arrive from Salerno to examine her body, and, mistrusting the appearance of death, seek to prove that she is alive by "beat[ing] her tender flesh until blood poured forth," pouring molten lead into the palms of her hands until it burns right through them, and are preparing to "stretch her over the fire to be roasted and grilled when more than a thousand ladies who had been waiting outside the great hall came to the door and saw through a small crack the torture and suffering being inflicted on the lady" and break down the door to stop them (196). Thessala is able to heal Fenice's wounds with an ointment after placing her back in her coffin, and she and Cligès are eventually able to marry after a long period of healing, after which Alis dies of grief. The social world in this poem seems to serve the interests of the corrupt Alis at first, creating a court in which the lovers must be very careful and can only be together through magical deception. But in the end, it is the social world of the court—and particularly the court's women, assembled together and acting as a crowd—that saves Fenice from being burned alive.

The role of communities of women is central to romance, as it is to fairy tales, from Sleeping Beauty's benevolent godmothers to Cinderella's evil stepsisters. Sometimes, as in *Cligès*, they appear both in the bonds of trust between specific women and in the interventions by larger communities of women where a single woman cannot succeed alone. As with other aspects of romance's social world, the role of female friends is often a positive one, but as romance increasingly depicts oversocialization toward the end of the Middle Ages it can also become a negative one. Friends can also introduce unwanted lovers into the lives of characters, particularly women characters. In Geoffrey Chaucer's "Franklin's Tale," the lady Dorigen misses her knight husband, who has left their home in Brittany to seek fame in Britain. She spends a lot of her time gazing in despair at the black rocks in the harbor, which she fears will impede her husband's safe return. Concerned for her well-being, her friends beg her to stop staring at the rocks and spend time with them instead, choosing activities away from the harbor so that she cannot fixate on the rocks:

Hire freendes sawe that it was no disport
To romen by the see, but disconfort,
And shopen for to pleyen somwher elles.
They leden hire by ryveres and by welles,
And eek in othere places delitables;
They dauncen and they pleyen at ches and tables.

(Her friends saw that it was no fun
to roam by the sea, but discomfort,
and decided to play somewhere else.
They led her by rivers and by springs,

and also in other delightful places;
They dance and they play chess and backgammon.)

(Chaucer 1987: lines 895–900)

Although the friends here are worried for Dorigen's health, their actions also suggest a discomfort with her solitude, which suggests that socialization is something of an imperative in the social world of this poem. Although men are frequently represented as seeking solitary adventures or meditations in medieval romance, women are represented in this way much less frequently. The parties and gatherings Dorigen's friends take her to, however, present their own dangers: they bring her into the orbit of a squire, Aurelius, who becomes obsessed with her and repeatedly propositions her (Figure 7.2), leading her to eventually answer him sarcastically with an impossible condition that must be met for her to grant him her love (he must eliminate/make disappear the rocks in the harbor). This rash promise nearly destroys her marriage when the rocks disappear and Aurelius comes to ask for her promised "love," causing her far more anguish than her solitary meditations on the dangers of the harbor. This romance shows us that even well-meaning friends can sometimes make a bad situation worse, demonstrating a negative aspect even of the seemingly positive social world of friendship. As more and more women found themselves

FIGURE 7.2: Warwick Goble, "Dorigen pledging Aurelius," *The complete poetical works of Geoffrey Chaucer* (1912).

moving away from their families without getting married in late medieval Western Europe due to changing economic conditions, the solitude and social relationships of women, especially young women, became a more central literary concern.[4]

Sometimes the friendships between women at court are depicted alongside friendships between men—both types of friendship are central to the narrative of Chrétien de Troyes's *Yvain, or the Knight with the Lion*. This is a romance that depicts the difficulties and triumphs of a number of friendships: that between the knights Yvain and Gawain while they are both away from the court; that between Yvain and the lion he meets while he is living in the wilderness; and that between his wife Laudine with her lady-in-waiting Lunet. Yvain's friendship with Gawain and Arthur is called into question repeatedly in the text due to his absence at crucial moments for the knightly community, which makes their final reconciliation, in which neither Gawain nor Arthur question Yvain's absence but instead simply welcome him back with open arms, all the more striking in its depiction of friendship as more than membership in the same chivalric community (Figure 7.3).

FIGURE 7.3: Yvain returns. Bibliothèque nationale de France, MS Français 1433, fol. 104r (1320[?]–1330[?]). Bibliothèque nationale de France, with permission.

In this same romance, the damsel Lunete's loyalty to her lady, Laudine, is called into question when Lunete persuades Laudine to marry Yvain after Yvain has defeated her husband in mortal combat. When Yvain leaves the court and disappears, Lunete's advice—and her intentions—are questioned by Laudine and her other advisors, leading to Lunete nearly being put to death as punishment. As Lunete explains to Yvain, who finds her imprisoned:

> But when it happened that you overstayed the year after which you should have returned here to my lady, she grew angry with me at once and felt very much deceived for having trusted me. And when the seneschal—a wicked, dishonest, disloyal man, who was extremely jealous of me because my lady trusted me more than him in many things—heard of this, he saw then that he could foment a real quarrel between us. In front of everyone assembled at court he accused me of betraying her for you.
> (Chrétien de Troyes [c. 1180] 1991: 341)

We can see here that the affection between Laudine and Lunete—what we might call the friendship that exists alongside their more formal relationship as lady and lady-in-waiting or advisor—causes jealousy among Laudine's other advisors and leads to accusations that Lunete has used this friendship to advance her own desires at the expense of Laudine's happiness and the welfare of her lands and people, demonstrating that friendship between women was something that raised fear and suspicion among men in courtly texts. Lunete and Laudine's ultimate reconciliation demonstrates that romance imagined the possibility of women's friendships surviving despite this disapproval.[5]

As with fairy tales, happy endings in romance are often achieved through the intervention of friends, magical elements, or encounters with non-human characters. But they are also only possible when characters recognize their errors or when social structures evolve. The many unhappy episodes or endings discussed here generally result from the rigidity of social structures, whether those structures are families, courts, or gendered expectations of behavior.

CONCLUSION

Although socialization and social bonds are only one of the major catalysts of action in medieval romance, romance's depiction of the rapidly evolving social and political words of the later Middle Ages makes socialization a significant part of even those romances that seem to focus on spiritual concerns, marvels, or heterosexual love. In romance, these forces never exist in a vacuum but are always contextualized, problematized, and understood in the context of the text's social world. Even romances about characters whose lives seem to take place largely away from social worlds, such as *Sir Degaré* and the Perceval romances, show the inevitable intrusion of real social concerns of the period into these isolated lives and demonstrate the dangers of pretending one can hide from society.

Romance demonstrates the simultaneous mutability and persistence of social bonds. The bonds between friends, between lovers, between family members, and between members of courtly communities are thrown into question by selfish acts, quests, magical objects, the revelation of hidden bloodlines and parentage, and characters' own ambitions. But when these bonds are flexible and forgiving enough to evolve along with their characters' identities and the changing social and material contexts in which they exist, they survive such tests. The depiction of reconciliation in many of the romances cited here may seem like a form of wishful thinking, but perhaps it is more fruitfully read as a depiction of possibility. Just as romance imagines a world in which magic or marvels or divine intervention can help solve conflicts as well as create them, it imagines a world in which forgiveness and reconciliation are possible, to a point. The social bonds in romance are often depicted as experiencing the most extreme tests one can imagine, and they were written in a time when famine, plague, political uncertainty, and migration did put many social bonds to the test. Perhaps, then, romance is asking us to imagine what social bonds would have to look like to survive under even the most extreme conditions.

CHAPTER EIGHT

Power

Patronage, Subversion, Seduction, and Challenge

MELISSA RIDLEY ELMES

INTRODUCTION

Power—and its subversion—are essential concerns in any fairy encounter, and that is certainly true of the fairies of medieval literature. Yet, critics in medieval studies traditionally have relegated fairy beings to the sidelines regarding both their power and their cultural significance, because the dominant viewpoint in scholarship on the period has been developed through a Christian lens with its insistence on either removing, or stripping of power and meaning, any figures not in accordance with that interpretation of the world beyond their appearance as counter-beings to the Catholic Church's hegemony in premodern Western Europe.[1] Recent studies such as those of Richard Firth Green and Tara Williams revise this understanding, arguing convincingly that a medieval audience would not recognize this attitude and, indeed, fairy folk in their various iterations performed myriad narrative functions and featured prominently in the medieval literary landscape regardless of text type: called variously elves (sing. "elf" and its variant spellings aelf and ylfe), faerie, ferli, and fay, or fey, they abound in Latin, Old English, Middle English, Anglo-Norman, Welsh, Irish, Norse, and Western European wonder tales and romances, sermons and philosophical and theological writings, charms, and even encyclopedias, chronicles, and other historical texts (see Green 2016; Williams 2018).[2] Setting aside the theological disdain that categorizes much of the modern world's received understanding of the fay, and examining fairies and their ilk in the literary texts in which they are preserved without the accompanying cumulative critical discourse focused on their ungodliness, reveals that medieval fairies operated in systems of power that, among their other purposes, both critiqued human power structures and offered important otherworldly alternatives to those structures and the sociopolitical worldview that depended upon them. Fairies were, and continue to be, among our most subversive imaginative acts as social creatures, as illustrated by the fairies of medieval romances and wonder tales—the kinds of stories that modern readers refer to as "fairy tales."

It is important to understand that in the medieval imaginary fairies are not a static category of homogenous figures sharing the same characteristics and deriving from the same origins.[3] While all fairy folk can be understood as supernatural beings with various powers, some fairies are euhemerized gods (such as the fairy king who takes the place of the mythic Greco-Roman god of the underworld in the early Middle English lay *Sir Orfeo*, a retelling of the story of Orpheus and Eurydice); some are the figures traditionally associated with Celtic otherworlds (such as Arawn, the lord of Annwn in the First Branch, and Rhiannon, the otherworldly wife of Pwyll in the First and Third Branches, of the Welsh *Mabinogion*); and with the myth traditions of pre-Christian Scandinavia (as with the Nordic *àlfar* and *disir*); some are humans who have acquired fairy power through the study of dark arts (such as Morgan le Fay in the Arthurian tradition); some fairies are immortal and others are not—although, if they are not immortal, most live for a very long time unless they are killed by someone; and some of the fairies found in the sprawling romance cycles of England and France are inconsistent in their presentation, sometimes immortal and other times not (for example, the Lady of the Lake in the Arthurian tradition).[4] Generally, except in the case of humans such as Morgan le Fay who acquire fairy powers rather than being born with them, the origins of fairy power are not explained and what powers a given fairy possesses are not usually explicitly mentioned—they simply exist, as the supernatural side of the natural order of things—leading to a range of ambiguous presentations of "power" in medieval fairy stories. Fairies, variously, are well educated and skilled in the magical arts; are preternaturally beautiful and thus, seductive; can, or do, variously manifest for themselves or bestow upon others wealth, healing, or other forms of prosperity (or, alternately, of adversity); can transport humans magically from one place to another or provide humans with some magical talisman; have the power of prophecy; or can hear what others say or think telepathically. Complicating matters still further, most fairies exhibit more than one of these powers and, although some presentations of fairy power are deeply gendered— in particular, that of fairy mistresses, which relies on the cultural frame of women's inherent seductiveness, and that of male fairy lovers, which embodies violent masculinity in the form of rape—in the main, fairy power is queer, in direct contrast to the typically heteronormative presentations of human power, and, as many scholars have noted, participates in a program of queerness in medieval texts.[5] The combination of a variety of origins and characteristics and their intrinsically queer nature means that any effort to read fairies and their powers in neatly categorical fashion can and will be met roundly with defeat—and that quality of being essentially unclassifiable, perhaps, might be understood as their primary meta-textual power.

LIMITS OF FAIRY POWER

Even in the fantastic, wish fulfillment-oriented world of medieval romance, fairy power is not unlimited; there are systems of power in place in which they participate, however invisible or inscrutable those systems are to readers, and those systems prevent fairies from being omnipotent. The most immediate evidence of the limited nature of fairy power lies in Melusine's story, wherein she variously has the power to curse her father, influence her husband's wealth, and exponentially improve her family's prosperity but not to break the curse (bestowed upon her by her mother) that binds her to her serpentine form, or to do anything to counter or diminish the repercussions she faces when her husband Raymond breaks his promise not to look in on her on Saturdays (Figure 8.1). Nor is Melusine either capable of renouncing her fairy nature on her own, or an immortal being in and of herself, although as a half-fairy she does possess longevity well beyond a human life span. It is only by marrying a human, bearing his children, and staying married to him that she can gain a mortal soul for her human half and from there, upon dying, ascend into heaven and attain salvation and thus immortality.[6] Loathly ladies—figures appearing to knights initially as unattractive but then transforming into beautiful women when the knights break the curses they are under, such as the fairy women in Geoffrey Chaucer's *Wife of Bath's Tale* and the Middle English romance *Sir Gawain and Dame Ragnell*—also exhibit conventional limitations in their power, being unable to avoid their physical transformation from beautiful to ugly and dependent upon the lover's intervention to break that cycle. However, although fairy power is limited, it is limited mainly in terms of what fairies can and cannot do with it regarding their own being; fairy power appears to be more or less limitless in terms of how, and for how long, it can be used upon and affect humans, with the caveat that there are also ways for humans to mitigate or deflect the fairy's intended outcome in a given situation. Fairy power is also often tied to a particular location—a realm (an otherworld), or an island (e.g., Avalon), or an ancestral castle (as in *Partonope de Blois*) where the fairy's powers are strongest—although this trait is not always or even usually

FIGURE 8.1: Melusine in her bath. Bibliothèque nationale de France, Rare Books, RES-Y2-400, fol. 142 (1478). Bibliothèque nationale de France, with permission.

specifically delineated, being more understood through intertextuality than necessarily stated outright in each individual story featuring a fairy.[7]

CLASS AND GENDER

While fairies occupy space in a broad range of textual genres and forms, in most of these the emphasis is on whether or not they exist, who believes in them, their nature as forces of good or evil, what kind(s) of magic or supernatural they signify, their relationship to the Christian God and His creations, and their classification and position in natural and supernatural world orders. Also, in most genres, fairies are among many other subjects and subject-figures described and categorized, and thus not allotted any specific or central narrative importance. It is only in the romance and wonder tale genres that fairies and their various powers come into play as an essential and driving narrative force at the heart of a given text. As James Wade points out, "romances are always concerned, first and foremost, with the lives of men and women" and it is in the context of their interactions with humans that fairies become narratively important (2011: 1). It is also in the context of their interactions with humans that the myriad ways that fairies embody, use, and engage with power become apparent and significant.

In the medieval European romance human power—who has it, how it is used, and for what purpose(s)—is tied regularly and inextricably to social status and biological sex. There is a clear hierarchy and distribution of power, beginning with the king and trickling down through knights, nobles, servants, and serfs, and, to a large extent, human power is a fickle thing, thanks to the concept of Fortune's Wheel.[8] Beyond the influence of fate, men wield, gain, and lose power based on their social position and their reputations and deeds, while women's power is based on their associations with these men and their reputations and patronage (typically, of men's deeds and literary production). There is no means in the medieval romance of disentangling a human woman's power from her sex and sexuality and, in fact, it is often through her sexuality that a woman, or a fairy in woman's form, aids a man in achieving his own status and power, as scholars such as Amy Vines (2014) have shown. This point highlights the most immediate difference in the relationships of humans to power and fairies to power in medieval romances. While fairy *desire* is typically linked to gender and/or sexuality—for example, with the fairy-mistress figures of Tryamour and of Mélusine, in the Arthurian tradition, and of Mélior in the various versions of *Partonope of Blois*[9]—and that desire results in a sexual relationship with a human man in which he can freely make use of her fairy power to develop his own power and status among humans as long as he adheres to some agreed-upon restriction of his agency demanded by the fairy lover, fairy *power* in itself has nothing to do with the gender, sex, or sexuality of the fairy (although *beauty* is a significant factor on which, more below) and nor is there any significant hierarchy in terms of the distribution of power among fairies, beyond there often being a fairy king or fairy queen and sometimes their servants or retinues involved in the narrative.[10] In medieval romance, the emphasis concerning fairy power is always on what that power can do for, or to, humans.

FAIRY–HUMAN INTERACTIONS

Medieval fairies are highly discriminating concerning which humans they interact with. They are not interested in using their powers to help humans of non-noble birth to acquire power in the form of status, and this is one significant way in which they distinguish themselves from fairies in later narratives (in the popular folktale rather than the literary fairy-tale tradition) or in modern adaptations of earlier tales, who occasionally will aid people of good and kind disposition who are also poor or not originally born into nobility, perhaps most famously in the modern version of *Cinderella*. One of the hallmarks of the medieval romance genre is that the protagonist is always a member of the noble classes, however unknown, distant, or lowly in position—a scion of a noble family, a bastard child raised away from court, or a secret child born of an illicit affair between a knight and a lady.[11] Even the squire of low degree—a young man who loves a king's daughter and must undertake a quest to prove his worth to marry her because of his lowly status—arguably the least well-positioned socially of the heroes of the fairy romance tradition, is already a squire and therefore technically a member of the nobility, on however low a rung of the social ladder (see "The Squire of Low Degree," in Kooper 2005: 135–59). In this unspoken (and unbroken) rule lies a suggestion of how fairy power operates philosophically: in every encounter in which a fairy is involved, power is attracted to power, or at least the potential for power. Fairies will happily consort with humans, but those humans must somehow be worthy; and while a potential human consort may be (and likely is, or soon becomes) renowned for his prowess and his fair form—as with Lybeaus Desconus ("The Fair Unknown") in that eponymous romance or Sir Gawain in *Sir Gawain and the Green Knight*—as noted above, worth is tied inextricably to social class on the human end of things (see Salisbury and Wheldon 2013). That understood, outside of the Irish and Welsh traditions, where fairy folk such as the Tuatha de Danaan almost exclusively interact with kings or their immediate family members, fairies also almost never engage with individuals at the very top of the social ladder in any meaningful way. In texts beyond the Celtic traditions (and *Sir Orfeo*, which is something of an anomaly being a fairy romance mapped onto a classical Greco-Roman myth) we almost never find fairies aiding kings and queens, with the notable exception of King Arthur, discussed below—suggesting that in medieval romance, fairies should be understood as actively using their power to disrupt and subvert the status quo in human society, but only within the parameters of the noble classes.[12] And in many cases—for example, *The Wife of Bath's Tale* and other loathly lady narratives, wherein a knight is faced with the decision as to whether he wants his wife to be beautiful and stupid or ugly and intelligent—they are also actively engaged in teaching the human and male protagonist an important lesson hinging on women's beauty, ethical in nature and tied to the agency of a human female. This is an interesting phenomenon given that fairies are overwhelmingly described as being preternaturally gorgeous, and therefore might not be expected to take an interest in human men's concerns over lesser physical attractiveness in a mortal sexual and/or life partner, since it is not a factor in their own relationship with the men, whom they ultimately intend to partner with as wives (see Chaucer, in Benson 1987). The reason for the embedded lesson in these narratives concerning human men's acceptance and appreciation of women regardless of appearance remains frustratingly opaque, as with so many other aspects of fairy nature and fairy power in medieval narratives.

While fairy folk in the form of the sovereignty goddess are essential to the rise in power and coronation of Irish kings, the only time we see fairies in the English tradition interfering directly in the life of a human king without another specific human also being involved in or affected directly by that interaction[13] is in the case of King Arthur. In Laȝamon's thirteenth-century Middle English *Brut*, fairies endow the newborn Arthur with strength surpassing that of all other knights, might as a ruler, longevity, and liberality:

> The time predestined came; then Arthur was born. As soon as he came upon earth, fairies took charge of him; they enchanted the child with magic most potent: they gave him strength to be the best of all knights; they gave him another gift, that he should be a mighty king; they gave him a third, that he should live long; they gave him, that royal child, such good qualities that he was the most liberal of all living men; these gifts the fairies gave him, and the child thrived accordingly.
>
> (*Layamon's Arthur, The Arthurian Section of Layamon's Brut* 2001: 21)

And, of course, Arthur also retires to the magical island of Avalon to be healed of his mortal wound at the end of every iteration of his life beginning with Geoffrey of Monmouth's *Historia regum Britanniae* (*History of the Kings of Britain*; Faletra 2008). The most famous passage depicting that scene is in Thomas Malory's *Le Morte Darthur*, wherein mortally wounded by Mordred, Arthur orders Sir Bedivere to throw Excalibur into the nearby lake; Bedivere hesitates, believing that throwing Excalibur away in this fashion can only lead to further harm and loss, but on his third attempt finally carries out Arthur's order. Bedivere then takes Arthur to the lake's side, and Malory writes:

> And whan they were there, evyn faste by the banke hoved a lytyll barge wyth many fayre ladyes in hit; and amonge hem all was a quene, and all they had blak hoodis, and all they wepte and shryked whan they saw Kynge Arthur.
> "Now put me into that barge," seyde the Kynge.
> And so he ded sofftely; and there resceyved hym thre quenys with grete mournyng. And so they sette hym downe, and in one of theire lappis Kyng Arthure layde hys hede.
> And than the quene seyde, "A, my dere brothir, why have ye taryed so longe from me? Alas, thys wounde on youre hede hath caught overmuch coulde."
> And anone they rowed fromward the londe ... seyde the kynge, ... I wyll into the vale of Avylyon to hele me of my grevous wounde.
> (2017: 926–7)[14]

Throughout King Arthur's life there is a fairy presence, and yet ultimately that presence does nothing to counter the fall of Camelot; this is a perfect example of how fairies bring great power and influence into human lives but do not hold sway over them. The only life-and-death alterations fairies make to human narratives is to take humans into their otherworlds, on which more below.

Fairy encounters can of course be accidental, but when fairies intentionally turn their attention to humans, their power is almost exclusively concentrated on aiding or thwarting individuals. It is certainly the case that their interactions with individuals can and often do involve and even affect other people, but that is not their intent or their focus; rather, it results from a clash between the circumstances of their interaction with the chosen individual and the human community that individual belongs to. This type of collateral damage occurs most often in Arthurian romances, such as Thomas Chestre's *Sir Launfal*, in which the fairy Tryamour focuses her power on helping Launfal rise in prominence. As in all of the versions of this story, Tryamour meets Launfal in private and declares her love for him, telling him that as long as he keeps their relationship a secret, she will shower him with wealth. At first, everything goes perfectly and upon his return from exile Launfal grows in status through the wealth bestowed upon him by the fairy; however, with his rise in prominence at court, Launfal catches the eye of Queen Guinevere, who attempts to seduce him. Launfal refuses Guinevere's advances, telling her he loves another woman who is more beautiful than she is. Guinevere retaliates by formally accusing Launfal of trying to seduce her, resulting in a trial. The only way Launfal can be found innocent is for him to produce the lovely maiden he has boasted of for comparison; he believes himself doomed, since he has broken his promise to keep the lady's existence secret. However, Tryamour and her retinue arrive at the trial to prove through their appearance that Launfal is telling the truth. In most versions of the story Launfal then joins the fairy on her horse and they ride off to the Land of Fairy; but in Chestre's version, Guinevere makes the rash statement during her accusation that "Yyf he [Launfal] bryngeth a fayrer thynge—/ Put out my eeyn gray!" (lines 809–10). After validating Launfal's words with her presence at court, Tryamour "to the Quene geth / And blew on her swych a breth / That never eft myght sche se" (lines 1006–8)—fulfilling the sentence Guinevere passed upon herself. While she does intentionally and directly breathe on Guinevere, rendering her blind, Tryamour's actions remain in defense and promotion of Launfal; she does not care about Guinevere.

This focus of a fairy's powers on an individual and the conflict that focus causes for that individual's community occur in almost meta-textual fashion in *Sir Gawain and the Green Knight*, in which ultimately it is revealed that the Green Knight's arrival in the Great Hall to interrupt the Christmas feast by proposing a game of ax-strokes was orchestrated by Morgan le Fay to frighten Guinevere to death and expose the corruption at Arthur's court. In the larger frame of the narrative, the Green Knight's interactions with Gawain are secondary or even incidental to Morgan's plot; her primary focus is on Arthur, and she seeks to use the knight, to frighten Guinevere, to get to Arthur. However, then Lord Bertilak's efforts at Hautdesert are turned to his own individual interaction with Gawain, making that young knight comfortable as his guest in an effort to thwart his quest. Lady Bertilak, as well, focuses her energies and efforts individually on seducing and then aiding Gawain by bestowing upon him the magical garter that prevents him from being killed, but also reveals his failure in not adhering to the letter of his agreement to share half of everything he receives during the day with his host upon Bertilak's return from the hunt each night (Figure 8.2).

The actions of Lord and Lady Bertilak are focused on and directly influence Gawain's outcome, and Gawain, in turn, is able to survive his ordeal and thus partially thwart Morgan's plan. While he is injured in the second half of the contest with the Green Knight, sustaining a nick to his neck, and that injury reveals his imperfections, when he returns to Camelot injured but alive, no one at that court is aware of Morgan's plan and thus no one knows that Gawain's injury is a sign of their community's failure. Rather, they all adopt the wearing of a garter themselves, concluding the story happily. This conclusion in which Gawain is altered for life through the revelation of his personal shortcomings, yet Morgan's ultimate plot to frighten Guinevere to death and expose the corruption of Arthur's court fails, is an excellent example of how fairy power can have marked effect on human lives but falls short of the ability to fully dictate the outcome of an encounter.

FIGURE 8.2: The Green Knight's Wife with Gawain. British Library, Cotton Nero A X, art3, fol. 129 (*c.* 1395–1400). British Library, with permission.

POWER AND GAMES

On the whole, fairies are not benevolent and generous: they expect a return on their investment in humans, and their demands and requests must be met to the letter if a human is to benefit from their power.[15] There is often a ludic quality to fairy relationships with humans, even as the game can be sinister and even deadly in nature. Fairies delight in using their powers to test humans through supernatural games, as with the game of strokes in *Sir Gawain and the Green Knight*, in which Sir Gawain uses the Green Knight's axe to cut off his head, and then has a year and a day to locate the Green Chapel and meet the Green Knight for a return blow. Fairy mistresses can seduce men outright through their otherworldly beauty; yet also willingly engage their knights in the lengthy flirtations of the lovers' game that grew out of the courtly love tradition. In Marie de France's *Lanval*, when the eponymous hero meets the fairy who has summoned him for an introduction, she greets him by stating that she has come from her own land to look for him because she loves him, presenting this as a straightforward situation in which she has come to offer him outright a claim on her affections as long as he proves himself to be "valiant and courteous" (line 113). In his (unprompted) response, Lanval addresses her according to the central tenets of the game of love—that a lover agree to do whatever his lady commands of him; that he foresake all other ladies and only serve her; and that he never seek to leave her:

> I will do what you command;
> For you I will give up everyone.
> I never wish to part from you:
> This is what I most desire.[16]

The fairy readily enters into the game by responding with the fourth essential tenet: that their love be kept secret from everyone else, or he loses it (and her):

> "Friend," she said, "Now I warn you,
> I command and beg you,
> Tell no one about this!
> I will tell you the whole truth:
> You would lose me forever
> If this love should be known;
> You could never see me again
> Or have possession of my body."
>
> (lines 127–30)[17]

Almost certainly, based on the near-ubiquity in these romances of fairies making demands on their lovers that must be met for the human to prosper from the relationship, she would have placed this or some other condition on him at some point in the scene; Lanval's employment of the language of courtly love opens the door for this demand to be handled in kind, presenting an opportunity for the fairy's pleasure to be increased by allowing her to participate in this mortal game.

When it is undertaken by a fairy knight in pursuit of a human woman in *Sir Degare*, this game of love is twisted and becomes sinister in nature. In that tale, on the anniversary of his wife's death the king and his retinue go to an abbey to hear Mass. Along the way, his daughter stops to rest, is separated from her ladies-in-waiting when she wanders off to gather flowers, and becomes lost in the wood. She comes across a "gentil, yong, and jolif man" (line 91) dressed in scarlet robes, who identifies himself as a fairy knight and tells her not to be afraid, he has come from afar because he has long loved her:

> "Damaisele, welcome mote thou be!
> Be thou afered of none wihghte:
> Iich am comen here a fairi knyghte;
> Mi kynde is armes for to were,
> On horse to ride with scheld and spere;
> Forthi afered be thou nowt:
> I ne have nowt but mi swerd ibrout.
> Iich have iloved the mani a yer."
>
> (lines 98–106)

This speech appears to be leading into the game of love; yet, after assuring her that he has come for love of her, suggesting some degree of safety or security of her person in his presence, the fairy knight promptly forces the princess to his will:

> "And now we beth us selve her,
> Thou best mi lemman ar thou go,
> Wether the liketh wel or wo."
> Tho nothing ne coude do she
> But wep and criede and wolde fle;
> And he anon gan hire at holde,
> And dide his wille, what he wolde.
> He binam hire here maidenhod.
>
> (lines 106–14)

Afterwards, he prophecies that the princess will bear him a son—"'Lemman,' he seide, 'gent and fre, / Mid schilde I wot that thou schalt be'" (lines 115–16)—and gives her his broken sword as a means by which his future son will know him when they meet, before leaving abruptly. Later, the fairy knight sends the princess a pair of magical gloves that only she can wear, which she leaves with the son she is forced to abandon, and who is raised by others. Years later, when the son inadvertently marries his mother, the gloves provide a recognition scene before the marriage is consummated. (Perhaps significantly, here the fairy knight is described as her lover, or "lemman,"[18] suggesting some intention that the fairy knight be read along similar lines as his fairy mistress counterpart, as more lover than rapist.[19])

Beyond demonstrating the ludic quality of some fairy–human relationships, juxtaposed against one another these two stories of fairy seduction highlight the overarching distinctions of female and male gender and power in medieval romance—Lanval's mistress uses her beauty to attract him, then enters the game of love and offers him her patronage in exchange for his vow of secrecy; the fairy knight by contrast coerces the king's daughter into a sexual union, using his physical beauty and gentle words to seduce her and his physical force to rape her. They also showcase the variety of fairy power—the fairy mistress in Lanval magically providing him with wealth, and the fairy knight demonstrating the preternatural power of prophecy and the possession and dispensation of magical objects from the otherworld.

The fairy folk of medieval romance can register as being fairly straightforward and transactional in their dealings with humans, but there is also often a great deal of deception, disguise, and trickery involved, particularly when it comes to the fairy figures in Celtic wonder tales, for instance, those of the Welsh *Mabinogion* and the Irish Ulster cycle. In what is called the *First Branch of the Mabinogion*, for instance, Pwyll, prince of Dyfed encounters Arawn, king of Annwn hunting in the woods. After declaring that Pwyll has insulted him by stealing the stag Arawn's hounds brought down to feed his own pack, Arawn proposes they enter into an alliance in which Pwyll will live in his kingdom and rule beside the most beautiful woman for a year. When Pwyll asks how his own realm will fare in his stead, Arawn responds, "I shall arrange that no man or woman in your realm realizes that I am not you, and I will take your place," and uses his power of glamour, or disguise, to trade physical appearances with Pwyll (Davies 2008: 6). In that same story, Pwyll is told that sitting on a mound will either result in personal injury or the witnessing of something wonderful. Pwyll takes on the challenge, seating himself on the mound, and a beautiful woman rides past on a stately horse at a steady pace. Determined to learn who she is, Pwyll sends one of the men accompanying him to follow her, but no matter how fast the man rides, he cannot catch up to her. Pwyll then sends for a horse and follows her on horseback himself; but again, no matter how fast he rides, he cannot draw close to her, even though "she was going at the same pace as when she had started" (9). Every man who pursues her is thus deceived into thinking he can catch her yet fails despite every effort to match her speed. The maiden exhibits the preternatural power of fairy travel, defying the physics of mortal physical movement; eventually, after several days of similarly fruitless pursuit, Pwyll realizes he cannot catch up to her and instead begs her to stop and speak with him, learning when she does that her name is Rhiannon and she has come to him because she loves him over all other men.[20] In the Irish *Cattle Raid of Cooley* (*Táin Bó Cúailnge*), the Morrigan, another Celtic otherworld woman, approaches the hero Cú Chulainn claiming to be a king's daughter and offering her love; when he refuses, she reveals her true identity and embarks upon a series of vengeful attacks upon him in various animal forms as he tries to honor his responsibility to defeat Queen Medb's champion, Lóch mac Mofemis, at a river ford, to prevent the theft of the titular bull (see Kinsella 2002).

DISPLACING/TRANSPORTING MORTALS

In addition to entering and exiting the mortal plane at will to interact with humans, fairies have the power to remove human beings from the human world entirely, temporarily or permanently. Typically, they exercise this power to preserve human lives when they are gravely injured, as in the case of King Arthur, taken to Avalon when he is mortally wounded by Mordred, or that of Floriant, brought to her castle by Morgan le Fay to avoid his impending death while hunting and joined there by his human beloved, representing a unique instance in medieval romance in which a fairy also permits the dead or dying individual's human beloved to be brought as well as to share eternity (see *Floriant et Florete* 2003). Fairies also exercise this power to separate the human from a corrupt, unappreciative, or otherwise-damaging courtly community (as with Lanval); to trade places with the human as a test (as when Arawn trades places with Pwyll in the *First Branch of the Mabinogion*); to bring humans into the otherworld for a test for which the fairy remains present (as in *Sir Gawain and the Green Knight*); or, in some cases, to abduct humans for an unspecified reason, as in the case of the humans turned into statues in *Sir Orfeo*.[21]

When this power is exercised for clearly benevolent aims, as in preserving the life of a dying human, this is explained, and often in detail, in the moment in which the human arrives into the otherworld. When the power is exercised in ways that can be construed as negative, sinister, or treacherous, as with *Sir Orfeo*'s human sculpture garden, no explanation is given for why or how the humans arrived or have come into their current state of being. When the power of Faerie is used to bring humans into the otherworld for a test, this is typically revealed toward the end of the narrative, when the test has either successfully or unsuccessfully concluded. While fairy power is intrinsic to the fairy's being, and the fairy's being is typically associated with a physical space, except in cases where human lives are being saved from imminent death by the magic of the fairy's realm or domicile, or where the invisible servants of a castle wait on the human visitor to showcase the fairy's supernatural largesse *in situ*, there is rarely any indication that fairies need to be in the otherworld to wield their powers or that their powers are substantially stronger there than in the human world; when fairies bring humans into the otherworld, that decision does not stem from some need to meet them on their own turf to retain their power over the mortals.

CONTROLLING BODIES

Where their attention is attracted to mortals, romance fairies are mostly interested in human bodies, and their efforts in relationship to humans almost exclusively hinge on some form of control upon those bodies, either through seduction, illusion, or coercion. Fairies of course have the power to seduce humans through their extreme beauty and promises of wealth and prosperity, as with Tryamour and Mélusine. Sometimes, they instead engage in illusory powers, such as disguising themselves or others through a glamour to look like someone else, as with Morgan le Fay and the Green Knight in *Sir Gawain and the Green Knight*, Pucelle aux Blanche Mains in *Le Bel Inconnu*, or the fairy mistress/wife in *The Wife of Bath's Tale*; or alternately, to fool the human into believing he is somewhere he is not, as with Dame D'Amour, who tricks Lybeaus into seeing himself in and thus, wishing to remain in paradise in *Lybeaus Desconus*. And sometimes, fairies and other fay creatures use their power to force humans into a test or other situation requiring them either to submit to the fairy's will or face significant personal loss or distress, as in Marie de France's *Guigemar*, in which a young nobleman out hunting mortally wounds a white hind and is himself wounded; as the hind dies, it curses Guigemar, so that his wound cannot be cured by any medicine but only through a love in which he, and the lady of his affections, are both willing to suffer for one another.[22] In some cases, the fairy exercises both control over and possession of the human's body but not for any discernible reason beyond simply to have it, as an object. This inscrutable desire for possession most notably occurs with the fairy king in *Sir Orfeo*, who abducts Dame Heurodis but then rather than physically assaulting her, as the fairy knight does the maiden in *Sir Degare*, simply adds her to his human sculpture garden.[23] In other cases, a fairy figure controls the body of a human by keeping it away from another member of the fay through magical means, as in the Irish *Wooing of Étain* (*Tochmarc Étaíne*): King Midir is accidentally blinded by a sprig of holly during a game while visiting his foster-son Aengus; healed by the Tuatha de Danaan's physician Dian Cecht, Midir demands recompense in the form of the hand of the most beautiful woman in the world—Étain, a mortal woman of the Ulaid tribe. Fúamnach, Midir's wife and also a member of the Tuatha de Danaan, then uses her magical powers to control Étain's body and prevent her from being with Midir, transforming her into a pool of water that evaporates into a large and beautiful fly, which Fúamnach then blows about the world with violent storms for many years. Eventually, Étain in fly form lands in the cup of another Ulaid woman, wife of the chieftain Étar; this woman drinks the contents of the cup, thereby becoming pregnant and birthing Étain back into the world (see "The Wooing of Étain," in Gantz 1981: 37–59). It is not uncommon for fay to combine two or more of these powers of bodily control and coercion in their efforts to bend humans to their will; for example, as already noted, in exchange for their patronage fairy mistresses almost always seduce their knightly lovers and then put them to a test of their loyalty and ability to keep the secret of their affair.

CONCLUSION

While fairy power ranges broadly in type and scope, in how it is used and how it is received, the essential power of every fairy in medieval literature is to attract the attention of mortals—both of the human characters who share space with them in texts and of the audiences of those texts. Fairies are seductive: their difference from humans—their beauty, their longevity, their magic, and their unpredictability; their ability to ignore conventions and rules, to make their own terms in relationships, and to engage in acts of wish fulfillment, are impossible to ignore. They bring with them promises of love and prosperity and can be harbingers of a positive change in an individual's fate; conversely, they are also sinister, capricious, and threaten adversity, danger, and loss alongside pleasure. They disrupt the status quo whenever they appear, either for an individual knight or lady, or for the community to which that knight or lady belongs, or for everyone involved. Their ambiguous, arbitrary, and idiosyncratic behaviors contrast importantly with the conventions of human courtly society and offer alternative ways of being and doing to those among their human counterparts who accept their calls to adventure, to tests and quests, and to love. They challenge humans to sharply question what they think, know, and feel, opening the door to opportunities only available to those who are willing and able to look past what and how things are, to what they might be. They require risk to attain success, offering the deal of "all or nothing" to those brave or foolhardy enough to engage them. Ultimately, regardless of how it manifests, the power of the fairy in medieval literature and culture subverts mundane reality and societal norms with limitless invention and imagined possibility.

NOTES

Introduction

1. Many scholars have grappled with the fairy tale genre; see Bottigheimer (2009, 2012, 2014), Tatar (1999, 2004, 2015), Ziolkowski (2007), and Zipes (2006, [2012] 2013, [2000] 2015).
2. Tolkien's influential essay, based on his 1939 lecture Andrew Lang, was one of the first to grapple seriously with defining the genre.
3. The tale of Patient Griselda entered the fairy-tale tradition through Boccaccio's *Decameron* and Chaucer's *Canterbury Tales*. It tells the tale of the peasant Griselda, whose virtue catches the eye of the kingdom's ruler. He marries her on the condition that she never disobeys him, in word, deed, or look. All seems to be well, until the ruler decides to test Griselda's patience. He tears her children—first a boy and then a girl—from her arms, reportedly sending them off to be killed, banishes her from the palace, and then asks her to come back and prepare the household to receive his new bride. Throughout all of these trials, Griselda keeps her promise of total obedience, and, in the end, the lord recognizes her patience, reveals that the new bride and her brother are actually Griselda's stolen children, restores her to her position and they live, the tale tells us, happily ever after.
4. For further discussion of the Grimms' academic work, see Ziolkowski (2007: 24–8) and Tatar (2004).
5. Cecire (2019) discusses several examples of current fantasy authors who seek to expand the genre beyond the limits of enchantment imposed by Lewis's and Tolkien's work. Other notable examples of fairy tale/fantasy works that create a non-Western fantasy Middle Ages include S. A. Chakraborty's *Daevabad Trilogy* (2017–20) and Ausma Zehanat Kahn's *The Bloodprint* (2017).
6. For a more detailed discussion of "factual" medieval discussion of fairies, see Green (2016: 33–41).
7. For details on the medieval Arabic magic tales, see Bottigheimer (2014: 84–120).
8. *Beowulf* is preserved in a single Old English manuscript, which scholars date to the late tenth century. For accurate and readable translations, see Heaney (2001) and Headley (2020).

9. The term "edda" refers to two Icelandic manuscripts, the *Prose* or *Younger Edda* dates to the early thirteenth century and the *Poetic* or *Elder Edda* to the end of that century.
10. For a discussion of and overview of these Arthurian tales, see Aronstein (2012).
11. For further discussion of the Wife of Bath, see Green (2016: 50–2) and Williams (2018: 108–15).
12. For further discussion of fairy mistresses in medieval romance, see Wade (2011: 109–46).
13. For a discussion of the connections between oral and written and the transmission of fairy tales in the Middle Ages, see Bottigheimer (2009: 1–8), Zipes (Zipes [2012] 2013: 3–7), and Ziolkowski (2007: esp. 1–8, 37–41, 53–60).

Chapter 1

1. Even the credulous James VI of Scotland writes of "the fourth kinde of Spirites called the Phairie" that "the deuil illuded the senses of sundry simple creatures, in making them beleeue that they saw and harde such thinges as were nothing so indeed" (1597: 74).
2. In the UK, when it comes to the marvelous, Cooper (2004) and her former students, Saunders (2010) and Wade (2011), have been chiefly concerned with motifs and themes, whereas in the United States, Cohen (1999, 2006), Ingham (2001), and Heng (2003) have concerned themselves primarily with political issues such as class, race, and gender.
3. For example, despite Todorov's explicit denial that he is using *l'étrange* in precisely Freud's sense (1970: 52), his English translator renders this term as "uncanny"— the standard English translation for Freud's *Unheimlich*; I have rendered it here as "weird" to dilute such an association.
4. It runs to fifty-nine closely printed double-column pages in the standard seventeenth-century printed edition.
5. A subsequent chapter, "On the Tricks of Demons" (124–37), is packed with fairy lore, some of it indebted to William of Auvergne.
6. Vivian, the lady of the lake, who had raised Lancelot, is once mentioned as a *fee* (Chrétien de Troyes [c. 1180] 2010: 138).
7. Ravenel, for instance, writes that the "[*Gowther*] poet may very well have thought to heighten the charm of his austere subject-matter by an admixture of the more highly spiced episodes [from T*ydorel*]" (1905: 161). More recently, Andrea Hopkins misses the fairy dimension of *Sir Gowther* by swallowing the author's own cultural prejudices hook, line, and sinker: "Sir Gowther is not a fairy but a fiend, and a particular type of fiend. He is in fact an incubus, a fiend which specializes in seducing mortal women" (1990: 162). Green even goes so far as to suggest that *incubus* was "probably the most widely used scholastic term for 'fairy' in the Middle Ages" (2016: 3). It is worth noting that when Sir Gowther undergoes penance by being fed with the emperor's dogs, the emperor's men mock him by calling him "Hob" (line 368), a common term for a fairy (cf. "Hobgoblin").
8. Its thirteenth-century French analogue, *Robert le diable* is doing very similar cultural work and may well also have been a source, though Ravenel suggests that there are several places where *Gowther* resembles *Tydorel* more closely than *Robert*; but see Hopkins (1990: 148–9).
9. For a measured treatment of this controversial figure, see Bertrand Bronson (1945); three other ballad versions (Child B, D, and E) also omit any specific reference to elves or Efland.

10. In the Cambridge MS the line reads, "a paire of gloues / That were sende hur owt of Elues lande" (Schleich 1929: 68).
11. Gower refers to the proverbial beauty of fairies in his *Balade 27* (line 22), written "Pour vous, q'avetz la bealté plus qe faie" ("for you, who is more beautiful than a fairy"; 1899: 360).
12. That is to say, "something *resembling [a tale about fairies] in being* unreal or incredible." Of course, the concept of a tale "having folkloric elements or featuring fantastic or magical events or characters" (OED Online 2020: extended Sense 1) would have been perfectly comprehensible in the Middle Ages, as Jan Ziolkowski's excellent *Fairy Tales from before Fairy Tales* (2006) demonstrates: "the special feature of this type is most definitely not the presence of a particular type (the fairy), but, rather, the salience of a particular content (the marvelous and/or the magical)" (46).

Chapter 2

1. For a more detailed discussion of Antoine Galland's translation of *The Thousand and One Nights*, see Bottigheimer (2012) and Mallette (2010).
2. See Akbari and Mallette (2013) for more about the complex literary histories of the medieval Mediterranean.
3. See Copeland (1991: ch. 7: "Translation as Rhetorical Invention").
4. Carol Hefferman catalogs the various possible sources of "The Squire's Tale" in *The Orient in Chaucer and Medieval Romance* (2003: ch. 4: "Chaucer's *Squire's Tale*: Content and Structure").

Chapter 3

1. On the equation of "fairy tales" and "the Middle Ages," see Ziolkowski (2009: 23).
2. On histories and anthologies of the Western fairy tale, see Ziolkowski (2009: 25–6).
3. For an overview of medieval romance, see Fuchs (2004: 37–65).
4. Legal scholar Kimberlé Crenshaw coined the term "intersectionality" in her article, "Demarginalizing the Intersection of Race and Sex" (1989). See also Crenshaw (1991).
5. On the performativity of gender, and the inevitability of variation within each performance, see Butler (1993: esp. 121–40).
6. While Fair Unknown stories were common in medieval romance, Eve Salisbury and James Weldon note in their introduction to *Lybeaus Desconus* that "the closest analogue to the Middle English *Lybeaus Desconus* is Renaut de Bâgé's 6,266-line, late twelfth-century Old French poem, *Li Biaus Descouneüs (Le Bel Inconnu)*, which perhaps explains why the story is repeatedly referred to as 'the Frensshe tale'" (Salisbury and Weldon 2013). James Weldon similar notes that "the exact nature of the relationship between French and German analogues [and the English romance] remains uncertain, but it is clear that *Lybeaus Desconus* bears some relation to Beaujeu's [Bâgé's] *Li Biaus Descouneüs*" (Weldon 2007: 75).
7. For both original Old French and Modern English translation, see Renaut de Bâgé, *Le Bel Inconnu (Li Biaus Descouneüs; The Fair Unknown)* (1992). All Modern English quotations of the poem are taken from this edition and are cited parenthetically by line number.
8. For the Middle English poem, see Salisbury and Weldon (2013). All Middle English quotations of the poem are taken from this edition and are cited parenthetically by

line number. On the attribution of authorship to Chestre, see Salisbury and Weldon, introduction to *Lybeaus Desconus*, "Authorship" (2013).
9. For a Modern English translation of the Middle French text, see d'Arras ([c. 1392] 2012). All Modern English quotations of the text are taken from this edition and are cited parenthetically by page number.
10. In arriving at *fin amor*, frequently translated as "courtly love," I arrive at a concept that is both crucially important to romance constructions of gender and sexuality and highly contentious within the field of medieval studies. *Amor courtois*, or "courtly love" was allegedly coined by the French philologist and medievalist Gaston Paris in the late nineteenth century, specifically in regard to Chrétien de Troyes's *Lancelet*. This romance features the earliest recorded story of Lancelot and Guinevere, whose love, at once adulterous and refined, requires Lancelot's absolute obedience to an often tyrannical queen. In the first half of the twentieth century, C. S. Lewis influentially codified courtly love in terms of four key characteristics: humility, courtesy, adultery, and the religion of love. As an adulterous love affair, courtly love transgressed feudal loyalties and Christian doctrine, but nonetheless transcended these social systems via mystification—Lewis's "religion of love" ([1936] 2013). The French historian Denis de Rougemont similarly describes courtly love as an adulterous, uncontrollable passion that elevates lovers beyond social structures. "Passion," as Rougemont notes, literally means suffering, and courtly love is a form of suffering passion that is aestheticized, eroticized, and celebrated. Taking the adulterous lovers Tristan and Isolde as his paradigm, Rougemont claims that courtly love is ultimately tragic, but the disaster in which it results is nonetheless "magnificent and desirable" (1982: 6). That lovers dare to defy society, even if their efforts fail, is what elevates courtly love, rendering it "freedom itself." Notably, these big claims about courtly love led to even bigger claims about the workings of gender and sexuality in Western cultures. As early as the 1960s, however, courtly love came under critique, with some skeptics going so far as to argue that courtly love was an invention of nineteenth- and twentieth-century philologists, who retrospectively imposed the concept upon medieval literature and culture. More recently, scholars have leaned toward the view that *fin amor* is an authentic construct of medieval literary culture, although one that cannot be rigidly defined and does not necessarily extend to actual social practice. For useful overviews of the history of the idea of courtly love, see Ruys (2014: 125–32) and O'Donoghue (2006: 7–24).
11. For influential studies on this point, see Burns (1993), Gaunt (1995: 71–121), and Krueger (1993).
12. For an overview of this representational tradition, see Burns (2008: 195–202).
13. On the tradition of natural magic and liberal arts education in the Middle Ages, see Saunders (2010: 104–5).
14. On medieval beliefs about human-fairy progeny, see Green (2016: 101).

Chapter 4

1. See, for instance, the *shedim*, *jinn*, and *aziza* of Hebrew, Islamic, and West African tradition, respectively, or the plethora of Japanese nature spirits who interact with people.
2. Jean d'Arras's *Mélusine* survives in ten manuscripts. Quotations of the original French are from the edition by Jean-Jacques Vincensini, *Mélusine, ou la Noble Histoire de Lusignan* (under d'Arras 2003); translations, unless otherwise indicated, are from

Melusine; or, the Noble History of Lusignan, translated by Donald Maddox and Sara Sturm-Maddox (under d'Arras [c. 1392] 2012). The poetic version by Coudrette, *Roman de Parthenay ou le roman de Mélusine,* survives in twenty manuscripts, and is assumed to be based on Jean's version or a common source. Quotations of Coudrette's original French are from the edition by Eleanor Roach, *Le Roman de Mélusine, ou Histoire de Lusignan* (see Coudrette 1982). Translations are my own.

3. "The Prologue of Sir Thopas" (Chaucer 2019: 393, line 712).
4. The first in their series of popular coffee-table books.
5. Welsh, "women of the un- or Otherworld," a realm variously depicted as an island or beneath water.
6. Literally, "re-greening." The *reverdie* in medieval French poetry was a poetic celebration of Spring and its natural beauties, adopted by other literary cultures, the most famous example being the opening to Chaucer's *Canterbury Tales.*
7. On the serpent/piscine biformity of Melusine and her analogues, see Bain (2018: 17–35).
8. Repeated by Gervase of Tilbury in *Otio Imperialia* (2002: 3.86: 729).
9. *Certainty of the Worlds of Spirits* (Baxtor 1691: 4, quoted in Briggs 1959): "Yea; we are not fully certain whether these Aeriel Regions have not a third sort of Wights, that are neither Angels, (Good or Fallen) nor Souls of Men, but such as have been placed as Fishes in the Sea, and Men on Earth; and whether those called Faeries and Goblins are not such."
10. Eleanor, or Alienor (1122–1204 CE), was both admired and condemned. Rumors about her infidelities abounded, fueled probably by jealousy of her beauty, intelligence, and "her ability to get and keep the upper hand" (Chapman 1955: 394).
11. For a modern French translation of the passage, see Lombard-Jourdan (2005: 121).
12. Antiquity and the Middle Ages teemed with mythologies about royal descent from supernatural ancestors, the most outstanding being Alexander the Great (said to be the son of Zeus who visited his mother in a bolt of lightning). In Arthurian tradition, the prophet Merlin was begotten by a demon or a fairy lover; so was Sir Degaré, and Lancelot was raised by a fairy mistress, the Lady of the Lake.
13. See also Urban's chapter "How the Dragon Ate the Woman: The Fate of Melusine in English" (2018: 368–87).
14. According to Paracelsus, Melusine, a nymph, had engaged the help of the Devil in securing a husband, and had she only stayed with him she might have freed herself from the fiend who exacted a penalty: her deformed shape on Saturdays (245–6).
15. Coudrette, German: Thüring von Ringoltingen (1456). Jean, Castillian: *La Historia de la linda Melosina* (1489). Jean, Middle Dutch: *Historie van Meluzine.* Coudrette, Middle English: title missing (c. 1590). Jean, early modern English, untitled (c. 1600). For Melusine's resurrection in the nineteenth century, see the novella *Undine* (1811) by Friedrich de la Motte Fouque; "Die neue Meluzine" (1817) by Johann Wolfgang von Goethe; John Keats's "The Lamia" (1820); the play *Pélleus et Mélisande* (1893) by Maurice Maeterlinck and the corresponding opera (1902) by Debussy. Finally, A. S. Byatt's award-winning novel *Possession* (1990) grants Melusine a fictional place in Victorian English literature, where two English scholars study the strange underpinnings of "The Fairy Melusine" by the imaginary Victorian poet Christabel La Motte.
16. Referencing Briggs: Sinistrari was born in 1627, but his *Daemonalitas* "remained in manuscript until it was found by Isidore Liseaux, who published it with a French translation in 1876. It cannot therefore have had a wide influence in

its own period, but it sums up a view which was held by a certain number of thinkers" (1959: 171–2).
17. Namely, "monsters." The original is *portentis*.
18. All further quotations of Jean's text in English come from the edition and translation by Maddox and Sturm-Maddox (d'Arras [*c*. 1392] 2012), unless noted. Quotations of the French come from the edition by Jean-Jacques Vincensini (d'Arras 2003: 113).
19. "They are called *lamias*, or rather *lanias*, from *laniare* (to mangle), because they mangle babies" (Gervase of Tilbury 2002: 717). Lamias in the Middle Ages were depicted as serpents with a woman's head who stole children.
20. This elevation may seem blasphemous, but Jean gives Melusine supernatural knowledge, inherited from her mother. In knowing Aimery's prophecy she enacts it.
21. For a thorough discussion of these debates, see Cole (2018: 247–50).
22. This term translates a common genre called *speculum principum*, a text for the instruction of a prince or a king, where virtuous behavior is outlined or exemplified, and unvirtuous behavior discouraged, often indirectly.
23. Maddox and Sturm-Maddox translate "including your own son who had found solace in religion?" (d'Arras [*c*. 1392] 2012). The original is more visceral: "ne ton filz ni s'estoit renduz au crucifix?" ("nor your son who was placed on the crucifix?") (d'Arras 2003: 692–4). The image portrays Fromont as a Christian martyr denied the opportunity, granted the sacrilegious Geoffroy, to repent.

Chapter 5

1. See, for instance, Vincent of Beauvais's *Speculum Naturale*, Thomas of Cantimpré's *De natura rerum*, and Bruno Latini's *Tresor*. Carolyn Walker Bynum's *Metamorphosis and Identity* (2001) explores in depth the fascination with hybridity and boundary crossing in the twelfth and thirteenth centuries.
2. See book eleven of Isidore's *Etymologiae* ([*c*. 560–636] 2006).
3. See the chapter "Cain's Kin" in Friedman ([1981] 2000).
4. Although in Genesis Noah technically directs his curse at Ham's son Canaan, in medieval literature and art the curse tends to be associated with Ham.
5. In the Middle Ages the Middle Irish word *luchrupán* refers to a small sprite-like supernatural being. An association with water that disappears from the later characterization of the leprechaun is evident in the *Adventure of Fergus son of Léti*, when the King of Ulster falls asleep on a beach and awakens to find himself being dragged into the sea by three *lúchorpáin* (Koch 2005: 1059, 1200).
6. The codex is the second of two codices making up British Library MS Cotton Vitellius A. xv. The manuscript was produced in the late tenth or early eleventh century. However, scholars do not assume that the scribe who copied the poem is necessarily its composer. For a detailed discussion of the Nowell Codex as a context for *Beowulf*, see Orchard ([1985] 1995).
7. The Book of Judith is part of the Catholic and Eastern Orthodox Bibles, but is excluded from Jewish scripture and assigned to the Apocrypha by Protestants.
8. All citations from *Beowulf* are from Roy Liuzza's translation (2000).
9. In fact, Tolkien observes that the term "*eoten*" is preserved in Old English only through its application to Grendel ([1936] 1964: 43).
10. For a discussion of Dante's monsters, see Jewiss (2001).

11. For more on the relationship between medieval culture and the fairy-tale tradition, see Clausen-Stolzenburg (1995) and Ziolkowski (2009).
12. The list of medieval genres that scholars have identified as contributing to the fairy-tale tradition exceeds those mentioned here. This discussion excludes those medieval genres (animal fable, fabliau, exemplum) that do not conventionally feature monsters. For an argument identifying the fairy tale as having its beginning in the Middle Ages, see Ziolkowski (2009).
13. See Mittman (2013: note 20) for additional theorists supporting this point.
14. It is a commonplace among scholars to observe that the definition of the monster refuses taxonomic categorization. See Cohen (1996), Asma (2009), and Mittman (2013).
15. The words "*Hic sunt dracones*" can be found (on the southeast coast of Asia) on the early modern Hunt-Lenox Globe (1510) now in the possession of the New York Public Library. Famous depictions of dragons on maps include a 1367 nautical chart by the Pizzigani brothers (Heidelberg, Biblioteca Palatina, Carta nautica no. 1612) and a *mappa mundi* in Andrea Vianco's 1436 atlas (Venice, Biblioteca Nazionale Marciana, MS It. Z. 76, map 9).
16. See "dragon" entry in *The Medieval Bestiary* (Badke 2011).
17. Rev. 12: 9 (Douay-Rheims Bible n.d.).
18. See Acker (2013: 54–5), Evans (2005: 217–18), and Tuczay (2006: 188). For more on the Indo-European dragon-slayer myth as cosmogony, see Dumézil (1970), Eliade (1971), de Vries (1959) and Watkins (1995).
19. For dragons and King Arthur, see Elmes (2017b) and Kordecki (1984).
20. See Dumézil (1983). For a summary of Dumézil's thought on the hero, see Littleton (1982). Evans (1985) makes a similar point.
21. ATU refers to the Aarne-Thompson Uther Tale Type Index.
22. Motif F582.1 in Thompson's *Motif-Index of Folk-Literature* (1959). See da Silva (2002) for a psychoanalytic approach to this theme in fairy tales.
23. This concept appears in folklore as well. See motif F582 (Poison Damsel) (Thompson 1959).

Chapter 6

1. In this chapter, I use the modern term "fairy" to describe inhabitants of the supernatural world or "otherworld," following Carey's definition of the latter as "a minimal designation for any place inhabited by supernatural beings and itself exhibiting supernatural characteristics" (1991: 1). It is worth noting that "otherworld" is a purely generic term: Sims-Williams points out that medieval Welsh and Irish writers did not use a single shared word for such a place or share a single coherent concept of the "otherworld," which is therefore a "useful, but probably misleading, modern term" (2011: 54).
2. *Lebor Gabála Érenn* is an eleventh-century compilation that survives in manuscripts from the twelfth century. It draws on a number of earlier sources, including the ninth-century *Historia Brittonum*, and an early written form is likely to have existed in the ninth century (Carey 1994: 17).
3. We can compare the description of the house in the Land of Promise with that of Ailill and Medb, king and queen of Connacht, in *Táin Bó Froích* ("The Cattle-Raid of Fróech"), where the hero is feasted for three days and three nights by the royal couple (Gantz 1981: 116–17). The larger-than-life nature of even the human world in Irish saga further complicates the division between the real world and the fairy world.

4. The tale has an overtly Christian purpose, with its prophecy of the birth of Christ and representations of a paradisal world. Proinsias Mac Cana commented that the author's purpose was "to create an aesthetic rapport between the pagan concept of the Otherworld and the Christian concept of Paradise" (1976: 95). Compare Walter Map's twelfth-century Latin tale (in *De Nugis Curialium*) of King Herla, who spends three days and nights at an otherworld feast, only to find on his return that hundreds of years have passed and he and his company will turn to ash if they touch the ground (James 1983: 26–31), a parable about the corruption of secular court life. Less didactic versions of the fairyland time warp occur in the Welsh prose tale, *Branwen uerch Lŷr* (Davies 2008: 33–4) and in the fifteenth-century Middle English *Romance and Prophecies of Thomas of Erceldoune* (Murray 1875: lines 93–286), where Thomas is saved by the fairy queen.
5. There are parallels here in the twelfth-century French romance by Chrétien de Troyes, *Yvain*, where the hero fulfills the knightly fantasy of marrying a woman with wealth and property and returns to her own land with her. Compare also the French romance by Marie de France, *Lanval*.
6. For the original Welsh text, see Bromwich and Evans (1992: 15; lines 412–15).
7. The word *gorsedd* meaning "assembly" occurs in the tenth-century Old Welsh poems found in a Latin text of works by Juvencus (McKee 2000a, b).
8. According to Davies there is a local place name in the area, Bedd Gronw ("Gronw's Grave"), indicating "very strong associations between this branch and local topography, perhaps more so than any other tale in the [*Mabinogion*] corpus" (2008: 244).
9. It is perhaps worth remembering Raymond Williams's (unflattering) description of modern-day advertising as "a system of organised magic" (Williams 1980: 186) in which narratives of fantasy and wish fulfillment "transform commodities into glamorous signifiers ... and these signifiers present an imaginary, in the sense of unreal, world" (During 1993: 320). Judith Williamson's formulation of magic as "the production of results disproportionate to the effort put in" (Williamson 1978: 141) is also relevant to medieval fairy worlds and their protagonists.
10. The reference is to "les Escoz e ... les Pis" in the Old French text (Rychner 1969: vv. 5–8). The French text names the city as "Carduel," a name that occurs in a number of French Arthurian romances including *Yvain* by Chrétien de Troyes. Carduel is generally taken to signify Carlisle (and the references to Picts and Scots in *Lanval* support this), though we also find confusion between Carlisle and Caerleon (in the southeast of Wales) in some romances, such as the *Alliterative Morte Arthure* (*c.* 1400).
11. Both *Guigemar* and *Partonopeus de Blois* are discussed by Cooper in her chapter on the theme of the "rudderless boat" (2004: 106–36).
12. See note 10 above. In the Welsh version of Chrétien's *Yvain*, the hero Owain sets out from Arthur's court at Caerleon (Davies 2008: 116).
13. For the description of the giant in the French text, see Roques (1965: vv. 269–89).
14. The relationship between three of Chrétien's romances (*Yvain*, *Erec et Enide*, and *Perceval*) and three Welsh prose tales (*Owain*, *Gereint uab Erbin*, and *Peredur*) has been much debated. The most likely explanation for the similarities between each of the three pairs of texts is that Chrétien drew on Welsh material transmitted to him via storytellers and interpreters and that his three verse romances were then conveyed back to Wales and adapted into Welsh texts which reworked the style and some of the plot details to suit the expectations of noble Welsh audiences.

Duggan argues for a strong element of oral transmission in both directions (2001: 196).
15. In Bliss's opinion, "the fairy mistress [in *Sir Launfal*] has little of the aura of enchantment which surrounds her in the work of Marie de France" (1960: 1). The element of wish fulfillment evident in popular romances such as *Sir Launfal* suggests a broad audience interested in the possibilities of social mobility, as Hahn has suggested (2000: 225).
16. The medieval Church tended to equate fairies with demons (Green 2016: 15–16), though as Green says, "In the popular mind fairy lore might have been reconciled with Christian teaching in ways that would have scandalized the more educated members of the clergy" (18).
17. There are a number of translations into modern English of *Sir Gawain and the Green Knight*. Reliable translations include Barron (1998) and Benson and Donoghue (2012). Recent literary translations have been made by poets Armitage (2008) and O'Donoghue (2006).
18. This critique is also evident in the French *Lanval*, which has been read as a rebuke of Arthur's treatment of the hero, working "to correct a fault in the central aristocratic society which it is itself unwilling or unable to correct" (Rider 2000: 120).

Chapter 7

1. For example, the fifteenth-century Wars of the Roses in England were fought between two branches of the same family for control of the throne. The Hundred Years War between England and France, fought in the fourteenth and fifteenth centuries, also involved cousins fighting each other. For more on the growing density of settlement in Western Europe by the fourteenth and fifteenth centuries, see Bartlett (1993).
2. As Elizabeth Archibald has written of medieval literature's frequent portrayal of incest, it "seems to be largely a plot mechanism—though a very serious one"; rather than reflecting a higher incidence of incest in the Middle Ages than today, which she notes that we have little evidence for (1996: 163, 157). Archibald argues that the rise of incest plots in the late Middle Ages may be the result of a complex intersection of cultural anxieties and political concerns (166).
3. For more on Chrétien's influences and sources, see Stahuljak et al. (2011). For example, Stahuljak and colleagues note that the literary and scholarly environment of Troyes in the twelfth century would have included a wide variety of influences, including translations of "Arabic treatises of astronomy and geometry" and translations of "Greek, Arabic and Judaic philosophy" (5).
4. For more on the changing social experiences of young women in this period, see Harris (2018).
5. For more on suspicions about women's relationships in medieval culture, see Lochrie (2003: 70–90).

Chapter 8

1. J. R. R. Tolkien is widely credited as being the first major scholar in medieval studies to take fairies seriously as subjects in their own right, and the stories featuring fairies seriously as literature worthy of critical study and adult attention; see "On Fairy Stories," an essay originally given as the Andrew Lang Lecture Series lecture at St. Andrews University in Scotland in March of 1939 and available as *Tolkien on*

Fairy-Stories (2014), edited by Verlyn Flieger and Douglas A. Anderson. Tolkien argues in this essay that "fairy stories" are a specific and discrete literary genre and that stories must feature fairy characters and/or take place in the realm of Faerie to be categorized as fairy tales, in direct contradiction of most folklorists both contemporary and prior to his own time, including Andrew Lang, himself, who subscribed to a much broader definition that included traveler's tales and folktales with magic, but no fairies, present within them. In addition to legitimizing fairy stories as their own genre, Tolkien discusses how such tales permit readers to view their own world through a different perspective; in the current chapter, I discuss this function of the fairy tale specifically in terms of what medieval fairy stories reveal to us about power structures and systems, class, and gender.

2. For space considerations, and in the interest of a general audience, this chapter focuses specifically on depictions of fairy power in the literatures and cultures of the medieval British Isles; supernatural beings with abilities and powers resembling those exhibited by these fairies are found throughout the folk traditions of the medieval world.

3. Green opts not to enter into discussion of fairy taxonomy at all: "I will have nothing to say on the vexed question of fairy taxonomy … all such questions are unanswerable, and attempt at a totalizing definition will prove illusory" (2016: 2). In general, I adopt a similar view that fairies and fairy folk (fay) comprise a wide range of figures and that the categorization of what is, and is not, actually a fairy, and of fairy relationships with regard to figures such as angels, demons, goblins, dwarves, pixies, nixies, and similar is a slippery subject best left alone. For the purposes of this chapter, because my topic is fairies and power, I exclude discussion of "devil's contract" figures such as Merlin or Sir Gowther whose powers can be argued as demonic through a primarily Christian rather than fairy lens, and limit myself to discussion of fairies specifically as they appear in romance and wonder tales and in relation to their human counterparts in those texts, as it is through those kinds of narratives that their various powers are most often activated and visible in the medieval literary imaginary.

4. See "Sir Orfeo" (Laskaya and Salisbury 1995: 26–41) and *The Mabinogion* (Davies 2008). Morgan le Fay is a recurring character in many Arthurian texts and, arguably, the best-attested of the medieval fairies; her most extensive narrative presence and depictions of her acquisition and use of fairy power are in the medieval romance tradition, being found, for example, in Robert de Boron's twelfth-century *Merlin* and its English translation *Prose Merlin* (Conlee 1998), *Sir Gawain and the Green Knight* (Borroff 2010), and *Le Morte Darthur* (Malory [1485] 2017). Morgan also has a significant presence in the chronicle tradition related to the Arthurian legend, beginning in the twelfth century with Geoffrey of Monmouth's *Vita Merlini* (the source for Boron's poem) and Stephen (Etienne) of Rouen's *Draco Normannicus*; see "The Life of Merlin" (2008) and "Stephen of Rouen, 'Draco Normannicus'" ([c. 1167–9] 1885). Pressine and Melusine appear in all versions of the Melusine legend; see note 9. The Lady of the Lake is killed by Balan in the "Balyn and Balan" episode in Thomas Malory's *Morte Darthur*, but she is conflated with Morgan, or known as Nimue, and characterized as one of the queens of Avalon and thus, immortal, in other iterations.

5. Medieval romances, and particularly Arthurian romances, have attracted the attention of many scholars working on queer theory and queerness in narratives in medieval contexts; see, for example, Dinshaw (1994), Boyd (1998), and Ashton

(2005); see also the scholarship of Karma Lochrie, Geraldine Heng, Louise Fradenburg, Tison Pugh, and Anna Klasowska.
6. See Elmes (2017a: 98) for discussion of this condition.
7. For example, examination of the various Arthurian tales in which it is featured reveal that the Isle of Avalon is tied to the powers both of Morgan le Fay and of the Lady of the Lake, see Wade (2011: ch. 1, esp. 11–13). Corinne Saunders also offers a brief overview of fairy otherworlds in chapter five of *Magic and the Supernatural in Medieval English Romance* (2010). Richard Firth Green discusses humans in fairyland in chapter 5 of *Elf Queens and Holy Friars* (2016); and Aisling Byrne's *Otherworlds: Fantasy and History in Medieval Literature* (2015) offers an engaging study of how authors use fairy worlds to explore and critique social concerns in England, Ireland, and the North Atlantic archipelago.
8. Fortune's Wheel (*Rota Fortunae*) was a philosophical symbol of the capricious nature of Fate that became popular following its inclusion in *The Consolation of Philosophy* (c. 524 CE), an important, highly regarded meditation on freedom and captivity, life and loss penned by the Roman senator and philosopher Boethius and popular throughout the medieval period. The wheel was spun by the goddess of fortune (Fortuna), and each spin altered the position of those humans who were on the wheel, some having their circumstances greatly improved, and some finding themselves experiencing terrible misfortunes. This concept was used to explain vexing problems, such as why mighty noblemen and kings could fall from power, and the overall temporality of earthly things. Perhaps the most famous literary depictions of Fortune's Wheel are two poems, "Fortune, Empress of the World" ("*Fortuna Imperatrix Mundi*") and "I Bemoan the Wounds of Fortune" ("*Fortune Plango Vulnera*") found in the *Carmina Burana*, a group of 254 "little songs" written in Latin and German between the eleventh and thirteenth centuries, collected in what is known as the Burana Codex, and popularized by Carl Orff's 1936 musical rendition, which is often excerpted in movies and other media. Fortune's wheel is regularly employed in medieval romances, especially Arthurian tales, and therefore sometimes even alongside fairy intervention in human affairs; for example, Sir Thomas Malory uses it to foreshadow the fall of Camelot in his *Morte Darthur*. See Patch (1972) and Boethius ([c. 524] 2010).
9. In Thomas Chestre's fifteenth-century "Sir Launfal"—and its earlier versions, the thirteenth-century anonymous "Sir Laundevale" and twelfth-century "Lanval" by Marie de France, in which she is not named but engages in the same narrative way—the fairy Dame Tryamour falls in love with Sir Launfal and grants him her body and riches in exchange for his promise to keep her a secret, promoting his improved position in Arthur's court. See "Sir Launfal" (Shepherd 1995: 190–218), "Sir Laundevale" (Shepherd 1995: 352–64), and Marie de France's "Lanval" (The Lais of Marie de France [n.d.] 2018: 162–95). In all the various versions of the Mélusine legend Mélusine, daughter of the fairy Pressine and a human king, falls in love with Duke Raymond, and agrees to marry him and use her power to found his family dynasty, as long as he agrees not to try to spy on her on Saturdays. See Jean D'Arras's *Mélusine; or, The Noble History of Lusignan* ([c. 1392] 2012), a modern English translation from the French; or *Mélusine compiled by Jean D'Arras, Englisht about 1500* (1895), the Middle English version. In the Old French and Middle English versions of the romance of Partonope of Blois the eponymous character becomes lost while hunting and finds himself wandering to the seashore, where he comes across an empty ship; boarding it, he arrives at Mélior's castle, where

invisible servants wait on him and, ultimately, he engages in a sexual encounter with an invisible woman, Mélior, who agrees to an affair with him during which she will fulfill all of his desires as long as he doesn't try to see her for a period of two-and-a-half years. See *Partonopeu de Blois: A French Romance of the Twelfth Century* ([n.d.] 1967); *The Middle English Versions of "Partonope of Blois"* ([n.d.] 1912).
10. As Helen Cooper notes, "If there is a single defining quality of the fairy monarch of either sex, it is not sexuality but power" (2004: 178).
11. Cooper remarks: "Throughout the first four centuries of romance, until the mid-sixteenth century, romance is inseparable from the ideas of chivalry, and from the primary exponent of chivalry, the knight. If the protagonist is not already a knight when his story opens, it will be concerned with his education in prowess, love, and just action that constitute his winning of his spurs" (2004: 41).
12. The Tuatha Dé Danaan, or "people of the goddess Danu" are variously understood to be deities of pre-Christian Ireland; distant historical individuals with preternatural powers that rendered them godlike; or the original figures that morphed eventually into the *aos si*, or fairy folk, in Gaelic folklore and literary representation. While they are often viewed as a pantheon of gods, they live in the otherworld that serves as the realm for all fairy folk and function in the same way as their elven and fairy counterparts in other folk traditions throughout the medieval British Isles; for example, in the eleventh-century *Adventure of the Sons of Eochaid Mugmedón* (*Echtra mac nEchach Muimedóin*) Niall Noígíallach, son of the High King of Ireland, is the only one among his brothers to properly kiss an old hag they encounter by a well; upon being kissed, she transforms into a beautiful woman and reveals herself to be the sovereignty goddess whose favor bestows the high kingship upon its receiver—a version of the loathly lady trope found in many fairy mistress stories, and also a narrative developed to explain the rise of a dynastic family's prominence through associations with powerful supernatural forces, in much the same way as Melusine does. For translations, see Carey (2003, 2012).
13. As, for example, in the case of Sir Orfeo, who interacts with the fairy king but on behalf of Heurodis.
14. The women in this barge are the nine fairy maidens of Avalon, and their queen is, of course, Morgan le Fay. See Malory ([1485] 2017: 926–7).
15. With the notable exception of *Pucelle aux Blanches Mains* (Maiden with the White Hands), the fairy mistress who aids the protagonist knight Guinglain in his tournament efforts even though he forsakes her love to enter into the tournament, then permits him to marry the human queen of Wales, Esmerée, in the twelfth-century French poem *Le Bel Inconnu* by Renaut de Beaujeu. See Renaud de Beaujeu (2003).
16. "Jeo frai vox comandemenz; / pur vus guerpirai tutes genz. / Jamés ne queor de vus partir: / ceo est la rien que plus desir" (lines 127–30).
17. "'Ami,' fet ele, 'ore vus chasti, / Si vus comant e si vus pri, / Ne vus descoverez a nul humme! / De ceo vus dirai ja la summe: / A tuz jurs m'avriëz perdue, / Se ceste amur esteit seüe; / Jamés ne me purriez veeir / Ne de mun cors seisine aveir'" (lines 143–50).
18. "And seththen she tok a paire glove / That here lemman here sente of fairi londe, / That nolde on no manne honde, / Ne on child ne on womman yhe nolde, / But on hire selve wel yhe wolde" (lines 194–8).
19. Rape occurs in many medieval romances, and its presence and often centrality to a knight's development over the course of romance tales has been the subject of a number of important and probing studies; see Kathryn Gravdal (1991); the essays

by Christine M. Rose, Monica Brzezinski Potkay, Christopher Cannon, and Beth Robertson in Robertson and Rose (2001), Edwards (2016: ch. 3), and Vines (2011: ch. 3, 2014).

20. Explicitly associated with the otherworld and therefore the fay, Rhiannon is one of the many figures in Welsh and Irish wonder tales who is variously understood as reflecting an ancient sovereignty goddess figure, typically Epona, the horse goddess, and a folkloric figure such as the calumniated wife. See Green (1996), Davies and Jones (1997).
21. Or, as Saunders puts it, "The otherworld can harm and heal, bestow or withdraw wealth, and shape love or revenge in extreme ways" (2010: 188).
22. See "Guigemar," in *The Lais of Marie de France* ([n.d.] 2018: 52–99).
23. As Saunders writes, "The King of Faery appears to be motivated by the desire to possess not souls but bodies, although this desire is not, as in *Sir Degarré*, constructed as sexual" (2010: 202).

REFERENCES

Acker, Paul (2013), "Dragons in the Eddas and in Early Nordic Art," in Paul Acker and Carolyne Larrington (eds.), *Revisiting the Poetic Edda: Essays on Old Norse Heroic Legend*, 53–75, New York: Routledge.

Akbari, Suzanne Conklin (2013), "Introduction: The Persistence of Philology: Language and Connectivity in the Mediterranean," in Suzanne Conklin Akbari and Karla Mallette (eds.), *A Sea of Languages: Rethinking the Arabic Role in Medieval Literary History*, 3–22, Toronto: University of Toronto Press.

Akbari, Suzanne Conklin and Karla Mallette, eds. (2013), *A Sea of Languages: Rethinking the Arabic Role in Medieval Literary History*, Toronto: University of Toronto Press.

Altschul, Nadia (2014), "Transfer," in Elizabeth Emery and Richard Utz (eds.), *Medievalism: Key Critical Terms*, 239–46, Cambridge: D. S. Brewer.

Ambrisco, Alan S. (2004), "'It lyth nat in my tonge': Occupatio and Otherness in the Squire's Tale," *Chaucer Review*, 38 (3): 205–28.

Anglo-Norman Dictionary (Online Edition) (2021), s.v. "fin2," Aberystwyth: Aberystwyth University. Available online: https://anglo-norman.net/entry/fin_2 (accessed January 12, 2021).

Apuleius (2017), "De Deo Socratis," in Christopher P. Jones (ed. and trans.), *Apuleius*, 349–61, Cambridge, MA: Harvard University Press.

Archibald, Elizabeth (1996), "The Appalling Dangers of Family Life: Incest in Medieval Literature," in Cathy Jorgensen Itnyre (ed.), *Medieval Family Roles: A Book of Essays*, 157–72, New York: Garland.

Aristotle (1963), *Generation of Animals*, trans. A. L. Peck, Cambridge, MA: Harvard University Press.

Armitage, Simon, trans. (2008), *Sir Gawain and the Green Knight*, London: Faber.

Aronstein, Susan (2012), *An Introduction to British Arthurian Narrative*, Gainesville: University of Florida.

Ashton, Gail (2005), "The Perverse Dynamics of Sir Gawain and the Green Knight," *Arthuriana*, 15 (3): 51–74.

Asma, Stephen T. (2009), *On Monsters: An Unnatural History of Our Worst Fears*, Oxford: Oxford University Press.

Augé, Marc (1995), *Non-Places: Introduction to an Anthropology of Supermodernity*, trans. John Howe, London: Verso.

Augustine ([fifth century] 1954), *The City of God*, bks. 17–22, vol. 8, trans. Gerald G. Walsh and Daniel J. Honan, Washington, DC: Catholic University of America Press.

Augustine of Hippo (2018), *The City of God Against the Pagans*, ed. and trans. Marcus Dodds, Peabody, MA: Hendrickson.

Awntyrs of Arthur (1995), in Thomas Hahn (ed.), *Sir Gawain: Eleven Romances and Tales*, Kalamazoo, MI: Medieval Institute Publications. Available online: https://d.lib.rochester.edu/teams/publication/hahn-sir-gawain (accessed January 14, 2021).

Badke, David, ed. (2011), "Dragon," in *The Medieval Bestiary: Animals in the Middle Ages*. Available online: http://bestiary.ca/beasts/beast262.htm (accessed October 1, 2019).

Bain, Frederika (2018), "The Tail of Melusine: Hybridity, Mutability, and the Accessible Other," in Misty Urban, Deva F. Kemmis, and Melissa Ridley Elmes (eds.), *Melusine's Footprint: Tracing the Legacy of a Medieval Myth*, 17–35, Leiden: Brill.

Barron, W. R. J., ed. and trans. (1998), *Sir Gawain and the Green Knight*, Manchester: Manchester University Press.

Bartlett, Robert (1993), *The Making of Europe: Conquest, Colonization and Cultural Change 950–1350*, Princeton, NJ: Princeton University Press.

Basile, Giambattista ([1634–6] 2007), *The Tale of Tales*, trans. Nancy Canepa, Detroit, MI: Wayne State University Press.

Benko, Georges (1997), "Introduction: Modernity, Postmodernity and the Social Sciences," in Georges Benko and Ulf Strohmayer (eds.), *Space and Social Theory: Interpreting Modernity and Postmodernity*, 1–44, Oxford: Blackwell.

Benson, Larry D., trans., and Daniel Donoghue, ed. (2012), *Sir Gawain and the Green Knight: A Close Verse Translation*, Morgantown: West Virginia University Press.

Bildhauer, Bettina and Robert Mills, eds. (2003), *The Monstrous Middle Ages*, Cardiff: University of Wales Press.

Bliss, A. J., ed. (1960), *Thomas Chestre, Sir Launfal*, London: Nelson and Sons.

Bliss, A. J., ed. (1966), *Sir Orfeo*, 2nd edn., Oxford: Clarendon Press.

Bloch, Howard (1991), *Medieval Misogyny and the Invention of Romantic Love*, Chicago: University of Chicago Press.

Boccaccio, Giovanni (1951), *Genealogie deorum gentilium*, vol. 1, ed. Vincenzo Romano, Bari: Laterza.

Boccaccio, Giovanni (1960), *The Nymph of Fiesole*, trans. Daniel J. Donno, New York: Columbia University Press.

Boethius ([c. 524] 2010), *Consolation of Philosophy*, trans. David R. Slavitt, Cambridge, MA: Harvard University Press.

Borroff, Marie, ed. and trans. (2007, 2010), *Sir Gawain and the Green Knight*, New York: Norton Critical Editions.

Bottigheimer, Ruth B. (2009), *Fairy Tales: A New History*, Albany: State University of New York Press.

Bottigheimer, Ruth B. (2012), *Fairy Tales Framed: Early Forwards, Afterwards, and Critical Works*, Albany: State University of New York Press.

Bottigheimer, Ruth B. (2014), *Magic Tales and Fairy Tale Magic: From Ancient Egypt to the Italian Renaissance*, London: Palgrave.

Boyd, David Lorenzo (1998), "Sodomy, Misogyny, and Displacements: Occluding Queer Desire in *Sir Gawain and the Green Knight*," *Arthuriana*, 8 (2): 77–113.

Braswell, Mary Flowers, ed. (1995), *Sir Perceval of Galles*, Kalamazoo, MI: Medieval Institute Publications.

Brewer, Derek S. (2003), "The Interpretation of Fairy Tales," in Hilda Ellis Davidson and Anna Chaudhri (eds.), *A Companion to the Fairy Tale*, 15–37, Woodbridge: D. S. Brewer.

Briggs, Katherine M. (1959), *The Anatomy of Puck: An Examination of Fairy Beliefs among Shakespeare's Contemporaries and Successors*, London: Routledge and Kegan Paul.

Bromwich, Rachel and D. Simon Evans, eds. (1992), *Culhwch and Olwen: An Edition and Study of the Oldest Arthurian Tale*, Cardiff: University of Wales Press.

Bromyard, John (1614), *Summa Praedicantium*, Antwerp: Nutius & Meursius.

Bronson, Bertrand H. (1945), "Mrs. Brown and the Ballad," *California Folklore Quarterly*, 4: 129–40.

Brownlee, Kevin (1994), "Mélusine's Hybrid Body and the Poetics of Metamorphosis," *Yale French Studies*, 86: 18–38.

Brownlee, Marina S. (1996), "Interference in Mélusine," in Donald Maddox and Sara Sturm-Maddox (eds.), *Melusine of Lusignan: Founding Fiction in Late Medieval France*, 226–40, Athens: University of Georgia Press.

Bruckner, Matilda Tomaryn (2016), "Natural and Unnatural Woman: Melusine Inside Out," in Laine E. Doggett and Daniel E. O'Sullivan (eds.), *Founding Feminisms in Medieval Studies: Essays in Honor of E. J. Burns*, 21–31, Cambridge: Boydell and Brewer.

Burger, Glenn D. (2018), *Conduct Becoming: Good Wives and Husbands in the Later Middle Ages*, Philadelphia: University of Pennsylvania Press.

Burgess, Glyn and Keith Busby, trans. (1986), *The Lais of Marie de France*, London: Penguin.

Burns, E. Jane (1993), *Bodytalk: When Women Speak in Old French Literature*, Philadelphia: University of Pennsylvania Press.

Burns, E. Jane (2008), "A Snake-Tailed Woman: Hybridity and Dynasty in the *Roman de Mélusine*," in E. Jane Burns and Peggy McCracken (eds.), *From Beasts to Souls: Gender and Embodiment in Medieval Europe*, 185–220, Notre Dame, IN: University of Notre Dame Press.

Butler, Judith (1990), *Gender Trouble: Feminism and the Subversion of Identity*, London: Routledge.

Butler, Judith (1993), *Bodies that Matter*, New York: Routledge.

Bynum, Caroline Walker (1997), "Wonder," *American Historical Review*, 102 (1) (February): 1–26.

Bynum, Caroline Walker (2001), *Metamorphosis and Identity*, New York: Zone Books.

Byrne, Aisling (2015), *Otherworlds: Fantasy and History in Medieval Literature*, Oxford: Oxford University Press.

Byrne, Aisling (2016), *Otherworlds: Fantasy and History in Medieval Literature*, Oxford: Oxford University Press.

Byrne, Francis John (1973), *Irish Kings and High-Kings*, London: Batsford.

Cannon, Christopher (2004), *The Grounds of English Literature*, Oxford: Oxford University Press.

Canton, Norman F. (1991), *Inventing the Middle Ages: The Lives, Works and Ideas of the Great Medievalists of the Twentieth Century*, New York: William Morrow.

Carasso-Bulow, Lucienne (1976), *The Merveilleux in Chrétien de Troyes' Romances*, Geneva: Droz.

Carbado, Devon W. (2013), "Colorblind Intersectionality," *Signs*, 38 (4): 811–45.
Carey, John (1987), "Time, Space, and the Otherworld," *Proceedings of the Harvard Celtic Colloquium*, 7: 1–27.
Carey, John (1991), "The Irish 'Otherworld': Hiberno-Latin Perspectives," *Éigse*, 25: 154–9.
Carey, John (1994), *The Irish National Origin-Legend: Synthetic Pseudohistory*, Cambridge: Department of Anglo-Saxon, Norse, and Celtic, University of Cambridge.
Carey, John, trans. (1997), "The Adventure of the Sons of Eochaid Mugmedón," in John T. Koch and John Carey (eds.), *The Celtic Heroic Age: Literary Sources for Ancient Celtic Europe and Early Ireland and Wales*, 192–7, Andover, MA: Celtic Studies Publications.
Carey, John (2001), "Did the Irish Come From Spain? The Legend of the Milesians," *History Ireland*, 9 (3): 8–11.
Carey, John (2003), "Echtra Mac nEchach," in John T. Koch and John Carey (eds.), *The Celtic Heroic Age: Literary Sources for Ancient Celtic Europe and Early Ireland and Wales*, 4th edn., 203–8, Celtic Studies Publications, 1, Aberystwyth: Celtic Studies Publications.
Carey, John, ed. (2009), *Lebor Gabála Érenn: Textual History and Pseudo-History*, Irish Texts Society, Subsidiary Series 20, Dublin: Irish Texts Society.
Carey, John (2012), "Tuath Dé," in John T. Koch (ed.), *The Celts: History, Life, and Culture*, 751–3, Santa Barbara, CA: ABC-CLIO.
Carney, James (1955), *Studies in Irish Literature and Language*, Dublin: Dublin Institute for Advanced Studies.
Carroll, Noel (1990), *The Philosophy of Horror: Or, Paradoxes of the Heart*, London: Routledge.
Cecire, Maria Sachiko (2019), *Re-Enchanted: The Rise of Children's Fantasy Literature in the Twentieth Century*, Minneapolis: University of Minnesota Press.
Chakraborty, S. A. (2017–20), *Daevabad Trilogy*, New York: Harper Voyager.
Chapman, Robert L. (1955), "A Note on the Demon Queen Eleanor," *Modern Language Notes*, 70 (6): 393–6.
Chaucer, Geoffrey (1987), *The Riverside Chaucer*, ed. Larry D. Benson, 3rd edn., Boston: Houghton Mifflin.
Chaucer, Geoffrey (2019), *The Norton Chaucer*, ed. David Lawton, New York: W. W. Norton and Company.
Chesterton, G. K. (1930), "Magic and Fantasy in Fiction," *The Bookman* (March): 27–30.
Child, Francis James, ed. (2001), *The English and Scottish Popular Ballads*, 1, 2nd corr. edn., Northfield, MN: Loomis.
Chrétien de Troyes ([c. 1180] 1990), "The Knight with the Lion," in David Staines (ed.), *The Complete Romances of Chrétien de Troyes*, 257–338, Bloomington: Indiana University Press.
Chrétien de Troyes ([c. 1180] 1991), *Arthurian Romances*, trans. William W. Kibler and Carleton W. Carroll, London: Penguin.
Chrétien de Troyes ([c. 1180] 2010), *Le chevalier de la charrette*, ed. Karl D. Uitti, Paris: Garnier.
Clausen-Stolzenburg, Maren (1995), *Märchen und mittelalterliche Literaturtradition*, Heidelberg: Universitätsverlag C. Winter.

Cohen, Jeffrey Jerome (1996), "Monster Culture (Seven Theses)," in Jeffrey J. Cohen (ed.), *Monster Theory: Reading Culture*, 3–25, Minneapolis: University of Minnesota Press.

Cohen, Jeffrey Jerome (1998), "The Order of Monsters: Monster Lore and Medieval Narrative Traditions," in Francesca Sautman, Diana Conchado Canadé, and Giuseppe Carlo Di Scipio (eds.), *Telling Tales: Medieval Narratives and the Folk Tradition*, 37–58, New York: St. Martin's Press.

Cohen, Jeffrey Jerome (1999), *Of Giants: Sex, Monsters, and the Middle Ages*, Minnesota: University of Minnesota Press.

Cohen, Jeffrey Jerome (2006), *Hybridity, Identity, and Monstrosity in Medieval Britain*, New York: Palgrave Macmillan.

Cole, Chera A. (2018), "Passing as a 'Humayne Woman': Hybridity and Salvation in the Middle English Melusine," in Misty Urban, Deva F. Kemmis, and Melissa Ridley Elmes (eds.), *Melusine's Footprint: Tracing the Legacy of a Medieval Myth*, 240–58, Leiden: Brill.

Colwell, Tania (2011), "Patronage of the Poetic Mélusine Romance: Guillaume L'Archevêque's Confrontation with Dynastic Crisis," *Journal of Medieval History*, 37 (2): 215–29.

Comfort, W. W., trans. (1975), *Chrétien de Troyes, Arthurian Romances*, London: Dent.

Conlee, John, ed. (1998), *Prose Merlin*, Kalamazoo, MI: Medieval Institute Publications.

Cooper, Helen (2004), *The English Romance in Time: Transforming Motifs from Geoffrey of Monmouth to the Death of Shakespeare*, Oxford: Oxford University Press.

Copeland, Rita (1991), *Rhetoric, Hermeneutics and Translation in the Middle Ages: Academic Tradition and Vernacular Culture*, Cambridge: Cambridge University Press.

Corbett, Richard (1955), *Poems*, ed. J. A. W. Bennett and H. R. Trevor-Roper, Oxford: Clarendon Press.

Coudrette (1982), *Le Roman de Mélusine, ou Histoire de Lusignan*, ed. Eleanor Roach, Paris: Klincksieck.

Crenshaw, Kimberlé (1989), "Demarginalizing the Intersection of Race and Sex: A Black Feminist Critique of Antidiscrimination Doctrine, Feminist Theory and Antiracist Politics," *University of Chicago Legal Forum*, article 8: 139–68.

Crenshaw, Kimberlé (1991), "Mapping the Margins: Intersectionality, Identity Politics, and Violence Against Women of Color," *Stanford Law Review*, 43 (6): 1241–99.

D'Arras, Jean ([c. 1392] 2012), *Melusine; Or, The Noble History of Lusignan*, trans. Sara Sturm-Maddox and Donald Maddox, University Park: Pennsylvania State University Press.

D'Arras, Jean (2003), *Mélusine ou la noble histoire de Lusignan*, ed. and trans. Jean-Jacques Vincensini, Paris: Livre de Poche.

Davies, Sioned, trans. (2008), *The Mabinogion*, Oxford: Oxford World Classics.

Davies, Sioned and Nerys Ann Jones (1997), *The Horse in Celtic Culture: Medieval Welsh Perspectives*, Cardiff: Wales University Press.

de Pizan, Christine (1999), *Epistre Othea*, ed. Gabriella Parussa, Paris: Droz.

Dinshaw, Carolyn (1994), "A Kiss is Just a Kiss: Heterosexuality and its Consolations in *Sir Gawain and the Green Knight*," *Diacritics*, 24 (2/3): 205–26.

Donaghue, Emma (1997), *Kissing the Witch: Old Tales in New Skins*, New York: HarperCollins.

Douay-Rheims Bible (n.d.), "The Apocalypse of St John (Revelation)." Available online: http://www.drbo.org/chapter/73012.htm (accessed January 2, 2021).

Dubost, Francis (1991), *Aspects fantastiques de la littérature narrative médiévale (XIIe–XIIIe siècles)*, 2 vols, Paris: Champion.
Duggan, Anne (2005), *Salonnières, Furies and Fairies: The Politics of Gender and Cultural Change in Absolutist France*, Newark: University of Delaware.
Duggan, Joseph J. (2001), *The Romances of Chrétien de Troyes*, New Haven, CT: Yale University Press.
Dumézil, Georges (1970), *The Destiny of the Warrior*, trans. Alf Hiltebeitel, Chicago: University of Chicago Press.
Dumézil, Georges (1983), *The Stakes of the Warrior*, trans. David Weeks, ed. Jaan Puhvel, Berkeley: University of California Press.
During, Simon, ed. (1993), *The Cultural Studies Reader*, London: Routledge.
Eco, Umberto ([1976] 1986), "The Return of the Middle Ages," in *Travels in Hyperreality*, trans. William Weaver, 59–85, New York: Harcourt Brace.
Edwards, Robert R. (2010), "Italy," in Suzanna Fein and David Raybin (eds.), *Chaucer: Contemporary Approaches*, 3–24, University Park: Pennsylvania State Press.
Edwards, Suzanne M. (2016), *The Afterlives of Rape in Medieval English Literature*, New York: Palgrave.
Eliade, Mircea (1971), *The Myth of the Eternal Return: Or, Cosmos and History*, vol. 46, Princeton, NJ: Princeton University Press.
Elmes, Melissa Ridley (2017a), "The Alchemical Transformation of Melusine," in Misty Urban, Deva F. Kemmis, and Melissa Ridley Elmes (eds.), *Melusine's Footprint: Tracing the Legacy of a Medieval Myth*, 94–105, Leiden: Brill.
Elmes, Melissa Ridley (2017b), "He Dreams of Dragons: Alchemical Imagery in the Medieval Dream Visions of King Arthur," *Arthuriana*, 27 (1): 73–94.
Emery Elizabeth and Richard Utz, eds. (2014), *Medievalism: Key Critical Terms*, Cambridge: D. S. Brewer.
Epstein, Marc Michael (1996), "Harnessing the Dragon: A Mythos Transformed in Medieval Jewish Literature and Art," in Laurie L. Patton and Wendy Doniger (eds.), *Myth and Method*, 353–89, Charlottesville: University of Virginia Press.
Evans, Jonathan (1985), "Semiotics and Traditional Lore: The Medieval Dragon Tradition," *Journal of Folklore Research*, 22 (2/3): 85–112.
Evans, Jonathan (2005), "'As Rare as They are Dire': Old Norse Dragons, Beowulf and the Deutsche Mythologie," in Tom Shippey (ed.), *The Shadow-Walkers: Jacob Grimm's Mythology of the Monstrous*, 207–69, Turnhout: ACMRS and Brepols.
Evans, Ruth, Andrew Taylor, Nicholas Watson, and Jocelyn Wogan-Browne (1999), "The Notion of Vernacular Theory," in Jocelyn Wogan Browne, Nicholas Watson, Andrew Taylor, and Ruth Evans (eds.), *The Idea of the Vernacular*, 314–30, University Park: Pennsylvania State University Press.
Faletra, Michael A., ed. and trans. (2008), *History of the Kings of Britain by Geoffrey of Monmouth*, Peterborough, ON: Broadview Press.
Flieger, Verlyn and Douglas A. Anderson, eds. (2014), *Tolkien on Fairy-Stories*, New York: HarperCollins.
Floriant et Florete ([n.d.] 2003), ed. and trans. Annie Combes and Richard Trachsler, Paris: Champion.
Fredrick, Sharonah (2016), "Disarticulating Lilith: Notions of God's Evil in Jewish Folklore," in Ian Frederick Moulton (ed.), *Eroticism in the Middle Ages and the Renaissance: Magic, Marriage and Midwifery*, 59–82, Turnhout: ACMRS and Brepols.

Friedman, John B. ([1981] 2000), *The Monstrous Races in Medieval Art and Literature*, Cambridge, MA: Harvard University Press.
Fuchs, Barbara (2004), *Romance*, London: Routledge.
Fulton, Helen, ed. (2012), *Urban Culture in Medieval Wales*, Cardiff: University of Wales Press.
Fulton, Helen (2013), "Magic and the Supernatural in Early Welsh Arthurian Narrative: *Culhwch Ac Olwen* and *Breuddwyd Rhonabwy*," *Arthurian Literature*, (30): 1–26.
Gantz, Jeffrey, trans. (1981), *Early Irish Myths and Sagas*, Harmondsworth: Penguin.
Gaunt, Simon (1995), *Gender and Genre in Medieval French Literature*, Cambridge: Cambridge University Press.
Gaunt, Simon (2000), "Romance and Other Genres," in Roberta L. Kreuger (ed.), *The Cambridge Companion to Medieval Romance*, 45–59, Cambridge: Cambridge University Press.
Gaunt, Simon (2013), "Linguistic Difference, the Philology of Romance and the Romance of Philology," in Suzanne Conklin Akbari and Karla Mallette (eds.), *A Sea of Languages: Rethinking the Arabic Role in Medieval Literary History*, 43–61, Toronto: University of Toronto Press.
Gerald of Wales (1891), *Liber de Principis instructione*, III.27, in George F. Warner (ed.), *Geraldi Cambrensis Opera*, vol. 8, London: Printed for her Majesty's Stationery Office, Eyre and Spottiswood.
Gerson, John (1706), *Joannis Gersonii Opera omnia nova ordine digesta, & in V. tomos distributa*, Antwerp: Sumptibus societatis.
Gervase of Tilbury (2002), *Otia Imperialia: Recreation for an Emperor*, ed. and trans. S. E. Banks and J. W. Binns, Oxford: Clarendon Press.
Gilmore, David (2003), *Monsters: Evil Beings, Mythical Beasts, and All Manner of Imaginary Terrors*, Philadelphia: University of Pennsylvania Press.
Gittes, Katherine (1983), "*The Canterbury Tales* and the Arabic Frame Tradition," *PMLA*, 98 (2) (March): 237–51.
Gower, John (1899), *French Works*, ed. G. C. Macaulay, Oxford: Clarendon Press.
Gower, John (1900–1), *The English Works of John Gower*, ed. G. C. Macaulay, 2 vols, London: Early English Text Society.
Grange, Huw (2017), *Saints and Monsters in Medieval Occitan Literature: Sublime and Abject Bodies*, Cambridge: Legenda.
Gravdal, Kathryn (1991), *Ravishing Maidens: Writing Rape in Medieval French Literature and Law*, Philadelphia: University of Pennsylvania Press.
Green, Miranda (1996), *Celtic Goddesses: Warriors, Virgins, and Mothers*, New York: George Braziller.
Green, Richard Firth (2016), *Elf Queens and Holy Friars: Fairy Beliefs and the Medieval Church*, Philadelphia: University of Pennsylvania Press.
Greenblatt, Stephen (1980), *Renaissance Self-Fashioning: From More to Shakespeare*, Chicago: Chicago University Press.
Haase, Donald (2016), "Wonder Tale," in Anne E. Duggan, Donald Haase, and Helen J. Callow (eds.), *Folktales and Fairy Tales: Traditions and Texts from Around the World*, 2nd edn., 1113, Santa Barbara, CA: ABC-CLIO.
Hahn, Thomas (2000), "Gawain and Popular Chivalric Romance in Britain," in Roberta L. Krueger (ed.), *Cambridge Companion to Medieval Romance*, 218–34, Cambridge: Cambridge University Press.

Hall, Alaric (2007), *Elves in Anglo-Saxon England: Matters of Belief, Health, Gender and Identity*, Woodbridge: Boydell Press.
Hanawalt, Barbara (1986), *The Ties that Bound: Peasant Families in Medieval England*, Oxford: Oxford University Press.
Harf-Lancner, Laurence (1984), *Les fées au moyen âge*, Paris: Champion.
Harris, Carissa (2018), *Obscene Pedagogies: Transgressive Talk and Sexual Education in Late Medieval Britain*, Ithaca, NY: Cornell University Press.
Haycock, Marged, ed. and trans. (2007), *Legendary Poems from the Book of Taliesin*, Aberystwyth: CMCS Publications.
Headley, Maria Dahvana, trans. (2020), *Beowulf: A New Translation*, New York: Farrar, Strauss and Giroux.
Heaney, Seamus, trans. (2001), *Beowulf: A New Verse Translation*, New York: Norton.
Hefferman, Carol F. (2003), *The Orient in Chaucer and Medieval Romance*, Cambridge: D. S. Brewer.
Heng, Geraldine (2003), *Empire of Magic: Medieval Romance and the Politics of Cultural Fantasy*, New York: Columbia University Press.
Higden, Ranulph, (2012), *Speculum Curatorum, A Mirror for Curates*, bk. 1, ed. and trans. Eugene Crook and Margaret Jennings, Paris: Peeters.
Honegger, Thomas (2017), "The Sea-Dragon—in Search of an Elusive Creature," in Gerlinde Huber-Rebenich, Christian Rohr, and Michael Stolz (eds.), *Wasser in Der Mittelalterlichen Kultur: Gebrauch-Wahrnehmung-Symbolik/Water in Medieval Culture: Uses, Perceptions, and Symbolism*, 521–31, Berlin: de Gruyter.
Hopkins, Andrea (1990), *The Sinful Knights: A Study of Middle English Penitential Romance*, Oxford: Clarendon Press.
Howard, Donald (1980), "The Four Medievalisms," *Stanford University Publishing*, (Summer): 4–5.
Hull, Vernam (1949), "Echtra Cormaic Maic Airt, The Adventure of Cormac Mac Airt," *Proceedings of the Modern Language Association*, 64 (4): 871–83.
Huot, Sylvia (2008), "Others and Alterity," in Simon Gaunt and Sarah Kay (eds.), *The Cambridge Companion to Medieval French Literature*, 238–50, Cambridge: Cambridge University Press.
Hutcheon, Linda (2006), *A Theory of Adaptation*, New York: Routledge.
Hutton, Ronald (2014), "The Wild Hunt and the Witches' Sabbath," *Folklore*, 125: 161–78.
Ingham, Patricia Clare (2001), *Sovereign Fantasies: Arthurian Romance and the Making of Britain*, Philadelphia: University of Pennsylvania Press.
Isidore of Seville ([c. 560–636] 2006), *The Etymologies of Isidore of Seville*, trans. Stephen A. Barney, Cambridge: Cambridge University Press.
Jaeger, Stephen C (1999), *Ennobling Love: In Search of a Lost Sensibility*, Chicago: University of Chicago Press.
[James VI of Scotland] (1597), *Daemonologie*, Edinburgh: Robert Waldegrave.
James, M. R., ed. and trans. (1983), *Walter Map, De Nugis Curialium*, rev. C. N. L. Brooke and R. A. B. Mynors, Oxford: Clarendon Press.
Jewiss, Virginia (2001), "Monstrous Movements and Metaphors in Dante's Divine Comedy," in Keala Jewell (ed.), *Monsters in the Italian Literary Imagination*, 179–90, Detroit, MI: Wayne State University Press.
Jones, Leslie Ellen (2002), "Fairies," in Carl Lindahl, John McNamara, and John Lindow (eds.), *Medieval Folklore: A Guide to Myths, Legends, Tales, Beliefs, and Customs*, 128–30, Oxford: Oxford University Press.
Kahn, Ausma Zehanat (2017), *The Bloodprint*, New York: Harper Voyager.

Kiessling, Nicholas (1970), "Antecedents of the Medieval Dragon in Sacred History," *Journal of Biblical Literature*, 89 (2): 167–77.

Kinoshita, Sharon (2013), "Beyond Philology: Cross-Cultural Engagement in Literary History and Beyond," in Suzanne Conklin Akbari and Karla Mallette (eds.), *A Sea of Languages: Rethinking the Arabic Role in Medieval Literary History*, 25–42, Toronto: University of Toronto Press.

Kinsella, Thomas (2002), *The Tain: Translated from the Irish Epic Tain Bo Cuailnge*, Oxford: Oxford University Press.

Kirk, Robert ([1692], 2008), *The Secret Commonwealth of Elves, Fauns, and Fairies*, ed. Andrew Lang, Mineola, NY: Dover Publications.

Koch, John T. (2005), *Celtic Culture: A Historical Encyclopedia*, Santa Barbara, CA: ABC-CLIO.

Koch, John T., and John Carey, eds. and trans. (1995), *The Celtic Heroic Age: Literary Sources for Ancient Celtic Europe and Early Ireland and Wales*, Malden, MA: Celtic Studies Publications.

Kooper, Erik, ed. (2005), *Sentimental and Humorous Romances*, Kalamazoo, MI: Medieval Institute Publications.

Kordecki, Lesley (1984), "Prophecy, Dragons and Meaning in Malory," *Proceedings of the Illinois Medieval Association*, 1: 62–75.

Krueger, Roberta L. (1993), *Women Readers and the Ideology of Gender in Old French Verse Romance*, Cambridge: Cambridge University Press.

Kreuger, Roberta L. (2000), "Introduction," in Roberta L. Kreuger (ed.), *The Cambridge Companion to Medieval Romance*, 1–12, Cambridge: Cambridge University Press.

Lady Sarashina (1971), *As I Crossed a Bridge of Dreams: Recollections of a Woman in Eleventh-Century Japan*, trans. Ivan Morris, London: Penguin.

Langland, William (1975), *Piers Plowman: The B-Version*, ed. George Kane and E. T. Donaldson, London: Athlone Press.

Langland, William (1997), *Piers Plowman: The C-Version*, ed. George Kane and George Russell, London: Athlone Press.

Larkin, Peter, ed. (2015), *Richard Coer de Lyon*, Kalamazoo, MI: Medieval Institute Publications. Robbins Library Digital Projects. Available online: https://d.lib.rochester.edu/teams/publication/larkin-richard-coer-de-lyon (accessed July 17, 2020).

Laskaya, Anne and Eve Salisbury, eds. (1995), *The Middle English Breton Lays*, Kalamazoo, MI: Medieval Institute Publications.

Latham, M. W. (1930), *The Elizabethan Fairies*, New York: Columbia University Press.

Layamon's Arthur, The Arthurian Section of Layamon's Brut (2001), ed. and trans. W. R. J. Barron and S. C. Weinberg, Exeter: University of Exeter Press.

Le Goff, Jacques (1980), "Ecclesiastical Culture and Folklore in the Middle Ages: Saint Marcellus of Paris and the Dragon," in *Time, Work & Culture in the Middle Ages*, trans. Arthur Goldhammer, 159–88, Chicago: University of Chicago Press.

Le Goff, Jacques (1985), *L'imaginaire médiéval*, Paris: Gallimard.

Le Goff, Jacques (1988), "The Marvelous in the Medieval West," in *The Medieval Imagination*, trans. Arthur Goldhammer, 27–44, Chicago: University of Chicago Press.

Lemay, Helen Rodnite, ed. and trans. (1992), *Women's Secrets: A Translation of Pseudo-Albertus Magnus' De Secretis Mulierum with Commentaries*, Albany: State University of New York Press.

Lerner, Alan Jay and Frederick Loewe (1962), [Musical] *Camelot*, New York: Chappell & Co. with Alfred Productions.

Lewis, C. S. ([1936] 1958), *The Allegory of Love*, New York: Oxford University Press.

Lewis, C. S. ([1936] 2013), *The Allegory of Love*, repr., Cambridge: Cambridge University Press.

Lewis, C. S. ([1964] 2012), "The Longaevi," in *The Discarded Image: An Introduction to Medieval and Renaissance Literature*, 112–38, Cambridge: Cambridge University Press.

Lewis, C. S. (1966), "*On Three Ways of Writing for Children*," in Walter Hooper (ed.), *Of Other Worlds*, 27–32, New York: Harcourt Brace Jovanovich.

Lippincott, Louise W. (1981), "The Unnatural History of Dragons," *Philadelphia Museum of Art Bulletin*, 77 (334): 2–24.

Littleton, C. Scott (1982), *The New Comparative Mythology: An Anthropological Assessment of the Theories of Georges Dumézil*, Berkeley: University of California Press.

Liuzza, Roy, trans. (2000), *Beowulf: A New Verse Translation*, Peterborough, ON: Broadview Press.

Lochrie, Karma (2003), "Between Women," in Carolyn Dinshaw and David Wallace (eds.), *The Cambridge Companion to Medieval Women's Writing*, 70–90, Cambridge: Cambridge University Press.

Lombard-Jourdan, Anne (2005), *Aux Origine de Carnaval: un dieu Gaulois ancêtre des Rois de France*, Paris: Odile Jacob.

Luft, Diana (2019), "Commemorating the Past after 1066: Tales from The Mabinogion," in Geraint Evans and Helen Fulton (eds.), *Cambridge History of Welsh Literature*, 73–92, Cambridge: Cambridge University Press.

Lynch, Kathryn (1995), "East Meets West in Chaucer's Squire's and Franklin's Tales," *Speculum*, 20: 530–51.

Macalister, R. A. Stewart, ed. and trans. (1938–56), *Lebor Gabála Érenn: The Book of the Taking of Ireland*, 5 vols, Irish Texts Society 34, 35, 39, 41, 44, London: Irish Texts Society.

Mac Cana, Proinsias (1970), *Celtic Mythology*, London: Hamlyn.

Mac Cana, Proinsias (1976), "The Sinless Otherworld of Immram Brain," *Ériu*, 27: 95–115.

Machaut, Gullaume de (1921), *Oeuvres de Guillaume de Machaut*, 3rd edn., ed. Ernest Hoepffner, Paris: Didot.

MacLeod, Sharon Paice (2012), *Celtic Myth and Religion: A Study of Traditional Belief, with Newly Translated Prayers, Poems and Songs*, Jefferson, NC: Macfarland and Co.

Mac Mathúna, Séamus, ed. and trans. (1985), *Immram Brain: Bran's Journey to the Land of the Women*, Tübingen: Niemeyer.

Mallette, Karla (2010), *European Modernity and the Arab Mediterranean: Toward a New Philology and a Counter-Orientalism*, Philadelphia: University of Pennsylvania Press.

Mallette, Karla (2013), "Reading Backward: The *1001 Nights* and Philological Practice," in Suzanne Conklin Akbari and Karla Mallette (eds.), *A Sea of Languages: Rethinking the Arabic Role in Medieval Literary History*, 100–16, Toronto: University of Toronto Press.

Malory, Sir Thomas ([1485] 2017), *Le Morte Darthur*, ed. P. J. C. Field, Woodbridge: D. S. Brewer.

Map, Walter (1983), *De Nugis Curialium: Courtiers' Trifles*, ed. M. R. James, rev. edn., Oxford: Clarendon Press.
McCone, Kim, ed. (2000), *Echtrae Chonnlai and the Beginnings of Vernacular Narrative Writing in Ireland: A Critical Edition with Introduction, Notes, Bibliography and Vocabulary*, Maynooth: Department of Old and Middle Irish.
McDonald, Nicola (2004), *Pulp Fictions of Medieval England: Essays in Popular Romance*, Manchester: Manchester University Press.
McKee, Helen (2000a), "Scribes and Glosses from Dark Age Wales: The Cambridge Juvencus Manuscript," *Cambrian Medieval Celtic Studies*, 39: 1–22.
McKee, Helen, ed. (2000b), *The Cambridge Juvencus Manuscript, Glossed in Latin, Old Welsh, and Old Irish: Text and Commentary*, Aberystwyth: CMCS Publications.
McKillip, Patricia (1982), *Stepping from the Shadows*, New York: Atheneum.
McKillip, Patricia (1999), "Introduction," in *Riddle-Master*, New York: Berkley Publishing.
Meid, Wolfgang, ed. ([1967] 1994), *Taín Bó Fraích*, Dublin: Dublin Institute for Advanced Studies.
Mélusine, compiled by Jean D'Arras, Englisht about 1500 (1895), ed. A. K. Donald, Early English Text Society ES 68, London: Kegan Paul, Trench, Trübner & Co.
Menocal, Maria Rosa (1987): *The Arabic Role in Medieval Literary History: A Forgotten Heritage*, Philadelphia: University of Pennsylvania Press.
Meyer, Kuno, ed. and trans. (1895), *The Voyage of Bran, Son of Febal, to the Land of the Living*, London: David Nutt.
Micha, Alexandre, ed. (1992), *Lais féeriques des XIIe et XIIIe siècles*, Paris: Flammarion.
Middle English Versions of "Partonope of Blois" ([n.d.] 1912), ed. A. Trampe Bödtker, Early English Text Society ES 109, London: Kegan Paul, Trench, Trübner & co.
Miller, Sarah A. (2010), *Medieval Monstrosity and the Female Body*, New York: Routledge.
Mills, Maldwyn, ed. (1973), *Six Middle English Romances*, London: Dent.
Mills, Robert (2003), "Jesus as Monster," in Bettina Bildhauer and Robert Mills (eds.), *The Monstrous Middle Ages*, 28–54, Cardiff: University of Wales Press.
Mirk, John (1974), *Instructions for Parish Priests*, ed. Gillis Kristensson, Lund: Gleerup.
Mittman, Asa Simon (2013), "Introduction: The Impact of Monsters and Monster Studies," in Asa S. Mittman and Peter Dendle (eds.), *The Ashgate Research Companion to Monsters and the Monstrous*, 1–15, Farnham: Ashgate.
Montoya, Alicia C. (2013), *Medievalist Enlightenment from Charles Perrault to Jean-Jacques Rousseau*, Cambridge: D. S. Brewer.
Morrison, Stephen, ed. (2013), *The Late Middle English Lucydarye*, Turnhout: Brepols.
Mouskès, Philippe (1838), *Chronique rimée*, ed. Baron de Reiffenberg, Brussels: Imprimeur de la commission royale d'histoire.
Murray, James A. H., ed. (1875), *The Romance and Prophecies of Thomas of Erceldoune*, London: Trübner.
Newman, Coree (2018), "The Good, the Bad, and the Unholy: Ambivalent Angels in the Middle Ages," in Michael Ostling (ed.), *Fairies, Demons, and Nature Spirits: "Small Gods" at the Margins of Christendom*, 103–22, Palgrave Historical Studies in Witchcraft and Magic, London: Palgrave MacMillan.
Ní Bhrolcháin, Muireann (2009), *An Introduction to Early Irish Literature*, Dublin: Four Courts Press.

Nichols, Stephen G. (1996), "Melusine Between Myth and History: Profile of a Female Demon," in Donald Maddox and Sara Sturm-Maddox (eds.), *Melusine of Lusignan: Founding Fiction in Late Medieval France*, 137–64, Athens: University of Georgia Press.

Nixon, Ingeborg, ed. (1980), *Thomas of Erceldoune*, Copenhagen: Akademisk Forlag.

Nolan, Robert J. (1974), "Origin of the Romance of Melusine: A New Interpretation," *Fabula*, 15 (3): 192–201.

O'Donoghue, Bernard, trans. (2006), *Sir Gawain and the Green Knight*, London: Penguin.

OED Online (2019), s.v. "monster, n., adv., and adj." Oxford: Oxford University Press. Available online: https://www-oed-com.ezproxy.emich.edu/view/Entry/121738?rskey=J09yUS&result=1 (accessed September 29, 2019).

OED Online (2020), s.v. "fairy tale, n. and adj." Oxford: Oxford University Press. Available online: https://www-oed-com.proxy.lib.ohio-state.edu/view/Entry/67750?redirectedFrom=fairy+tale (accessed January 12, 2021).

Ogden, Daniel (2013), "10. Lamia, Slain by Eurybatus and Others," in *Dragons, Serpents, and Slayers in the Classical and Early Christian Worlds: A Sourcebook*, 97–108, Oxford: Oxford University Press.

Orchard, Andy, ed. ([1985] 1995), *Pride and Prodigies: Studies in the Monsters of the Beowulf-Manuscript*, Toronto: University of Toronto Press.

Orchard, Andy (1995), "Liber Monstrorum," in Andy Orchard (ed. and trans.), *Pride and Prodigies: Studies in the Monsters of the Beowulf-Manuscript*, 255–317, Cambridge: D. S. Brewer.

Ostling, Michael (2018), "Introduction: Where've All the Good People Gone?," in Michael Ostling (ed.), *Fairies, Demons, and Nature Spirits: 'Small Gods' at the Margins of Christendom*, 1–53, Palgrave Historical Studies in Witchcraft and Magic, London: Palgrave MacMillan.

Oswald, Dana (2004), *Monsters, Gender and Sexuality in Medieval English Literature*, Woodbridge: D. S. Brewer.

Owen, D. D. R. (1975), "Introduction," in W. W. Comfort (trans.), *Chrétien de Troyes, Arthurian Romances*, London: Dent.

Owst, G. R. (1957), "Sortilegium in English Homiletic Literature of the Fourteenth Century," in J. Conway Davies (ed.), *Studies Presented to Sir Hilary Jenkinson*, 272–303, Oxford: Oxford University Press.

Pancaroğlu, Oya (2004), "The Itinerant Dragon-Slayer: Forging Paths of Image and Identity in Medieval Anatolia," *Gesta*, 43 (2): 151–64.

Paracelsis (1941), "On Nymphs, Sylphs, Pigmies, Salamanders and on Other Spirits," in Henry E. Sigerist (ed. and trans), *Four Treatises by Theophrastus von Hohenheim, Called Paracelsus*, 213–53, Baltimore: Johns Hopkins University Press.

Partonopeu de Blois: A French Romance of the Twelfth Century ([n.d.] 1967), ed. Joseph Gildea, Villanova: Villanova University Press.

Patch, Howard Rollin (1972), *The Goddess Fortuna in Medieval Literature*, Cambridge, MA: Harvard University Press.

Patterson, David J. (2013), "Adversus Paganos: Disaster, Dragons, and Episcopal Authority in Gregory of Tours," *Comitatus: A Journal of Medieval and Renaissance Studies*, 44: 1–28.

Pluskowski, Aleks (2003), "Apocalyptic Monsters: Animal Inspirations for the Iconography of Medieval North European Devourers," in Bettina Bildhauer and

Robert Mills (eds.), *The Monstrous Middle Ages*, 155–77, Cardiff: University of Wales Press.
Poirion, Daniel (1982), *Le merveilleux dans la littérature française du moyen âge*, Paris: Presses Universitaire de France.
Pretty Woman (1990), [Film] Dir. Garry Marshall, USA: Touchstone Pictures.
Propp, Vladimir ([1928] 1968), *Morphology of the Folktale*, ed. Louis A. Wagner, 2nd rev. edn., Austin: University of Texas Press.
Putter, Ad and Myra Stokes, eds (2014), *The Works of the Gawain Poet*, London: Penguin.
Radulescu, Raluca and Cory James Rushton, eds. (2009), *A Companion to Medieval Popular Romance*, Woodbridge: D. S. Brewer.
Ravenel, Florence Leftwich (1905), "Tydorel and Sir Gowther," *PMLA*, 20: 152–78.
Rees, Alwyn and Brinley Rees (1961), *Celtic Heritage: Ancient Tradition in Ireland and Wales*, London: Thames and Hudson.
Renaud de Beaujeu (2003), *Le Bel Inconnu*, trans. and ed. Michèle Perret, trans. Isabelle Weil, Paris: Champion.
Renaut de Bâgé (1992), *Le Bel Inconnu (Li Biaus Descouneüs; The Fair Unknown)*, ed. Karen Fresco, trans. Colleen P. Donagher, New York: Garland Publishing.
Resnick, Irven M. and Kenneth Kitchell Jr. (2007), "'The Sweeping of the Lamia': Transformations of the Myths of Lilith and Lamia," in Brian Britt and Alexandra Cuffel (eds.), *Religion, Gender, and Culture in the Pre-Modern World*, 77–104, New York: Palgrave.
Riches, Samantha J. E. (2003), "Encountering the Monstrous: Saints and Dragons in Medieval Thought," in Bettina Bildhauer and Robert Mills (eds.), *The Monstrous Middle Ages*, 125–37, Cardiff: University of Wales Press.
Rider, Jeff (2000), "The Other Worlds of Romance," in Roberta L. Krueger (ed.), *The Cambridge Companion to Medieval Romance*, 115–31, Cambridge: Cambridge University Press.
Rieger, Angelica (1994), "'Dame plus bele que fée': Une expression proverbiale et son histoire dans les littératures française et occitane du moyen âge," in Danielle Buschinger and Wolfgang Spiewok (eds.), *Die Welt der Feen im Mittlealter/ Le monde des fées dans la culture médiévale*, 143–61, Greifswald: Greifswalder Beiträge zum Mittelalter.
Robertson, Elizabeth and Christine M. Rose, eds. (2001), *Representing Rape in Medieval and Early Modern Literature*, New York: Palgrave.
Roblin, Sylvie (1985), "Le Sanglier et la serpente: Geoffroy la Grand Dent dans l'histoire des Lusignan," in Laurence Harf-Lancner (ed.), *Métamorphose bestiaire fantastique au Moyen Age*, 247–85, Paris: École normale supérieure de jeunnes filles.
Roques, Mario, ed. (1965), *Le Chevalier au Lion (Yvain)*, Paris: Honoré Champion.
Rougemont, Denis de (1982), *Love in the Western World*, trans. Montgomery Belgion, Princeton, NJ: Princeton University Press.
Ruys, Juanita Feros (2014), "Love," in Elizabeth Emery and Richard Utz (eds.), *Medievalism: Key Critical Terms*, 125–32, Cambridge: D. S. Brewer.
Rychner, Jean, ed. ([1966] 1969), *Les Lais de Marie de France*, Paris: Honoré Champion.
Salisbury, Eve (2014), "'Lybeaus Desconus': Transformation, Adaptation, and the Monstrous-Feminine," *Arthuriana*, 24 (1): 66–85.
Salisbury, Eve and James Weldon, eds. (2013), *Lybeaus Desconus*, METS, Kalamazoo, MI: Medieval Institute Publications.

Saunders, Corinne (2010), *Magic and the Supernatural in Medieval English Romance*, Woodbridge: D. S. Brewer.
Scala, Elizabeth (1999), "Pretty Women: The Romance of the Fair Unknown, Feminism, and Contemporary Romantic Comedy," *Film and History: An Interdisciplinary Journal of Film and Television Studies*, 29 (1–2): 34–45.
Schleich, Gustav, ed. (1929), *Sire Degarré*, Heidelberg: Carl Winter.
Schultz, James (2006), *Courtly Love, the Love of Courtliness, and the History of Sexuality*, Chicago: University of Chicago Press.
Scot, Reginald (1972), *The Discoverie of Witchcraft*, ed. Montague Summers, New York: Dover.
Scrope, Stephen (1970), *The Epistle of Othea*, ed. Kurt Bühler, London: Early English Text Society.
Shepherd, Stephen H. A., ed. (1995), *Middle English Romances*, New York: W. W. Norton.
Shikibu, Murasaki (2015), *The Tale of Genji*, trans. Dennis Washburn, New York: Norton.
Shippey, Thomas (2005), "Alias Oves Habeo: The Elves as a Category Problem," in Thomas Shippey (ed.), *The Shadow Walkers: Jacob Grimm's Mythology of the Monstrous*, 157–87, Tempe: Arizona Center for Medieval and Renaissance Studies.
Silva, Francisco Gentil Vaz da (2002), *Metamorphosis: The Dynamics of Symbolism in European Fairy Tales*, New York: Peter Lang.
Sims-Williams, Patrick (2011), *Irish Influence on Medieval Welsh Literature*, Oxford: Oxford University Press.
Soja, Edward (1980), "The Socio-Spatial Dialectic," *Annals of the Association of American Geographers*, 70 (2): 207–25.
Spenser, Edmund ([1590–1609] 1987), *The Faerie Queene*, ed. Thomas P. Roche Jr. and C. Patrick O'Donnell Jr., London: Penguin Books.
Spyra, Piotr (2020), *The Liminality of Fairies: Readings in Late Medieval English and Scottish Romance*, New York: Routledge.
Stahuljak, Zrinka, Virginie Greene, Sarah Kay, Sharon Kinoshita, and Peggy McCracken (2011), *Thinking Through Chrétien de Troyes*, Cambridge: D. S. Brewer.
Staines, David, ed. (1991), *The Complete Romances of Chrétien de Troyes*, Bloomington: Indiana University Press.
"Stephen of Rouen: 'Draco Normannicus'" ([c. 1167–9] 1885), in Richard Howlett (ed.), *Chronicles of the Reigns of Stephen, Henry II., and Richard I*, vol. 2, 589–786, London: Longman.
Tatar, Maria, ed. (1999), *The Classic Fairy Tales*, New York: Norton.
Tatar, Maria, ed. (2004) *The Annotated Brothers Grimm*, intro. A. S. Byatt, New York: Norton.
Tatar, Maria, ed. (2015), *The Cambridge Companion to Fairy Tales*, Cambridge: Cambridge University Press.
Tatlock, J. S. (1933), "The Dragons of Wessex and Wales," *Speculum*, 8 (2): 223–35.
Taussig, Michael (1993), *Mimesis and Alterity: A Particular History of the Senses*, New York: Routledge.
Taylor, Jane H. M. (1996), "Melusine's Progeny: Patterns and Perplexities," in Donald Maddox and Sara Sturm-Maddox (eds.), *Melusine of Lusignan: Founding Fiction in Late Medieval France*, 165–200, Athens: University of Georgia Press.
Thomas of Cantimpré (1627), *Thomae Cantipratani ... Bonum Universale de Apibus*, Douai: Beller.

Thomas, Keith (1971), *Religion and the Decline of Magic*, London: Weidenfeld & Nicholson.
Thompson, Stith (1959), *Motif-Index of Folk-Literature; a Classification of Narrative Elements in Folktales, Ballads, Myths, Fables, Mediaeval Romances, Exempla, Fabliaux, Jest-Books, and Local Legends*, rev. and enl. edn., Bloomington: Indiana University Press.
Thomson, Derick S., ed. (1976), *Branwen Uerch Lyr*, Dublin: Dublin Institute for Advanced Studies.
Tisset, Pierre, ed. (1960), *Procès de condamnation de Jeanne d'Arc*, vol. 1, Paris: Klincksieck.
Todorov, Tzvetan (1970), *Introduction à la littérature fantastique*, Paris: Éditions du Seuil.
Todorov, Tzvetan (1975), *The Fantastic: A Structural Approach to a Literary Genre*, trans. Richard Howard, Ithaca, NY: Cornell University Press.
Tolkien, J. R. R. ([1936] 1968), "Beowulf: The Monsters and the Critics," in Donald K. Fry (ed.), *The Beowulf Poet: A Collection of Critical Essays*, 8–56, Englewood Cliffs, NJ: Prentice-Hall.
Tolkien, J. R. R. (1964), "On Faerie Tales," in *Tree and Leaf*, 3–73, Boston: Houghton Mifflin.
Tuczay, Christa (2006), "Drache und Greif—Symbole der Ambivalenz," *Mediaevistik*, 19: 169–211.
Urban, Misty (2010), *Monstrous Women in Middle English Romance: Representations of Mysterious Female Power*, Lampeter: Edwin Mellen Press.
Urban, Misty (2018), "How the Dragon Ate the Woman: The Fate of Melusine in English," in Misty Urban, Deva F. Kemmis, and Melissa Ridley Elmes (eds.), *Melusine's Footprint: Tracing the Legacy of a Medieval Myth*, 368–87, Leiden: Brill.
Urban, Misty, Deva F. Kemmis, and Melissa Ridley Elmes, eds. (2017), *Melusine's Footprint: Tracing the Legacy of a Medieval Myth*, Leiden: Brill.
Urban, Misty, Deva F. Kemmis, and Melissa Ridley Elmes, eds. (2020), *The Melusine Romance in Medieval Europe: Translation, Circulation, and Material Contexts*, Woodbridge: D. S. Brewer.
Verner, Lisa (2014), *The Epistemology of the Monstrous in the Middle Ages*, New York: Routledge.
Vines, Amy N. (2011), *Women's Power in Late-Medieval Romance*, Cambridge: D. S. Brewer.
Vines, Amy N. (2014), "Invisible Woman: Rape as a Chivalric Necessity in Medieval Romance," in Amanda Hopkins, Robert Allen Rouse, and Cory James Rushton (eds.), *Sexual Cultures in the Literature of Medieval Britain*, 161–80, Woodbridge: D. S. Brewer.
Vries, Jan de (1959), *Heroic Song and Heroic Legend*, trans. B. J. Timmer, London: Oxford University Press.
Waddell, John (1983), "Rathcroghan—A Royal Site in Connacht," *Journal of Irish Archaeology*, 1: 21–46.
Wade, James (2011), *Fairies in Medieval Romance*, New York: Palgrave Macmillan.
Walter Map (2002), *De nugis curialium: Courtiers' Trifles*, trans. M. R. James, rev. ed. C. N. L. Brooke and R. A. B. Minors, Oxford: Clarendon Press.
Warner, Marina (1998), *No Go the Bogeyman: Scaring, Lulling, and Making Mock*, New York: Farrar, Straus and Giroux.

Warner, Marina (2018), *Forms of Enchantment: Writings on Art and Artists*, London: Thames and Hudson.
Waters, Claire M., ed. and trans. (2018), *The Lais of Marie de France*, Peterborough, ON: Broadview Press.
Watkins, Calvert (1995), *How to Kill a Dragon: Aspects of Indo-European Poetics*, Oxford: Oxford University Press.
Weber, Max ([1922] 1956), *The Sociology of Religion*, trans. Ephraim Fischoff, London: Methuen.
Weldon, James (2007), "'Naked as she was bore': Naked Disenchantment in *Lybeaus Desconus*," *Parergon*, 24 (1): 67–99.
William of Auvergne (1674), *Guiliemi Alverni … Opera Omnia*, 2 vols, Paris: Praelard.
William of Newburgh (1988), *The History of English Affairs*, vol. 1, ed. and trans. P. G. Walsh and M. J. Kennedy, Warminster: Aris & Phillips.
Williams, David (1996), *Deformed Discourse: The Function of the Monster in Mediaeval Thought and Literature*, Montreal: McGill-Queen's University Press.
Williams, Raymond (1980), "Advertising: The Magic System," in *Problems in Materialism and Culture: Selected Essays*, 170–95, London: Verso.
Williams, Tara (2018), *Middle English Marvels: Magic, Spectacle, and Morality in the Fourteenth Century*, University Park: Pennsylvania State University Press.
Williams, Tara (forthcoming 2021), "Merveille," in Stephanie L. Batkie, Matthew W. Irvin, and Lynn Shutters (eds.), *A New Companion to Critical Thinking on Chaucer*, Leeds, UK: Arc Humanities Press.
Williamson, Judith (1978), *Decoding Advertisements: Ideology and Meaning in Advertising*, London: Boyars.
Woodcock, Matthew (2004), *Fairy in* The Faerie Queene*: Renaissance Elf-Fashioning and Elizabethan Mythmaking*, Farmington, VT: Ashgate Publishing.
Workman, Leslie J. (1995), "Medievalism," *The Year's Work in Medievalism*, 10: 227.
Workman, Leslie J. (1999), "The Future of Medievalism," in John Gallant (ed.), *Medievalism: The Year's Work for 1995, Studies in Medievalism*, 7–18, Baltimore: Johns Hopkins University Press.
Ziolkowski, Jan M. ([2006] 2007, 2009), *Fairy Tales from before Fairy Tales: The Medieval Latin Past of Wonderful Lies*, Ann Arbor: University of Michigan Press.
Zipes, Jack ([1983] 1991), *Fairy Tales and the Art of Subversion*, New York: Routledge.
Zipes, Jack ([2000] 2015), *Oxford Companion to Fairy Tales*, Oxford: Oxford University Press.
Zipes, Jack (2006), *Why Fairy Tales Stick*, New York: Routledge.
Zipes, Jack ([2012] 2013), *The Irresistible Fairy Tale: The Cultural and Social History of a Genre*, Princeton, NJ: Princeton University Press.

CONTRIBUTORS

Susan Aronstein is Professor of English and Honors at the University of Wyoming, United States. Her research focuses on medievalism, Arthurian legend, Disney, and transmedia storytelling. She is the author of *Hollywood Knights: Arthurian Cinema and the Politics of Nostalgia*, *British Arthurian Narrative* (2005), and *The Road to Wicked: The Marketing and Consumption of Oz from Baum to Broadway* (with Kent Drummond and Terri Rittenberg, 2018), as well the coeditor (with Tison Pugh) of *Disney's Middle Ages: A Fairy Tale and Fantasy Past* (2012) and *The United States of Medievalism* (2021).

Melissa Ridley Elmes is Assistant Professor of English at Lindenwood University, United States. Her research examines post-Conquest, fifteenth-century English, Celtic, Anglo-Norman, and Old Norse literatures and cultures and women's and gender studies. She is the coeditor of *Melusine's Footprint: Tracing the Legacy of a Medieval Myth* (2017) and has articles published or forthcoming on the Arthurian and Robin Hood legends, Chaucer, the *Mabinogion*, *Beowulf*, medieval literature pedagogy, and medievalisms. She is currently working on two monographs on violence and feasting in medieval British and Arthurian texts, alongside projects in Arthurian ethics and violence and gender on the premodern stage.

Helen Fulton is Professor of Medieval Literature at the University of Bristol, UK. She works at the interface between medieval English and Welsh literatures, with a focus on the social and political significance of medieval texts, transnational influences, and manuscript transmission. She is the coeditor of the *Cambridge History of Welsh Literature* (2019).

Richard Firth Green is Academy Professor of English at the Ohio State University and the author of three monographs: *Poets and Princepleasers* (1980), *A Crisis of Truth* (1998), and *Elf Queens and Holy Friars* (2016).

Sarah L. Higley is Professor of English at the University of Rochester, United States. She has written articles and books on Old English and Middle Welsh poetry (*Between Languages*, 1993); film studies, the occult, and the "monstrous feminine" (*Millennial Cinema and* The Blair Witch *Controversies*, 2004); and her exploration of divine and invented words led to her third book on the *Lingua ignota* of Hildegard of Bingen: *An Edition, Translation, and Discussion* (2007). She is working on an edition of an anonymous Middle-English poetic translation of Coudrette's *Roman de Parthenay*, or "The Tale of Melusine."

Christine M. Neufeld is a Professor in the Department of English Language and Literature at Eastern Michigan University, United States. She is the coeditor of the *Journal of Narrative Theory*, the author of *Avid Ears: Medieval Gossips, Sound and the Art of Listening* (2019), as well as a coeditor of *Writing Beyond Pen and Parchment: Inscribed Objects in Medieval European Literature* (2019). In addition to numerous publications on cinematic medievalism, Neufeld's scholarship on witches in medieval and early modern literature has led to a variety of public lectures on the social stakes of "medieval" monsters.

Shyama Rajendran is Assistant Professor of Literature at Krea University, India. Her research is centered on late medieval literature and explores varied forms of cultural and linguistic belonging and how demarcations of difference are culturally reproduced. She brings together medieval literature, sociolinguistics, critical race theory, disability theory, and gender studies to develop productive conversations that exist at the intersections of these fields. Her research also situates English multilingual authors within the context of the global Middle Ages and draws on methodologies from scholars working in non-European contexts.

Lynn Shutters is Assistant Professor of English at Colorado State University, United States. Her research encompasses feminist approaches to medieval literature, late medieval narratives of marital affection, and the medieval reception of classical antiquity. Recent publications include articles in *Comparative Literature* and the *Chaucer Review* and a chapter in the edited collection *Medieval Futurity: Queering Time and Space*. She works extensively as an editor, having recently edited a special issue of the *Chaucer Review* on Chaucer's *Legend of Good Women* (with Betsy McCormick and Leah Schwebel; 2017), as well as *A New Companion to Critical Thinking on Chaucer* (with Stephanie Batkie and Matthew Irvin; 2021).

Usha Vishnuvajjala holds a PhD from Indiana University, United States, and is a lecturer in English literature at Cardiff University in Wales. Her research focuses on Arthurian literature, medievalism, gender, and emotion, and her current projects include the monograph *Feminist Medievalisms* and the collection *Women's Friendship in Medieval Literature*, coedited with Karma Lochrie.

INDEX

Note: *n* = endnote.

Acker, Paul 123–5
adaptations 45–61
adultery
   as product of court setting 167–9, 196*n*10
   dangers of 71, 169–71
Adventure of Fergus son of Léti (anon.) 198*n*5
"The Adventures of the Sons of Eochaid Mugmedon" (anon.) 105
Aislinge Óenguso (The Dream of Óengus, anon.) 138–9
Akbari, Suzanne Conklin 48, 50
"Aladdin and his Magic Lamp" 56
Albertus Magnus, St 29, 125
   see also *De secretis mulierum*
Aleph-Bet of Ben Sirah (anon.) 130
Alexander the Great 113, 197*n*12
Alexander's Letter to Aristotle (anon.) 117
Alfonsi, Petrus, *Disciplina Clericalis* 121
"Ali Baba and the Forty Thieves" 56
Alliterative Morte Darthur (anon.) 18, 167, 200*n*10
Altschul, Nadia 13
Ambrisco, Alan 60–1
animals, magical 17, 57–61, *58*
Anjou, (1st) Count/Countess of 98

Annwfn (Welsh Otherworld) 142–5, 178
   geographical location 143–5
   human visits to 142–3
Apuleius 121
   De Deo Socratis 95
The Arabian Nights see *The Thousand and One Nights*
Arawn (legendary figure) 142–3, 178
Archibald, Elizabeth 201*n*2
Ariosto, Ludovico, *Orlando Furioso* 47
Aristotle 131
   On the Generation of Animals 122
   Metaphysics 102
Armitage, Simon 201*n*17
Arthur, King (legendary character) 18, 27, 145, 181, 183–4, 190
   see also titles of Arthurian works
Augé, Marc 136
Augustine of Hippo, St 41, 113
   The City of God 115
Aulnoy, Marie-Catherine d' see d'Aulnoy
The Awntyrs off Arthur (anon.) 18, 165–8
Aymeri de Narbonne (anon.) 152

Barron, W. R. J. 201*n*17
Bartholomaeus Anglicus, *De proprietas rerum* 125

Basile, Giambattista 120
  "The Dragon" 130
  Tale of Tales 1
Baxtor, Richard, *Certainty of the Worlds of Spirits* 96, 197n9
beauty
  as incitement to rape 84
  male/female, similarity of 68–9
  as marker of virtue 86
  overlap with courtliness 67–8
  role of clothing 68
  as source of power 181–2
  as temptation 74–5
Le Bel Inconnu (Renaut de Bâgé/Beaujeu) 18, 65, 131, 191, 195nn6–7, 204n15
  "fearsome Kiss" episode 78–80
  and *fin amor* 69–71
  and gender/courtliness 68–71
  plot summary 66
  treatment of lineage 83
  treatment of marvels/eroticism 78–82
  treatment of masculine/feminine virtue 71–3, 79
Bendigeidfran (legendary figure) 146–7
Benko, Georges 136
Benson, Larry D. 55, 201n17
Beowulf (anon.) 12, 14, 17–18, 93, 117–18, 129, 193n8, 198n9
Bernger von Horheim 70
Berry, Jean, duc de 34, 67, 91
Bersuire, Pierre, *Reductorium morale* 99, 112–13
Bliss, A. J. 201n15
Bloch, Howard 74
Boccaccio, Giovanni 54, 121
  De Genealogia deorum 41–2
  Decameron 47, 193n3
  Il ninfale esolano 42
  relationship with *The Thousand and One Nights*/Chaucer 48–50, 53, 55
Boethius, *The Consolation of Philosophy* 203n8
The Book of Sir John Mandeville (anon, ?de Langhe) 126, 132
Boron, Robert de, *Merlin* 202n4
Bottigheimer, Ruth B. 1–2, 16, 158
Bran (legendary figure) 18, 92, 138, 139–41

Branwen uerch Lŷr (*Branwen daughter of Lŷr,* anon.) 154, 200n4
Breton lays 35–9, 121
Brewer, Derek 27
Brocéliande, forest of (Brittany) 31–3
Bromyard, John, *Summa Predicantium* 33
Brown, Anna, Mrs 39
Brownlee, Kevin 132
Brownlee, Marina S. 108
Bruckner, Matilda 94
Burchard of Worms 95
Burger, Glenn 77
Burns, E. Jane 76
Butler, Judith 73
Byatt, A. S., *Possession* 34, 197n15
Bynum, Caroline Walker 77–8, 79
  Metamorphosis and Identity 198n1
Byrne, Aisling, *Otherworlds: Fantasy and History in Medieval Literature* 203n7

Caesarius of Heisterbach 95–6
Cain (biblical character) 116–17
Cannon, Christopher 160
Cantor, Norman 12, 13
Carey, John 199n1
Carmina Burana (anon.) 203n8
Carney, James 117
Carroll, Noel 16–17
Cassian, John 41
Cecire, Maria Sachiko 12, 13, 193n5
Certeau, Michel de 24
Chakraborty, S. A., *Daevabad Trilogy* 193n5
Chandragupta, Emperor 113
chansons de geste 16, 152
Chapelain, Jean 6
Chapman, Robert L. 99
Chaucer, Geoffrey 14, 121
  The Canterbury Tales 47, 92, 193n3, 197n6
  The Franklin's Tale 171–3, 172
  The Merchant's Tale 43, 96
  The Nun's Priest's Tale 43
  The Tale of Sir Thopas 43
  The Wife of Bath's Tale 19–20, 24–5, 27, 39, 43, 179, 183
  referencing of earlier works 54
  relationship with *The Thousand and One Nights*/Boccaccio 48–50, 53, 55

scepticism regarding fairies/tales 40,
    42–3, 44
  visits to Italy 49–50, 54
  see also *The Squire's Tale*
Chesterton, G. K. 29
Chestre, Thomas 66
  Sir Launfal 184–5, 201*n*15, 203*n*9
  see also *Lybeaus Desconus*
Chourne, William 24, 25
Chretien de Troyes 154
  Cligés 18, 170–1
  Le Conte du Graal 162–3
  Erec and Enid 18, 162, 200*n*14
  Lancelot or The Knight of the Cart 18,
    35, 162, 196*n*10
  Perceval 18, 19, 174–5, 200*n*14
  Yvain or the Knight of the Lion 18, 31,
    126, 147–8, 152, 155, 159, 162,
    163, 165, 167, 168–9, 173, 173–4,
    200*n*5, 200*n*10, 200*n*14
  influences/sources 200*n*14, 201*n*3
Christian Church
  demonization of fairies 29–34, 35,
    38–9, 40–1, 95–6, 201*n*16
  hostility to belief in fairies 33–4, 44,
    94–5
  misogynistic teachings 38–9, 74
  saints' lives 121
  view on monsters/monstrosities 114–20,
    125–6
Christine de Pizan, *Epistre Othea* 41, 42
Cinderella, tale/figure of 182
Clarke, Susannah, *Jonathan Strange and
    Mr. Norrell* 20, 27
class (social), power linked to 181–2
classical mythology 41–3, 91–2, 127
  ecclesiastical re-transmission 121
Cohen, Jeffrey J. 115–16
  Monster Theory: Reading Culture 122–3
Cole, Chera A. 101–2
Cooper, Helen 159, 204*nn*10–11
Copeland, Rita 54
Corbett, Richard, Bishop 24
Cormac mac Airt (legendary figure) 139
Coudrette, *Le Roman de Parthenay* 91, 94,
    98, 99, 103, 106, 107, 109
  English translation 99–100
  surviving manuscripts 196–7*n*2
court/court life 162–74

competing demands of 164
disruption of family 162–3, 164
female communities 171–3
jealousy, problem of 167–8
oversocialization/excess 164–5
problems of romantic consummation
    168–71
as site of close/familial ties 163
see also courtliness
courtliness 64–5, 67–71, 70
  and beauty 67–9
  and *fin amor* 69–71
  see also court/court life
Creed, Barbara 132–3
Crenshaw, Kimberlé 195*n*4
Ctesias 113
Cuchulain (legendary character) 18,
    189–90
Culhwch ac Olwen (anon.) 142, 145, 154,
    200*n*4
Cupid and Psyche, legend of 121

Dante (Alighieri), *Inferno* 120
d'Aulnoy, Marie-Catherine 1, 7, 15, 20,
    63, 121
  Tales of the Fairies 8
  dedication of Tales 7
David I of Scotland 26
Davies, Sioned 200*n*8
Dawkins, Richard 5
Dbussy, Claude, *Pélleus et Mélisande*
    197*n*15
De secretis mulierum (attrib. Albertus
    Magnus) 131
de Vries, Jan 126
deformity, as symbol of evil/cursed state
    105, 107–8, 132
Die, comtesse de 7
Disney, Walt/Disney Studios 1, 45
The Distaff Gospells (fifteenth-century
    collection) 26
Diyab, Hanna 55–6
Donoghue, Daniel 201*n*17
Donoghue, Emma, *Kissing the Witch: Old
    Tales in New Skins* 133
dragons 123–33, *124*, 199*n*15
  as battle standards 126–7
  doubts as to existence 125
  "fearsome Kiss" motif 78–80, 132

    in fictional narratives 126
    iconic place in medieval culture 125
    saints' battles with 125–9
    'scientific' descriptions 125
    slaying, as heroic/theological motif 126–30, 131–2
    theological appropriations 125–6
    woman-dragon hybrids 128–33
    see also serpents
Dryden, John 40
Dubost, Francis 28–9
Duggan, Anne E. 6, 7, 8
Dumézil, Georges 126, 129

Echtra mac nEchach Muimedóin (*Adventure of the Sons of Eochaid Mugmedón*, anon.) 204n12
Echtra Nerai (*The Adventure of Nera*, anon.) 141
Echtrae Chonnlai (*The Adventure of Connla*, anon.) 141, 145, 155
Eco, Umberto 5, 111
Eddas (anon.) 9, 14, 18, 194n9
Edward IV of England 98
Edwards, Robert R. 49–50
Eleanor of Aquitaine, Queen 97–8, 99, 197n10
Eliade, Mircea 126
Elizabeth, Queen Consort *see* Woodville, Elizabeth
Elizabeth I of England 97, 98
Elmes, Melissa Ridley 100
Elucidarium (theological handbook, anon.) 30–1
Erceldoune, Thomas of *see* 'Thomas the Rhymer'
Eve (biblical character) 131

Fadin, Francois 105
'Faerie' 2–3, 12, 21, 93
    faerie adventures, defined 18–19
Fafnir (legendary figure) 129–30
fairies
    alleged sightings 25–6
    appearance/behaviour, perceptions of 26–7
    artistic depictions 93
    association with classical mythology 41–3

    belief in 15–16, 26, 29–30, 194n1
    deletion from later versions of tales 39–40
    demonization 29–34, 35, 38–9, 40–1, 44, 95–6, 201n16
    diminishing belief in 23–4
    distancing in place and time 24–5, 34–5, 63–4, 111–12
    etymology 92–3
    games/trickery 187–90
    medieval commentaries 16
    natural/unnaturalness 93–4
    powers 178–9, 182–92; linked to place 179–80
    (presumed) habitation 135 (*see also* Otherworld)
    prevalence in medieval imagination 177–8
    (problems of) definition 90, 91–3
fairy lovers 20, 37, 179
fairy mistresses 19–20, 80–1, 178–9
    see also "Woman in the Wood" motif
fairy offspring 83, 197n12
fairy tales
    cultural history 20–1
    dictionary definition 27, 44
    late medieval developments 34–44
    medieval engagement with 16–17
    perceived post-medieval origins 63–4
    relationship with belief 27–9
    taxonomy 17–20
fairy-wives *see* "Woman in the Wood" motif
family/family life 160–3
    class differences 160–1
    threats to 161, 162–3
Fates, in classical mythology 92
"fearsome Kiss" motif 78–80, 132
fin amor 69–71, 196n10
    defined 69
    linked to adultery 71
Flint, W. Russell *172*
Floriant et Florete (anon.) 190
Fortune's Wheel, trope of 203n8
French romances, geography/social ambience 137, 147–8, *149*
    see also chansons de geste; romance; *specific titles*

Froud, Brian, and Allen Lee, *Fairies* 93, 101
Fuchs, Barbara 64
Fulton, Helen 16
Fyleman, Rose 135

Galland, Antoine, *Les Mille et une nuits* 46
  transformation of source material 45–7, 55–6
games, relationship with power 187–90
Gaunt, Simon 47–8, 52
gender/sexuality 63–87
  and female autonomy 38–9
  male/female differences 71–2
  male/female similarities 68–9
  power linked to 181–2
  traditional roles 64
  tropes 64–5
  see also courtliness; "the marvellous"; rape; virtue; women
Genghis Khan 56
Geoffrey of Monmouth
  History of the Kings of Britain 18, 127, 183
  Life of Merlin 202n4
Geoffroy II of Lusignan 105
George, St, feats ascribed to 127
Gerald of Wales, *Liber de Principis instructione* 98
Gereint uab Erbin (anon.) 200n14
Germany, cultural nationalist projects 8–10
Gerson, Jean 33–4
Gervase of Tilbury 102, 103
  Otia Imperialia 92–3, 98–9, 121
Gesta Romanorum (anon.) 121
giants 84–5, 145
Gilmore, David 113
Ginzburg, Carlo 26
God, visual representations 120
Goethe, Johann Wolfgang von, "Die neue Meluzine" 197n15
Gower, John 42–3
  Balade 27 195n11
  Confessio Amantis 43
  Tale of Narcissus 43
Grange, Huw 121
Gravdal, Kathryn 84
Green, Richard Firth 16, 80, 177, 194n7, 201n16, 202n3
  Elf Queens and Holy Friars 94–5, 203n7
Greenblatt, Stephen, *Renaissance Self-Fashioning: From More to Shakespeare* 97
Gregory IX, Pope 105
Grimm, Jacob/Wilhelm 5, 8–10, 14, 21, 45
  Ancient German Law 9
  Children's and Household Tales 1–2, 9–10
  Das Schlangenmädchen (The Snake Girl) 130
  German Dictionary 9
  German Grammar 9
  German nationalist project 8–10
  Lay of Hildebrand (eds) 9
  source material 17
guardian knights, motif of 159
Guest, Lady Charlotte 142
Guillaume de Machaut, *Fontaine Amoureuse* 41
Guy of Warwick (legendary figure) 129
Gwragedd Annwn (fairy race, Welsh) 93

Ham (biblical character) 117, 198n4
Hanawalt, Barbara 161
Hansel and Gretel, tale/figure of 155
Harf-Lancner, Laurence 33
Hell/Hell mouth
  guarded by dragons 126
  visual representations 119, 120
Henry I of England 26
Henry II of England 26, 97, 99
Henry of Marsburg 31–2
"hidden people" 91
Higden, Ranulph, *Speculum Curatorum* 33
Holy Grail, as focus of romances/later stories 162–3
Homer, *Odyssey* 113
Hopkins, Andrea 194n7
Howard, Donald 3
Hundred Years War (1337–1453) 100, 201n1
Huon of Bordeaux (anon.) 26, 34, 96
Hutcheon, Linda 53–4, 55, 61

Immram Brain mac Febail (The Voyage of Bran son of Febal, anon.) 139
incest, as plot feature 201n2

Irish tales/culture 18, 91, 96, 105, 136, 137–42, 198*n*5, 199*n*3
　founding myths 137–8
　influence on later cultures 141–2
　see also Otherworld; Tuatha Dé Danann
Isidore of Seville, Archbishop 113, 115–16, 122

Jaeger, Stephen 71
James VI of Scotland/I of England 194*n*1
James, Henry 28
James, M. R. 28
Japanese tales/culture 158–9, 162
Jean d'Arras 26
　see also Mélusine
Jerome, St 102, 130
Jerusalem, siege of (1099) 127
Joan of Arc 25, 29
Jones, Leslie Ellen 96
Judith (anon.) 117–18
Julius Caesar 34

Kahn, Ausma Zehanat, *The Bloodprint* 193*n*5
Keats, John, "The Lamia" 197*n*15
"Kemp Owyne" (anon.) 130
Kinoshita, Sharon 50
Kirk, Robert 90, 91
Kramer, Heinrich, *Malleus Maleficarum* 131

la Force, Charlotte-Rose Caumont de, "L'Enchanteur" 6–7
La Motte Fouque, Friedrich de, *Undine* 197*n*15
"Lai de Guingamor" (anon.) 35
Lai de Tydorel (anon.) 35–9, 194*n*7
lais féeriques 35, 43
Lamia, mythical figure of 103, 130–1, 198*n*19
Lancelot-Graal cycle (anon.) 29, 32, 36, 71
Lang, Andrew 45
Langland, William, *The Vision of Piers Plowman* 43–4
L'Archeveque, Guillaume de Parthenay/ L'Archeveque family 91, 105
Latham, M. W. 24
Laȝamon, *Brut* 183
Le Goff, Jacques 24, 28, 41, 126

Lebor Gabála Érenn (*Book of Invasions of Ireland*, anon.) 137, 199*n*2
Lee, A. C. 48
Lee, Allen *see* Froud, Brian
Lemay, Helen R. 131
Lerner, Alan Jay, and Frederick Loewe, *Camelot* 112
Lewis, C. S. 5, 10–14, 15, 196*n*10
　The Allegory of Love 12
　Chronicles of Narnia 29
　The Discarded Image 12, 92
　"On Three Ways of Writing for Children" 13
L'Héritier de Villandon, Jeanne-Marie
　Apothéose de Mademoiselle de Scudéry 7
　"The Enchantments of Eloquence" 6–7
　"Letter to Madame D. G***" 6–7
Liber monstrorum de diversis generibus (anon.) 96, 114–15
Life of Marcellus (anon.) 127
Lilith (legendary figure) 130–1
Lippincott, Louise 126
Llyn y Fan Fach (Welsh folktale) 92
Loewe, Frederick *see* Lerner, Alan Jay
Louis XIV of France 7
Lovecraft, H. P. 28, 34
Luther, Martin 23
Lybeaus Desconus (anon., poss. Chestre) 65, 182, 191, 195–6*nn*6–8
　divergence from source material 66–7, 73, 83
　"fearsome Kiss" episode 78–80, 132
　plot summary 66–7
　treatment of femininity/virtue 73–5
Lynch, Kathryn 55, 56

Maas, Sarah J., *Court of Thorns and Roses* 20
Mabinogion 18, 142–7, 144, 178, 200*n*8, 202*n*4
　First Branch *see Pwyll Pendeuic Dyuet*
Mac Cana, Proinsias 200*n*4
Maeterlinck, Maurice, *Pélleus et Mélisande* 197*n*15
magic/wonder tales 17
"magical naturalism" 16–17
Mallette, Karla 45–7, 50–2
Malory, Thomas, *Morte Darthur* 14, 159, 167, 183–4, 202*n*4
Map, Walter 25, 29, 98, 102

De nugis curialium (Courtiers' Trifles) 26, 99, 121, 200*n*4
Margaret, St 121, 127, *128*
Marie de France 7, 14, 147, 161
  Les Deuz Amanz (The Two Lovers) 161
  Equitan 169–70
  Le Fresne (The Ash Tree) 161–2
  Guigemar 147, 148, 191
  Lanval 19–20, 147, 148, 150, 155, 187–8, 201*n*18, 203*n*9
  Laüstic 169
  Yonec 17, 20, 96, 147
marriage, roles within 76–7
"the marvellous" 64–5, 77–83
  defined 77–8
  definitions 77–8
  embodied by women 77, 78
  encountered by men 77
Math vab Mathonwy (Math son of Mathonwy, anon.) 143
McDonald, Nicola 160
McKillip, Patricia
  Riddle Master trilogy 14
  Stepping from the Shadows 14–15
Mediterranean, medieval trade/cultural exchanges 50–3, *51*
Megasthenes 113
Melusine (mythological character) 15, 20, 34, 37, 91, 94, 98–109, 131, 179, 181, 197*n*14
  absence of English accounts 99–100
  accounts preceding Jean d'Arras 98–9
  common features of tales 202*n*4, 203*n*9
  modern versions/reinterpretations 197*n*15
  versions in various languages 100
  see also following entry
Mélusine, ou La Noble Histoire de Lusignan (Jean d'Arras) 26, *34,* 37, 44, 65, 90, 91, *101,* 102–8, *108,* 109, *180,* 198*n*23, 203*n*9
  (claimed) sources 98–9
  English translation 99–100
  historical background 105
  moral ambiguity 104–5
  plot summary 67, 103–4
  surviving manuscripts 196–7*n*2
  treatment of beauty/virtue 75–7, 82–3
  treatment of half-human state 94, 109, 132
  treatment of heredity 83, 105–7, 132
  treatment of mortal women 83
  treatment of the marvellous 82–3
Menocal, Maria Rosa 48, 53
Michael, St, feats ascribed to 127
Middle Ages
  academic visions of 10–14
  as construct 3–5
  genuine belief in fairy-tale world 15–16
  modern associations with fairy-tale settings 3, 63–4, 111–12
Middle English romance 137, 148–53, 159–75
  divergence from French sources 150, 151–2, 159, 163
  linguistic significance 150
Moises De Leon, Rabbi, *Zohar* 130–1
monsters/monstrosities 17–18, 111–33
  ancient Greek/Roman accounts 113
  early medieval theories/theology of 113, 114–20
  etymology 112
  prevalence in medieval imagination 112
  (problems of) definition 112–13, 123, 199*n*14
  saints' battles with 121
  and the wonder tale 120–3
  see also dragons; serpents; witches
Montoya, Alicia C. 6
Morgan le Fay (legendary figure) 27, 167, 178, 185, 202*n*4, 203*n*7, 204*n*14
mounds/hills, association with Otherworld 139, 146
Mouskès, Philippe, *Chroniques rimées* 97–8

nature, Classical/medieval conceptions 93–4
Nibelungenlied (anon.) 9
Nichols, Stephen J. 108
nineteenth century, literary studies in 47–8
non-human characters 89–109
  divine mission 102–3
  salvation denied to 101–2
  see also animals; fairies; the marvellous; monsters
Nowell Codex 117–18, 198*n*6

O'Donoghue, Bernard 201*n*17
Orff, Carl 203*n*8
Orléans, Philippe I, duc d' 7
Ostling, Michael 91
Otherworld(s), in Irish/Welsh mythology 96, 136, 137–47, 178, 199*n*1
　boundary markers 139, 145
　human visits to 139–41, 142–3
　linked to above-ground locations 139, 141–2, 143, 200*n*8
　mapped 144
　materiality 139
　see also Annwfn
Ovid (P. Ovidius Naso) 121, 150–1
Owein, neu Chwedyl Iarlles y Ffynanwn (*Owain, or the Lady of the Fountain,* anon.) 148, 155, 200*n*14
Owst, Gerald R. 33
Oxford University, English Literature syllabus 14

Paien de Maisieres, *La Mule sans frein* 35
Palatine, Elisabeth Charlotte, Princess 7
Pancaroğlu, Oya 127–9
Paracelsus (Theophrastus von Hohenheim) 100, 101, 197*n*14
Paris, Gaston 196*n*10
Parrish, Maxfield
　"The Enchanted Forests of Medievalism" 11
　"Medievalism and Fairy Tale Castles" 4
Partonope de Blois (anon.) 179, 181, 203–4*n*9
The Passion of Saint Christopher (anon.) 117
Patient Griselda, tale/figure of 8, 193*n*3
Patterson, David 127
Pearl (anon.) 12
Peredur (anon.) 200*n*14
Perrault, Charles 6, 14, 15, 45, 121
　Tales and Stories of Mother Goose 8
　Tales and Stories of the Past 1
　criticism of contemporaries 7–8
Plato 95
Pliny the Elder (C. Plinius Secundus)/Plinian races 113, *114*, 117
Poe, Edgar Allan 28, 34
Poirion, Daniel 29
power, representations of 177–92

　control of human bodies 191–2
　of displacement/transportation 190
　exercised through games/trickery 187–90
　in fairy–human interactions 182–5
　linked to class/gender 181–2
　linked to specific locations 179–81
Pretty Woman (1990) 86–7, *87*
Propp, Vladimir 122
Pwyll (legendary figure) 142–3, 145, 146–7, 178, 189
Pwyll Pendeuic Dyuet (*Pwyll Prince of Dyfed,* anon.) 142–3, 145, 146–7, 189, 190

queer theory 202–3*n*5
quests, and masculine virtue 71–4, 84–5

rape 64–5, 84–6, 161, 179, 204–5*n*19
　ambiguous depictions 85–6
　as class marker (of victim/attacker) 84–5
　prevention, as marker of chivalry 84–5
Ravenel, Florence Leftwich 194*n*7
reception theory 27
Renaut de Bâgé/Beaujeu see *Le Bel Inconnu*
reverdie (poetic genre) 94, 197*n*6
Rhiannon (legendary figure) 205*n*20
Richard Coer de Lyon (*Richard the Lion-Heart,* anon.) 20, 97
Robert le Diable (legendary figure) 37, 194*n*8
Roblin, Sylvie 105
Romance and Prophecies of Thomas of Ercledoune (anon.) 200*n*4
romance (genre) 64–87
　celebration of beauty/devotion 74–7
　centrality of chance/*aventure* 165–7
　contemporary social relevance 174–5
　focus on conspicuous consumption 137, 148, 151, 153, 154–5
　French vs. English 137
　gender tropes 64–5, 74
　geographical settings 137, 147–8
　influence of saints' lives 129
　intertextuality 65
　non-European influences 158
　standard gender roles 64
　treatments of family 160–2
　treatments of space 147–53

urban settings 148, *149*
see also court/court life; courtliness; "the marvellous"; Middle English romance; rape; virtue; *titles of texts*
Rougemont, Denis de 196*n*10
Rowling, J. K., *Harry Potter* series 29
royalty, alleged supernatural background 97–8
Rumpelstiltskin, tale/figure of 155

Saïd, Edward 55
saints, battles with monsters/dragons 121, 125–9
Salisbury, Eve 79, 132–3, 195*n*6
Sarashina, Lady, *As I Crossed a Bridge of Dreams* 162, 163, 168
Saunders, Corinne, *Magic and the Supernatural in Medieval English Romance* 203*n*7, 205*n*23
Scala, Elizabeth 87
Schultz, James 68–9
Scot, Reginald 24
Scott, Walter, *Minstrelsy of the Scottish Borders* 39–40
Scrope, Stephen 41
Second Lucidaire see *Elucidarium*
Sedgwick, Eve 73
Sercambi, Giovanni, *Novella* 47
serpents
    alluring/feminine nature 79–80
    woman-serpent hybrids 75–7 (see also Melusine)
    women transformed into 78–81
    see also dragons
Shahnameh (*The Book of Kings,* anon.) 158
Shakespeare, William 135
    A Midsummer Night's Dream 26, 39, 93, 100
    Romeo and Juliet 26
Shikibu, Murasaki, *The Tale of Genji* 158–9, 162, 168
Shippey, Tom 90, 102
Sigurd/Siegfried (legendary figure) 18, 129
Sims-Williams, Patrick 199*n*1
Sinistrari, Louis Marie 102, 197–8*n*16
Sir Bevis of Hampton (anon.) 129
Sir Degaré (anon.) 20, 40, 94, 161, 174–5, 188–9, 191, 197*n*12, 205*n*23
Sir Gawain and Dame Ragnell (anon.) 179

Sir Gawain and the Green Knight (anon.) 14, 18, 59, 96, *166*, 186, 202*n*4
    fairy–human interactions 182, 185, 187, 190, 191
    modern English translations 12, 201*n*17
    sense of place 152–3, 154
    treatment of court life 164–7
Sir Gowther (anon.) 35–9, 194*n*7
Sir Landevale (anon.) 150, 153, 203*n*9
Sir Orfeo (anon.) 14, 20, 34–5, 150–2, 154, 178, 182, 190, 191, 202*n*4, 204*n*13
Sir Perceval of Galles (anon.) 157–8, 163, 174–5
Snow White, tale/figure of 155
society/socialization 157–75
"Solomon's Daughter in the Tower" (anon.) 17
space, treatments of 135–55
    fairy powers linked to 179–80
    social construction 135–6
    see also court; family; Otherworld; urban settings
speculum principum ('mirror for princes'), literary genre 198*n*22
Spenser, Edmund 135
    The Faerie Queene 24, 97, 98
The Squire's Tale (Chaucer) 47, 55, 56–61, *58*
    Arthurian motifs 58–9
    "magic horse" motif (from *The Thousand and One Nights*) 57, 59–61
    storyteller's self-deprecation 57, 59
    treatment of exoticism 56–7, 59, 60–1
St. Patrick's Purgatory (anon.) 126
Stahuljak, Zrinka 201*n*4
Stanzaic Morte D'Arthur (anon.) 167
Stephen of Rouen, *Draco Normanicus* 34, 202*n*4
Straparola, Giovanni Francesco 120
    Pleasant Nights 1

Táin Bó Cúailnge (*The Cattle-Raid of Cooley,* anon.) 190
Táin Bó Froích (*The Cattle-Raid of Fróech,* anon.) 139, *140*, 141, 199*n*3
The Tale of Genji see Shikibu, Murasaki

Tales of the Marvellous (medieval Arabic collection) 17
Taliesin (legendary poet) 142
Tatar, Marie 2–3, 8
Tatlock, J. S. 125
Taussing, Michael 61
Taylor, Jane H. M. 107–8
Thomas, Keith 23, 24
Thomas of Cantimpré
   Bonum Universale de Apibus (The Universal Good of Bees) 31–3
   De natura rerum 198n1
Thomas of Ercledoune (anon.) 39–40, 96
'Thomas the Rhymer' (historical/legendary figure) 20, 39–40, 96
Thompson, Stith 121
Thousand and One Nights, The 15, 45
   "The Enchanted Horse" 57–61
   earliest surviving manuscript 17
   European adaptations 45–7
   influence on Boccaccio/Chaucer 48–50, 53, 55, 57, 59–61
Tochmarc Étaíne (The Wooing of Étaín, anon.) 138, 191
Todorov, Tzvetan, *Introduction à la littérature fantastique* 28–9, 34, 194n3
Tolkien, J. R. R. 5, 10–14, 15, 17, 21, 93, 198n9
   "*Beowulf:* The Monsters and the Critics" 12, 118, 193n2
   The Lord of the Rings 29
   "On Fairy Stories" 193n2, 201–2n1
   Pearl (trans.) 12
   Sir Gawain and the Green Knight (trans.) 12
   theoretical writings 2–3, 12–13
translation, medieval practices of 53–4
Tristan and Isolde, legend of 9, 71, 129, 196, 196n10
Tuatha Dé Danann (fairy race, Irish) 91, 137–42, 204n12
   interactions with humans 139–41, 182, 191
   rules of conduct/abilities 138–9
   social organization 138

urban settings, in romance 148, *149*
   rejection 150–1

Verner, Lisa 115
Vienna Genesis (Bibilcal codex) 116
Villiers, Pierre de, abbé 7–8
Vincent of Beauvais, *Speculum Naturale* 198n1
Vines, Amy 181
Virgil (P. Vergilius Maro) 14
   Aeneid 113
virtue 64–5, 71–7
   beauty as marker of 86–7
   feminine forms 71–2, 74–7
   lapses from 75
   masculine forms 71–4
   and the quest 71–4
The Vision of Tundale (anon.) 126
The Voyage of Bran (anon.) 92, 96
The Voyage of Saint Brendon (anon.) 96, 126

Wade, James 16, 80, 96, 109, 181
   Fairies in Medieval Romance 92
Warner, Marina 67
   No Go the Bogeyman 122–3
Warner, Sylvia Townsend, *Kingdoms of Elfin* 27
Wars of the Roses (1461–85) 201n1
Washburn, Dennis 158–9
Weber, Max 23
Weldon, James 195n6
Welsh tales/culture 18, 92, 136, 142–7
   division of Otherworlds 143–5, *144*
   fairy–human interactions 146
   political implications 146–7, 154
   relationship with French 147–8
wilderness, fears/symbolism of 93–4
William I of England "The Conqueror" 25
William of Auvergne, Bishop 95
   De Universo 31
William of Newburgh 25–6, 29
Williams, David 115, 120
Williams, Raymond 200n9
Williams, Tara 16, 77, 79, 177
Williamson, Judith 200n9
witches 130, 131–3
"Woman in the Wood" motif 89, *90*, 91, 97–8, 100–1, 103
women
   communities of, consolations/pitfalls 171–3

domestic role 76–7
empowerment 38–9
as fallen/sinful 74
mortal, contrasted with magical 83
as objects of devotion 74–7
subjugation 8
as temptresses 74–5, 84, 130–1
woman-serpent/dragon hybrids 75–7, 128–33 (see also Melusine)
see also gender/sexuality

wonder tales 120–3
Wonders of the East (anon.) 117
Woodcock, James 97, 98
Woodville, Elizabeth, Queen 98
Workman, Leslie 3–4

Ziolkowski, Jan M. 1–2, 3, 5, 9, 17, 64
  Fairy Tales Before Fairy Tales 52–3, 195n12
Zipes, Jack 1, 5, 7, 53, 122–3, 159, 160